LONE WOLF
TERRORISM

ALSO BY JEFFREY D. SIMON

The Terrorist Trap: America's Experience with Terrorism

LONE WOLF
TERRORISM

UNDERSTANDING THE GROWING THREAT

JEFFREY D. SIMON
FOREWORD BY BRIAN MICHAEL JENKINS

 Prometheus Books

59 John Glenn Drive
Amherst, New York 14228

Published 2016 by Prometheus Books

Prometheus Books recognizes the following registered trademarks mentioned within the text: Celexa®, Facebook®, Glock®, Google®, iPod®, MySpace®, Twitter®, Tylenol® PM, YouTube®

Cover image © 2013 Media Bakery
Cover design by Grace M. Conti-Zilsberger
Cover design © Prometheus Books

Inquiries should be addressed to
Prometheus Books
59 John Glenn Drive
Amherst, New York 14228
VOICE: 716–691–0133 • FAX: 716–691–0137
WWW.PROMETHEUSBOOKS.COM

20 19 18 17 16   5 4 3 2 1

Library of Congress Cataloging-in-Publication Data

Names: Simon, Jeffrey D. (Jeffrey David), 1949- author.
Title: Lone wolf terrorism : understanding the growing threat / Jeffrey D. Simon.
Description: Amherst, New York : Prometheus Books, [2016] | Originally published
    in hardback version in 2013. | Includes a new preface by the author. |
    Includes bibliographical references and index.
Identifiers: LCCN 2016014589 (print) | LCCN 2016023761 (ebook) |
    ISBN 9781633882379 (pbk.) | ISBN 9781616146474 (ebook)
Subjects: LCSH: Terrorists. | Internet and terrorism. | Terrorism—Prevention.
Classification: LCC HV6431 .S524 2016 (print) | LCC HV6431 (ebook) |
    DDC 363.325—dc23
LC record available at https://lccn.loc.gov/2016014589

Printed in the United States of America

CONTENTS

PREFACE TO THE PAPERBACK

Lone wolf terrorism—the Boston Marathon bombing, the shooting of church folk in South Carolina, the massacre of innocent people in San Bernardino, the attack on a gay nightclub in Orlando. Each of these events and others in recent years have dominated the news and sent an increasing shudder through the American public, raising a host of questions: Why is this happening now? How safe are we really? Is this the world we can expect to live in?

These tragic events were yet another reminder of how one or two individuals, working alone without any outside assistance, can wreak havoc on unsuspecting victims and create fear and anxiety throughout a nation. The threat of lone wolf terrorism has emerged as one of the most bewildering, frustrating, and dangerous forms of violence for our times. Bewildering because seemingly anyone can become a lone wolf, inspired by extremist ideology posted on the Internet, or through face-to-face contacts with supporters of various militant causes, or by even just deciding to commit a terrorist act for personal or other reasons. Frustrating because these types of terrorists often fly under the radar, making the job of law enforcement extremely difficult in terms of trying to prevent these violent acts. And dangerous because there are no constraints on their level of violence, as lone wolves only answer to themselves and can therefore act upon any scenario they dream up without worrying, as would some terrorist groups, about the reactions or repercussions of a particular type of attack.

The Boston Marathon bombing, which occurred in April 2013, was an example of lone wolves who perpetrate their violence in the name of Islamic extremism. Tamerlan Tsarnaev and his younger brother Dzhokhar set off pressure-cooker bombs that killed three people and injured more than 260 others. There have been many more incidents of Islamic lone wolf terrorism these past few years, including attacks in Canada, Australia, Britain, France, and other countries around the world. In the US, an Islamic militant opened fire on a military recruiting station and a Navy Operational Support Center in Chattanooga, Tennessee, in July 2015, killing four Marines and fatally wounding a navy sailor, while a husband and wife team, Syed Rizwan Farook and Tashfeen Malik, who had a six-month-old baby girl, launched a shooting spree at a disability center in San Bernardino, California, in December 2015, killing fourteen people and injuring more than twenty others. Shortly after the attack began, a post on a Facebook page associated with the female terrorist, Tashfeen Malik, pledged allegiance to Abu Bakr al-Baghdadi, the leader of the terrorist group Islamic State in Iraq and Syria (ISIS). Then, in June 2016, Omar Mateen burst into a gay nightclub in Orlando, Florida, and massacred forty-nine people and injured more than fifty others. Mateen also pledged allegiance to ISIS during the attack.[1]

The rise of ISIS has been one of the major recent developments in the world of terrorism. After capturing large areas of territory in Syria and Iraq in 2014, the group declared an Islamic "caliphate" and called upon Muslims everywhere to come join the fight. The group also used social media to encourage lone wolves to strike within their home countries. ISIS has indeed proven quite savvy in their Internet blogs, tweets, and other social media tools to attract various individuals to their cause. In one respect, it is the jihadist equivalent of sending spam messages to millions of people. You only need a small percentage to take the bait to be effective.

Yet it would be wrong to assume that lone wolf terrorism is the exclusive domain of Islamic extremists. A major theme in my book is that lone wolf terrorism is a diverse phenomenon that cuts across the political and religious spectrum. Events since publication of the hardcover in February 2013 have borne this out. In addition to lone wolf attacks by Islamic extremists, there was an attack by an anti-abortion militant on a Planned Parenthood clinic in Colorado Springs, Colorado, in November 2015 that killed three people, a massacre of nine African-American churchgoers in Charleston, South Carolina, in June 2015 by a white supremacist sympathizer who wanted to start a race war, and the killing of a Transportation Security Administration agent at Los Angeles International Airport in November 2013 by an anti-government militant.[2]

The Internet has proven to be the game changer in the world of lone wolf terrorism. Lone wolves no longer have to feel truly "alone" as they can fantasize about being part of an extremist movement by just reading blogs, tweets, or entering into chat rooms. One of the key challenges will be to determine what the "tipping" points are that propel an otherwise nonviolent individual who may be expressing radical and extremist views or just venting on the Internet to actually follow through with an attack.

For a long time, lone wolves were ignored by policy makers, intelligence officials, and terrorism experts. Even today, despite the prevalence of lone wolf attacks throughout the world, the idea that the individual terrorist can be as dangerous as large-scale terrorist organizations is still a difficult concept for some people to accept. It is important, however, to remember that terrorist attacks are not always complex operations that require detailed planning, resources, training, and leadership directed by a group. Lone wolves, whether motivated by political, religious, or idiosyncratic reasons, have proven numerous times that they can have profound effects on governments and societies by their acts of violence. Unfortunately, we are likely to see more of these types of attacks in the coming years. It is a threat that shows no signs of abating anytime soon.

Jeffrey D. Simon
Santa Monica, California
June 2016

FOREWORD

Jeffrey D. Simon has been among the most creative thinkers in the study of terrorism. He warned about overreactions to terrorism and the problems in declaring a "war" on terrorism back in the 1980s in an article for *Foreign Policy* that became the genesis for his first book *The Terrorist Trap: America's Experience with Terrorism.* He was also among the first to systematically assess the threat of terrorists using biological weapons in an essay he wrote while at RAND in the 1980s. Now he has once again broken new ground in this first, comprehensive, and fascinating journey into the world of the lone wolf terrorist.

In nature, a lone wolf hunts outside of the pack. Deprived of company, relying on his own cunning and ferocity, he is a determined and dangerous predator. In popular literature, a lone wolf is the archetypal antihero—tough, self-reliant, and ruthless as required. Unconstrained by feckless politicians or cautious bureaucrats, he does what is necessary to get the job done—rescue innocent victims, save civilization. The annals of crime also record lone wolves—stalkers, serial killers, mad bombers—driven by grievance, cause, or madness.

Lone wolves recently have come to be viewed as a growing terrorist threat. Unprecedented unilateral intelligence efforts and growing cooperation among intelligence services and law-enforcement organizations worldwide have rendered the terrorists' operating environment more hostile. While still not optimal, domestic intelligence collection in the United States since 9/11 has uncovered and thwarted all but three terrorist plots inspired by al Qaeda's ideology. Those three plots were carried out by lone operators: Carlos Bledsoe, who killed one army recruiting officer and wounded another in Little Rock, Arkansas; Nidal Malik Hasan, who killed thirteen of his fellow soldiers and wounded thirty-two others at Fort Hood, Texas*; and Faisal Shahzad, who attempted to set off an explosive device in Times Square, New York.

There is greater confidence today that large terrorist conspiracies will be identified. Tiny conspiracies, however, remain hard to detect. Lone operators, unless they reach out to others for moral reinforcement or material support, are almost impossible to know about, and they have proved themselves capable of carrying out large-scale violence and sustaining long campaigns.

Technological advances have increased the lethality of the lone wolf. Guns have made murder easier. Today's mass killers have access to ever-greater firepower. The invention of dynamite further enhanced the destructive power of the individual. With a single bomb, an individual can bring down an airliner, killing hundreds. Chemical and biological weapons also increase the capacity of the individual to kill in quantity. At the time of his capture, the Alphabet Bomber was working on the production of nerve gas. The anthrax letters, which terrorized the country in 2001, are believed to have been sent by a single individual. The Internet can be a source of inspiration, moral reinforcement, and practical instruction for potential killers.

America's principal current concern continues to be al Qaeda's global terrorist campaign. Under continuing pressure, al Qaeda today is more decentralized and more dependent on its affiliates and allies and on its ability to radicalize and recruit individuals to carry out terrorist attacks at home.

Approximately two-thirds of the homegrown al Qaeda–inspired terrorist plots in the United States since 9/11 have involved a single individual. Only a few of these individuals actually had physical contact with al Qaeda abroad. Having traveled to training camps run by al Qaeda or its allies, these individuals received instruction and were sent back to the United States to prepare and carry out terrorist attacks. A greater number were inspired by one-way contact with al

Qaeda websites or by online correspondence with al Qaeda communi-
cators. Some of the plotters thought they were in contact with al Qaeda
operatives, but these turned out to be police undercover agents—a
majority of the most advanced plots were FBI sting operations.

The term *lone wolf* would apply only to a few of these terrorist
plotters. The behavior of many resembled more that of stray dogs.
They sniffed at the edges of al Qaeda's extremist ideology, participated vicariously in its online jihad, exhorting each other to action,
carelessly throwing down threats, boasting of their prowess as war-
riors, of the heroic deeds they were ready to perform, barking,
showing their teeth, hesitating, then darting forward until ensnared
by the law. What drives them?

When I was testifying before the Senate Homeland Security
Committee shortly after Major Hasan's murderous attack at Fort
Hood, committee chairman Joe Liebermann asked, "Some have
called Major Hasan a terrorist while others have described him as
a deeply troubled man. Where do you come down, Mr. Jenkins?" I
responded that "the two descriptions are not mutually exclusive—
terrorism is not an activity that attracts the well-adjusted." Can we
make a distinction?

To achieve consensus on a definition of terrorism in the 1970s,
it was necessary to maintain sharp boundaries. Terrorism was politically motivated violence. While terrorists committed crimes in the
classic sense, terrorism differed from ordinary crime in its objectives.
Political content was a criterion of terrorism. Crime might produce
terror, but ordinary criminals were not terrorists.

Just as we sought to draw a line between the terrorist and the
ordinary criminal, we also tried to distinguish terrorists from violent
lunatics. Crazies, by definition, could not be terrorists.

Some governments were prone to attach the pejorative label "terrorist" to all their political foes. But the United States achieved its
independence through force of arms and recognized the right of
armed rebellion. Armed rebellion is not itself terrorism, although
rebels might carry out acts of terror. So might governments.

These distinctions are easy to make when considering an individual who is a member of a terrorist group, but they become much harder in the case of lone operators who lack obvious terrorist connections, whose motives can be inferred only from their choice of targets, or who may be motivated by extreme political views, sometimes of their own invention. They all consider themselves avatars of a greater cause.

Hesham Mohamed Hadayet, who in 2002 opened fire on passengers at the El Al counter at Los Angeles International Airport, was depressed and clearly hostile toward Jews, but absent evidence of membership or connection with a political cause, was he a terrorist? Under pressure from the victims' families, the authorities finally concluded that Hadayet hoped by his action to influence US policy (the necessary political content), and he therefore was labeled a terrorist.

Muharem Kurbegovic, the so-called Alphabet Bomber, carried out his campaign on behalf of the "Aliens of America," a group that existed only in his mind. He also claimed to be the Messiah. Initially considered insane, he spent more than five years in the state institution for the criminally insane. He was later judged mentally fit to stand trial.

Theodore Kaczynski, the Unabomber, carried on a seventeen-year terrorist bombing campaign. To explain why, he wrote a thirty-five-thousand-word manifesto. He was diagnosed as suffering from paranoid schizophrenia but was judged fit to stand trial.

Anders Breivik, who detonated a massive vehicle bomb in Oslo, then opened fire on a youth camp, killing seventy-seven persons in all, published a fifteen-hundred-page manifesto on the Internet. He was judged to have been legally sane and stood trial. So was Timothy McVeigh, whose bomb killed 168 people in Oklahoma City in a war of his own imagination on the federal government. Both are considered terrorists.

While distinctions, in my view, remain important, Simon—I think sensibly in this context—takes a broader view of his subject matter. To carry out extreme acts of violence without a military mandate, societal sanction, or reinforcement by comrades requires a level of determination edging on madness. To those who must fathom the motives or respond to the threat, the distinctions may be meaningless.

As evidenced from the few examples cited, the boundaries between violent extremism and psychopathology are blurry. The boundaries of terrorism are invented, while the construct of mental disorder is being continuously revised.

There have been numerous studies of suicide terrorists, most of whom are lone operators recruited, equipped, and deployed by larger organizations. And there is a growing volume of studies of the process of radicalization and self-recruitment to terrorism. But until now, there has been no study of lone wolf terrorism. Jeffrey D. Simon's book opens the door to this new domain.

Brian Michael Jenkins,
senior advisor to the president of the RAND Corporation,
advisor to the National Commission on Terrorism,
and author of *Will Terrorists Go Nuclear?*

---

*As we go to press, Nidal Malik Hasan has not gone to trial and the author and publisher acknowledge that under American jurisprudence he is presumed innocent until proven guilty in a court of law. The text reflects the opinion of both Brian Michael Jenkins (foreword writer) and Jeffrey D. Simon (author), after careful consideration of the known facts, that Mr. Hasan carried out the shooting for reasons he has not yet explained.

ACKNOWLEDGMENTS

Writing a book is an exhilarating journey. One of the best parts is when it is time to acknowledge all those who helped along the way. I would like to particularly thank David Rapoport and John Mueller for our frequent and informative meetings, during which we discussed the issue of lone wolf terrorism. Jean Rosenfeld was an early believer in my ideas about lone wolf terrorism, and I am grateful to her for her support. I am also indebted to Ken Chin, who was invaluable in providing feedback and encouragement throughout this project.

I would also like to thank the following colleagues, friends, and others who helped in many different ways: Richard Antony, Martin Balaban, James Bondurant, David Boren, Molly Boren, William Casey, Melinda Catlett, Sandy Chin, Joe Cirillo, Phil Edney, Jenifer Elzea, Steven Emerson, Bill Fargo, Stephen Fischer Jr., Mark Giuliano, Betsy Glick, Cathy Gonzalez, Theresa Hart Barry, Sharon Hayes, Robert Hitsous, Michael Intriligator, Steven Kafka, Eddie Kamiya, Janet Kamiya, Erica Kelly, Chris Kemp, Ed Kobak, Sherm Lamb, Ira Latto, Sue Moran, Bennett Ramberg, Kathy Schreik, Lorron Snell, Cindy Forrestal-Snell, Douglas Snyder, Shoshana Snyder, Jodi Solomon, Travis Sorrows, Warren Spencer, Nkenge Stocks, Meg Sullivan, Bill Teachworth, Kevin Terpstra, James Tong, Donna Wald, Carole Wood, and Ted Zwicker.

Catherine L. Hensley provided superb editing skills and was a pleasure to work with.

Special thanks goes to Brian Michael Jenkins, who wrote the foreword and who was my mentor when I began studying terrorism many decades ago.

I would also like to thank everybody at Prometheus Books, led by Steven L. Mitchell, the editor in chief, for their enthusiasm for a book on lone wolf terrorism. This includes Jade Zora Ballard, Bruce Carle, Grace M. Conti-Zilsberger, Mark Hall, Jill Maxick, Brian McMahon, Lisa Michalski, Catherine Roberts-Abel, Laura Shelley, and Melissa Raé Shofner.

Nobody could ask for a better agent than Jill Marsal. She championed this book from the beginning and was a constant source of support and encouragement.

Finally, I want to thank Ellen, Richard, Julie, Penya, Jack, Eric, Elijah, Justine, Caleb, and Oscar for being a special part of my life.

INTRODUCTION

Just before noon on September 16, 1920, a man drove a horse and wagon along Wall Street in New York City. He parked it across the street from the J. P. Morgan and Company bank headquarters and then vanished from the area, never to be seen again. Hidden in the wagon was a bomb comprised of one hundred pounds of dynamite and five hundred pounds of heavy, cast-iron slugs, along with a timing device. When the bomb exploded, it killed thirty-eight people and injured more than two hundred others. At the time, it was the worst terrorist act ever on US soil, in terms of casualties.

That infamous record stood for more than thirty-five years until November 1, 1955, when a young man placed his mother aboard a plane in Denver after hiding several sticks of dynamite in her luggage, killing her and forty-three other people when the plane exploded in midair. He was executed a little more than a year later. Then, on April 19, 1995, another young man drove a bomb-laden rental truck up to the front of the Alfred P. Murrah Federal Building in Oklahoma City at around 9 a.m., lit two fuses, and sped away in another car. When his 4,800-pound bomb, made from a mixture of ammonium nitrate fertilizer and fuel oil, exploded, 168 people lost their lives. The man responsible was apprehended a few days later and eventually executed for his crime.

That three of the worst terrorist attacks in US history, with the exception of the 9/11 attacks, were the work of lone wolves, or at least individuals working with minimum assistance from others, indicates the significance of this type of terrorist threat. Mario Buda (the perpetrator of the Wall Street bombing), John Gilbert Graham (the man responsible for the first major midair plane bombing in US history), and Timothy McVeigh (the individual responsible for the Oklahoma City bombing) were as different as three people could possibly be. Buda was an Italian anarchist, one of the last remaining members of the Galleanists, an anarchist group active in the United States during the early part of the twentieth century. The Galleanists were responsible for some of the most audacious terrorist attacks in the United States, including the sending of thirty package bombs across the country over a three-day period in April 1919. The targets included members of President Woodrow Wilson's administration, federal law-enforcement officials, members of Congress, judges, mayors, governors, local police officials, and prominent businessmen. Then, on the evening of June 2, the Galleanists struck again, this time setting off bombs less than an hour or two apart from each other in seven US cities, including New York and Washington, DC. Soon after these attacks, Luigi Galleani was deported to Italy along with several of his close aides. By September 1920, the Galleanists were in disarray, having seen their ranks decimated with arrests, detentions, and deportations. Many members fled the country before they could be arrested.[1]

Buda, "who had appointed himself the avenging angel of the imprisoned and deported anarchists," decided to stay and launch one more attack.[2] He sprang into action shortly after two of his close friends and fellow Galleanists, Nicola Sacco and Bartolomeo Vanzetti, were indicted for murders committed during a robbery of a shoe factory. It didn't bother him that innocent people would be killed in the Wall Street bombing. Like many anarchists, he believed in the slogan "There are no innocent." He fled to Italy soon after the attack, never to be heard from again. As one historian noted, "It was his final act of reprisal in America. The biggest of them all, it had gone off without a hitch."[3]

While Buda could be described as a man who believed in a "cause," Graham could only be described as someone who believed in money. Already having served time in jail for bootlegging, and having received a suspended sentence for check forgery, Graham decided to try to hit the jackpot by collecting on a $37,500 insurance policy on his mother's life that he purchased at the airport. He also was anxious to share part of his mother's estate, which was worth $150,000. Putting a bomb in his mother's suitcase before she boarded a United Airlines flight out of Denver seemed to be the perfect plan. He knew how to build a dynamite bomb, since he had worked for construction and logging companies, where dynamite was used. After saying good-bye to his mother, Graham calmly waited at an airport coffee shop until he heard word that the plane had crashed. He later called the airline's office to confirm that his mother was dead. He remained stoic and unremorseful throughout his trial, conviction, and execution. Because there was no federal law at that time to cover his offense, he was executed for murder under Colorado law in 1957. The first major midair plane bombing in America was therefore not the work of a political or religious extremist, but rather that of a greedy young man.[4]

McVeigh, a homegrown American terrorist who blew up the federal building in Oklahoma City, was not greedy, but he was certainly angry. His anger was directed at the US government, which he blamed for the deaths of more than eighty members of the Branch Davidian cult, whose compound in Waco, Texas, burst into flames during a government raid in 1993. Federal authorities claimed that cult members possessed large numbers of illegal weapons. The Oklahoma City bombing occurred on the second anniversary of that raid.

McVeigh had attended meetings of the Michigan Militia, which was one of several antigovernment, right wing militia groups throughout the country. The militia movement believed that the government intended to confiscate all citizens' weapons, thereby abrogating the Second Amendment's guarantee of the right of citizens to keep and bear arms. The Waco raid was viewed as evidence that this was now occurring. McVeigh was also influenced by a novel, *The Turner Diaries*, which was "based on the premise that the United States has already succumbed unwittingly to a conspiracy of global control from which it needs to be liberated through terrorist actions and guerilla bands."[5] McVeigh had sold copies of the book at gun shows.

Both McVeigh and Terry Nichols, who helped McVeigh prepare the bomb, were arrested for the Oklahoma City bombing. Nichols was convicted in June 1998 and sentenced to life in prison without the possibility of parole while McVeigh was found guilty in June 1997 and executed for his crime in June 2001.

Buda, Graham, and McVeigh all demonstrated one of the main characteristics that separates terrorism from all other types of conflicts—namely, the ability of a single individual to commit a violent act, or threaten to do so, and at times receive the same degree of attention, reaction, and fear that larger, more established terrorist groups usually attain. The lone wolf, however, until recently, was often overlooked in assessing the terrorist threat, since many definitions of terrorism require that an act of violence be committed by a group with a political, social, or religious objective. The media and government officials also tended to talk about the terrorist threat in terms of groups such as al Qaeda or other large-scale violent organizations.

Yet in terms of the effect a violent act committed by a single individual can have upon society and government, there is sometimes little difference between the actions of the lone wolf and those of larger, more organized terrorist groups. For example, the reaction after the Wall Street bombing was shock and anger, with the New York Chamber of Commerce labeling the bombing "an act of war" and Attorney General A. Mitchell Palmer stating it was part of a major plot to overthrow the capitalist system.[6] The Denver plane bombing also shocked the nation, as most Americans were outraged by this new form of violence. The public now had to fear midair plane bombings in addition to accidental plane crashes. Federal agencies began conducting studies on identifying the best security measures that could be used at airports to detect explosives in luggage. The Oklahoma City bombing, coming just two years after the World Trade Center was bombed by Islamic extremists, caused people to worry that terrorism was now spreading into the heartland. It seemed as though no place in America would be safe from terrorist attacks, including those committed by homegrown American terrorists.

Other lone wolves who have elicited major reactions include Theodore Kaczynski, the infamous "Unabomber," who held an entire nation in fear for seventeen years beginning in 1978 by planting or sending package bombs to victims throughout the United States; and Bruce Ivins, who sent letters filled with anthrax spores to members of Congress and the media in 2001, creating a crisis atmosphere in America concerning the threat of bioterrorism. The anthrax letter attacks were indicative of the innovative nature of the lone wolf. Prior to those attacks, it was not believed that anthrax spores could survive being sent through the mail. Lone wolves have been responsible for other attacks that represented the first time a particular tactic was used, such as the first vehicle bombing (the Wall Street bombing), a major midair plane bombing (the Denver bombing), hijacking, and product-tampering attacks in the United States. The lone wolf has long been among the most innovative and creative in terms of terrorist tactics, introducing new forms of violence that the more established terrorist groups eventually adopt as their own.

The United States is not alone in experiencing the effects of lone wolf terrorism. In July 2011, Anders Breivik, a thirty-two-year-old Norwegian man, set off a car bomb near government buildings in Oslo and then traveled to an island to massacre youths attending a summer camp run by the ruling Labor Party. The attacks represented the worst act of terrorism in Norwegian history and sent shockwaves throughout the country. Meanwhile, Italy had its own version of the Unabomber, when a suspected lone wolf planted more than thirty bombs over a twelve-year period beginning in 1994.

There have also been recent cases of lone wolves linking up with organized groups or trying to form their own terrorist networks in order to carry out attacks. Colleen LaRose, who used the pseudonym "Jihad Jane" on her MySpace page, tried to recruit extremists online through e-mails during 2008 and 2009. She was also involved in a plot to assassinate a Swedish cartoonist who had portrayed the Prophet Muhammad in a derogatory manner in one of his cartoons. LaRose traveled to Europe in an effort to form her own terrorist cell.

In another instance, a Nigerian man, Umar Farouk Abdulmutallab, was recruited by a Yemen-based branch of al Qaeda and sent on a lone wolf mission to the United States to blow up an airliner. Abdulmutallab was overpowered by passengers and crew as he tried to ignite a bomb hidden in his underwear as the plane flew over Detroit, Michigan, on Christmas Day in 2009.

The lone wolf threat is destined to grow in the coming years, as the technological and information revolutions will no doubt assist those individuals interested in perpetrating virtually any type of terrorist attack. Terrorism has long been linked to the irreversible march of technology. Technological advancements in all fields do not discriminate among their users. Innovations in weapons, communications, information systems, and so forth are there for all to take advantage of, including lone wolf terrorists.

The Internet will grow to contain even more reports, websites, and other information than it does today for lone wolves to use in researching, planning, and implementing an attack. Lone wolves can learn about sophisticated weapons, how to make various explosives, and even how to build a homemade biological weapon. They will have technology at their fingertips as they fly under the radar in conducting online surveillance of targets. More individuals are also likely to become self-radicalized as they read terrorist webpages and communicate with other like-minded people via e-mail, Twitter, Facebook, chat rooms, and other social-networking tools. And terrorist groups will undoubtedly search for these lone wolf types, since they can be easily recruited, quickly trained, and sent off on various missions.

While there have been many books and articles published on different aspects of terrorism in the post-9/11 era, there has been very little systematic study of the lone wolf phenomenon.[7] This book is an attempt to bridge that gap by providing an in-depth look at this important aspect of terrorism. Three central themes emerge in the following pages. The first is how the lone wolf is changing the dynamics of international terrorism. No longer can theories on terrorism and strategies on how to deal with the terrorist threat exclude the role of lone wolves, since they are capable of matching, and sometimes exceeding, the impact that "regular" terrorist groups can have upon a nation. The lone wolf is forcing us to revise our thinking about terrorism and shift away from an almost exclusive focus on terrorist groups and organizations toward a new appreciation for the importance of the individual terrorist. From the analysis of the causes of terrorism and the motivations of terrorists to the identification of policies and measures that need to be taken to combat this global threat, the lone wolf is now an integral part of the discussion.

The second theme of this book, mentioned earlier, is the key role that technology, particularly the Internet, is playing in the rise of the lone wolf. While there were significant lone wolves before the Internet was invented, the cyber world has undoubtedly been a godsend for the individual terrorist. It has led to a proliferation of lone wolves around the world and allowed for anybody with a laptop to quickly become knowledgeable about terrorist tactics, targets, and weapons, including how to launch a terrorist attack. The role of the Internet in the radicalization of potential lone wolves is also a key part of this trend.

The third theme of this book is the creative and innovative nature of the lone wolf terrorist. Because these individuals work alone or with just one or two other people, lone wolves are not burdened by any group decision-making processes or intergroup dynamics that can sometimes stifle creativity in formulating plans and operations. Lone wolves are therefore free to think up any type of scenario they want and then try to act upon it, because they are accountable only to themselves. Related to this is the fact that, because they are not part of a group, lone wolves will not be concerned, as would be some terrorist groups, about potential government and law-enforcement crackdown following an incident that could lead to the virtual elimination of the group through arrests and other measures. And if a lone wolf is suffering from a mental illness, then he or she will not think rationally about the risks and consequences of a particular terrorist tactic. Furthermore, because they do not rely upon any segment of the population for financial, logistical, or political support, lone wolves, unlike many terrorist groups, do not have to worry about negative reactions by the public to a particular attack.

The world of the lone wolf is indeed a fascinating one. This book is intended to take the reader on a journey into that world. The lone wolf terrorist threat clearly demonstrates why combating terrorism is an endless struggle. We cannot expect to "defeat" terrorism, when terrorism can be viewed as just one person with one bomb and one cause. Perhaps the best description of the difficult task we face in dealing with terrorism was made by the Irish Republican Army (IRA). Following a failed attempt to assassinate British prime minister Margaret Thatcher in 1984, the IRA issued the following chilling statement: "Today, we were unlucky! But remember, we only have to be lucky once. You will have to be lucky always!"[8] Unfortunately, we can't always expect to be lucky in the battle against terrorism. We are living in an age in which all types of terrorists, including lone wolves, can gain access to weapons, including weapons of mass destruction, and commit horrendous terrorist attacks. Yet while it is unrealistic to expect that we can ever totally defeat terrorism, it is not unrealistic to believe that we can be better prepared to deal with all types of terrorist contingencies, including those centered on lone wolves. It is crucial, therefore, that we do not ignore the lone wolf threat in the ongoing battle against terrorism and that we be as committed to understanding and combating it as we are with respect to all the other forms of global terrorism.

CHAPTER 1

THE GROWING THREAT OF LONE WOLF TERRORISM

"The biggest concern we have right now . . . is the lone wolf terrorist," President Barack Obama said in 2011.[1] Central Intelligence Agency (CIA) director Leon Panetta told Congress a year earlier that "it's the lone-wolf strategy that I think we have to pay attention to as the main threat to this country."[2] India's home secretary, G. K. Pillai, echoed those sentiments, warning that "terrorists can be anywhere. The real challenge is the lone wolf, someone who is not known."[3] Australian foreign minister Stephen Smith joined the list of concerned public officials when he said in a radio interview that "we are now seeing emerging the potential so-called lone wolf escapade where we don't have sophisticated planning but an individual is seduced by the international jihad and as a lone wolf does extreme things."[4] Whether it is homegrown terrorists influenced by jihadist websites and chat rooms or individuals bent on terrorist activity for a wide range of causes or issues, the threat of lone wolf terrorism is growing around the world.

It is understandable, however, if one is skeptical of anybody who writes that the terrorist threat is "growing" or "increasing" in any shape or form. Haven't we had enough warnings about terrorism over the years, often fueled by self-interested politicians, government officials, terrorism experts, and others? The Department of Homeland Security's ill-conceived "color-coded alert" system is still fresh in many minds, and its only effect was scaring people about terrorist threats that never materialized. Keeping the terrorist threat high in the public's mind and on the government's agenda is good for business, both for terrorists, who thrive on the psychological fear that terrorism evokes, and for those who talk, write, or consult about terrorism. But there is enough evidence to indicate that the lone wolf threat is real and is not likely to fade away anytime soon.

A dizzying array of recent lone wolf attacks and plots illustrates the diversity of this threat, as noted in the introduction. The twin terror attacks in Norway by an anti-Islamic extremist were among the worst lone wolf incidents in history. In the United States, lone wolf attacks in recent years have ranged from terrorists motivated by single issues and antigovernment ideology to those inspired by Islamic extremism and white supremacy. Britain has also experienced a diverse array of lone wolf incidents. A lone wolf Islamic extremist was arrested in April 2008 before he could carry out a suicide attack on a shopping center in Bristol. Among the items police found in a search of the man's apartment were the unstable explosive hexamethylene triperoxide diamine (HMTD), an electrical circuit capable of detonating the explosive, and a suicide vest. Just over a month later, another lone wolf terrorist sympathetic to Islamic extremism was injured in a failed suicide attack in a restaurant in Exeter. He was preparing three nail bombs in the restaurant's bathroom when one accidently exploded in his hands. Lone wolf incidents in Britain also included a plot by a neo-Nazi to wage a violent campaign against "non-British" people using shrapnel bombs. When the man was arrested on the platform of a Suffolk train station in October 2008, police found two homemade explosives in his possession. A search of his home uncovered explosive ingredients and white supremacist and neo-Nazi literature. He also reportedly idolized Timothy McVeigh, the Oklahoma City bomber, and David Copeland, another lone wolf neo-Nazi, who became known as the "London Nailbomber."

Lone wolf terrorism is not limited to just a few incidents and places. Rather, it is increasingly occurring in countries throughout the world. How, then, can we explain the rise of lone wolf terrorism? Explanations for any type of terrorism are fraught with difficulties. The study of terrorism is a speculative endeavor at best, with cultural and personal biases potentially affecting explanations as to why individuals or groups may resort to violence against a wide range of targets. There have been explanations posited that range from poverty, alienation, and humiliation as the root causes of terrorism to explanations that focus on foreign state sponsorship of terrorist activity. The diverse nature of terrorism precludes any overall theory from being capable of explaining this phenomenon. It is difficult, for example, to argue that terrorism is due to specific conditions or situations when terrorism exists in virtually every country around the world. As Norwegian scholars Brynjar Lia and Katja H-W Skjolberg correctly point out, "We find terrorists among deprived and uneducated people, and among the affluent and well educated; we find terrorists among psychotic and 'normal' healthy people; and among people of both sexes and of all ages. Terrorism occurs in rich as well as in poor countries; in the modern industrialised world and in less developed areas; during a process of transition and development, prior to or after such a process; in former colonial states and in independent ones; and, in established democracies as well as in less democratic regimes."[5]

One way, however, to explain the rise in lone wolf terrorism is to view it as part of an emerging trend in terrorism that can best be described as the "Technological Wave." This wave permeates all aspects of terrorism and is of immense value to the individual who wants to embark upon a campaign of terrorist violence.

THE TECHNOLOGICAL WAVE OF TERRORISM

The concept of "waves" of terrorist activity was first formulated by pioneering terrorism scholar David C. Rapoport to explain the history of modern terrorism.[6] A wave can be thought of as a "cycle of activity in a given time period—a cycle characterized by expansion and contraction phases. A crucial feature is its international character; similar activities occur in several countries, driven by a common predominant energy that shapes the participating groups' characteristics and mutual relationships."[7] According to Rapoport, there have been four basic waves of terrorism since the late 1880s. The first wave began with the anarchist movement of the late-nineteenth and early-twentieth centuries. The Anarchist Wave was followed by the Anti-Colonial Wave, which began in the 1920s; the New Left Wave, which began in the 1960s; and the Religious Wave, which began in 1979. While there can be overlap in the waves, as one ebbs and another emerges, the lifespan of a wave is a generation, or about forty years, "a suggestive time frame closest in duration to that of a human life cycle, in which dreams inspiring parents lose their attractiveness for children."[8]

If Rapoport is correct, then we can expect the current Religious Wave to end, or at least be overtaken by a new wave of terrorism, by 2020. While it might be hard to imagine religious-inspired terrorism by organized, decentralized, or ad hoc groups not being the main form of terrorism for several more decades, given the numerous attacks perpetrated by Islamic extremists around the world, the history of terrorism has been characterized by the changing of the guard at different periods. Each of Rapoport's four waves, for example, was launched into a global movement by some type of grand event or incident. Rapoport points out that the wounding of a Russian police commander who had mistreated political prisoners in 1878 by Vera Zasulich inspired the Russian anarchist movement, particularly her proclamation that she was a "terrorist, not a killer," after she threw her weapon to the floor.[9] She was acquitted at her trial and treated as a heroine after she was freed. German newspapers reported that the pro-Zasulich demonstrations meant a revolution was imminent in Russia.[10]

The Treaty of Versailles, which ended World War I, precipitated the Anti-Colonial Wave, as the "victors applied the principle of national self-determination to break up the empires of the defeated states."[11] The third wave, the New Left Wave, found its inspiration in the Vietnam War and the effective role of the Viet Cong in its battles with American and South Vietnamese troops. The war led to the formation of radical groups in the Third World and the West, where "the war stimulated enormous ambivalence among the youth about the value of the existing system. Many Western groups—such as the American Weather Underground, the West German Red Army Faction (RAF), the Italian Red Brigades, the Japanese Red Army, and the French Action Directe—saw themselves as vanguards for the Third World masses. The Soviet world encouraged the outbreaks and offered moral support, training, and weapons."[12]

The fourth wave, the Religious Wave, was launched after the 1979 Iranian Revolution, which, along with the Soviet invasion of Afghanistan that same year, led to religious extremism in many parts of the world. The Iranian Revolution "was clear evidence to believers that religion now had more political appeal than did the prevailing third-wave ethos because Iranian Marxists could only muster meager support against the Shah."[13] The Ayatollah Khomeini regime in Iran "inspired and assisted Shiite terror movements outside of Iran, particularly in Iraq, Saudi Arabia, Kuwait, and Lebanon."[14]

While terrorist groups with religious agendas will undoubtedly be active for many years to come, a new wave, the Technological Wave, is emerging and making for a more level playing field among terrorists with different ideologies and agendas.[15] No single type of terrorist ideology will dominate this new wave in the same way that anarchism, anticolonialism, "New Left" ideology, and religious fundamentalism dominated the preceding four waves. Instead, technology is there for all to take advantage of, offering any group or individual the opportunity to compete in the world of terrorism. We can see technology's influence in all aspects of terrorism, from the rapid growth in the use of technology by governments and militaries for surveillance, detection of weapons, counterterrorist operations, and other purposes to its use by a wide variety of terrorists.

No one type of terrorist movement has a monopoly on the use of technology. For example, virtually every terrorist group has a website and is utilizing the Internet for recruitment, spreading its message, communications, and a variety of other purposes. In terms of weapons, insurgents in Iraq have used sophisticated improvised explosive devices (IEDs) in their attacks. The insurgents have proved to be technologically adaptable, as they switched from first using remote-controlled IEDs to then using long wires buried in the ground (also known as "command wires") in order to detonate the bombs after US troops acquired the ability to successfully jam the remote-controlled devices. Another indication of the technological savvy of the Iraqi insurgents is their use of explosively formed penetrators (EFPs). The EFPs "fire a slug of high density metal at between 4,000 and 6,500 miles per hour with much more energy than roadside bombs made from artillery shells. The penetrator's high velocity punches a relatively small hole in a vehicle's armor, then sprays occupants inside with a stream of shrapnel."[16]

IED and EFP technology is likely to be exported around the world as many insurgents leave Iraq and Afghanistan and take their terrorist campaigns to other countries. The Technological Wave will not only witness extremists from Iraq and Afghanistan using sophisticated IEDs and EFPs in different countries but will also include other terrorists, including lone wolves, who have their own agendas and who learn how to make the latest IEDs and EFPs from veterans of the Iraqi and Afghan insurgencies. They may also acquire the knowledge even without the cooperation of the militants from Iraq and Afghanistan, since it is difficult in the world of terrorism for one group or cell to keep weapons technology a secret from other extremists. Furthermore, there won't be the billion-dollar effort in other countries that the United States used in Iraq and Afghanistan to neutralize and defeat the IED and EFP threat. That will make it easier for extremists to use these and other technologically sophisticated weapons in their attacks.

THE INTERNET AND THE LONE WOLF

The most important aspect of the Technological Wave that helps explain the growing prominence of the lone wolf terrorist is the Internet. In fact, the Internet can be considered the grand event that helped launch the wave. The Internet is the "energy" for this new wave, continually revolutionizing the way information is gathered, processed, and distributed; the way communications are conducted and social networks are formed; and the way single individuals, such as lone wolves, can become significant players by using the Internet to learn about weapons, targets, and techniques.

By the first decade of the twenty-first century, the Internet was an integral part of everyday life for many people. One could find information on virtually any topic and feel connected to the world at large with a laptop computer or a smartphone. For the individual interested in perpetrating a terrorist attack, everything from how to build homemade bombs to maps and diagrams of potential targets were available on the Internet. So, too, were detailed accounts of terrorist incidents around the world, which lone wolves could study in order to determine what might work for them. In addition, the Internet provided a mechanism for lone wolves to become infatuated with extremist ideologies through the reading of websites, blogs, Facebook pages, and other tools available online. Lone wolves could also find other like-minded individuals on the Internet and obtain help from one or two other people in perpetrating an attack.

We only have to look at some of the recent lone wolf incidents to see the significant role that the Internet is playing for the individual terrorist. Anders Breivik, the Norwegian lone wolf who perpetrated the dual terrorist attacks in Norway, posted a fifteen-hundred-page manifesto on the Internet shortly before he embarked on his campaign of terror. The manifesto called for an end to "the Islamic colonisation and Islamisation of Western Europe" and blamed Norwegian politicians for allowing that to happen. He hoped his attacks would bring attention to his manifesto, which it certainly did, as his document suddenly became known throughout the world. Breivik was also influenced by anti-Islamic bloggers and writers in the United States whom he found on the Internet and whose quotations he used in his manifesto.[17]

Another lone wolf who posted a manifesto on the Internet before his terrorist attack was Joseph Stack. After setting fire to his home in Austin, Texas, on the morning of February 18, 2010, Stack flew his single-engine plane into a downtown Austin office building in which nearly two hundred people worked for the Internal Revenue Service (IRS). One person besides Stack was killed in the attack. Stack was motivated by a hatred for the IRS, which he blamed for ruining his life. He was particularly upset with a 1986 change in the tax law that prevented contract software engineers like him from taking certain deductions. The new law made it difficult for information-technology professionals to work as self-employed individuals. This forced many of them to become company employees.[18] In his manifesto, Stack wrote about the new tax law, saying that "they could only have been more blunt if they would have came out and directly declared me a criminal and non-citizen slave."[19] Stack's manifesto revealed the frustration that was building up inside him. He wrote, "I would only hope that by striking a nerve that stimulates the inevitable double standard, knee-jerk government reaction that results in more stupid draconian restrictions people wake up and begin to see the pompous political thugs and their mindless minions for what they are. Sadly, though I spent my entire life trying to believe it wasn't so, but violence not only is the answer, it is the only answer."[20]

Richard Poplawski, a white supremacist who killed three police officers in Pittsburgh, Pennsylvania, in April 2009, used the Internet to frequent a neo-Nazi chat room, "Stormfront," where he shared his racist, anti-Semitic, and antigovernment views with other like-minded individuals. Finding kindred souls on the Internet seemed to embolden Poplawski. His postings from November 2008 until March 2009 revealed an increasingly confrontational nature. He urged other white supremacists not to "retreat peaceably into the hills," but rather to strive for "ultimate victory for our people [by] taking back our nation." He also wrote that he would likely be "ramping up the activism" in the near future.[21] Poplawski surfed the Internet to order the AK-47 assault-style rifle that he used in his attack. The Internet seller delivered the rifle to a store, where Poplawski purchased the weapon.[22]

Another example of a lone wolf who used the Internet was Colleen LaRose (who is discussed in further detail in chapter 4), also known as "Jihad Jane," one of the few female lone wolves. She was attracted to the global reach of the Internet and hoped it would aid her in forming a terrorist network in 2008 and 2009 for high-profile attacks in Europe and South Asia. Meanwhile, a US Army major, Nidal Malik Hasan (who is discussed in further detail in chapter 2) opened fire at a soldier-processing center in Fort Hood, Texas, in November 2009, killing thirteen people and wounding thirty-two others. Hasan used the Internet to communicate with an American-born radical Islamic cleric who at the time was living in Yemen, Anwar al-Awlaki.

The Internet has been indispensable for lone wolves interested in learning about potential weapons. David Copeland, the British neo-Nazi mentioned earlier, who set off three bombs packed with nails in April 1999, discovered how to make the nail bombs after searching the Internet for information. Among the Internet sources he used were *The Terrorist's Handbook* and *How to Make Bombs: Book Two*. He acquired the bomb-making materials from shops and hardware stores but was not able to effectively assemble the necessary ingredients that were detailed in the web-based guides. He therefore used less-sophisticated bombs comprised of fireworks material and nails that were still powerful enough to kill three people and injure 139 others.[23]

Another British lone wolf terrorist, Nicky Reilly, who had converted to Islam, downloaded videos from YouTube in order to learn how to make nail bombs. His attempt in May 2008 failed, as noted earlier, when one of the three nail bombs he was preparing in the restroom of a restaurant in Exeter exploded in his hands. Reilly was in contact over the Internet with two men believed to be living in Pakistan who encouraged Reilly to perpetrate a suicide terrorist attack. The men, who were never located, discussed with Reilly potential targets, including an attack on police, civil servants, or the general public. They ultimately persuaded him to commit an attack on the public.[24]

The Internet also provides lone wolves with an easy means for conducting surveillance of potential targets, including detailed maps of airports and buildings, flight and train schedules, and even computer images of the inside of a specific plane, indicating how many passengers will be on a flight and the exact location of available seats. This could be valuable information for a lone wolf hijacker, who would not want to seize a plane with too many passengers on board, since that could make controlling the passengers difficult. Knowing the seating chart would also be an advantage because the hijacker would know exactly where everyone is located and could choose a seat that works to his or her advantage. For example, there have been plots by terrorists to use liquid bombs on a plane that require the terrorists to assemble the bomb while onboard due to the unstable nature of the explosives (which could explode prematurely). A lone wolf could, therefore, use the Internet to choose a seat in the rear of the plane by the bathroom in order to not be noticed missing for an extended period of time as he or she assembles the bomb.

The Internet not only offers lone wolves a convenient way to conduct surveillance of a target, but it also can be the target itself. The lone wolf cyberterrorist threat includes using the Internet and other communication and information systems that are linked by computers to cause disruptions and chaos in government, businesses, and everyday life. The threat of cyber attacks has received increased attention in recent years. Most of this attention, however, has focused on foreign governments and terrorist groups launching cyber attacks, not on lone wolves. Yet lone wolves have demonstrated throughout history that they should not be ignored. A computer-savvy lone wolf could be as dangerous as the most sophisticated terrorist group or cell in using the Internet to perpetrate a major cyberterrorist attack. Cyberterrorism may also be a natural fit for lone wolves who prefer to stay at home and perpetrate their attacks over the Internet, whether that be sending computer viruses or hacking into government databases and deleting or altering files. The lure of never having to venture out into the "real world" but instead being able to launch an attack from the comfort and privacy of their own home is something that isolated and socially maladjusted lone wolves may find appealing.

Perhaps one of the most obvious and yet overlooked reasons for why the Internet is the lifeblood for many potential lone wolf terrorists is the same reason it is the lifeblood for many scholars, professionals, and the curious public—namely, the addictive appeal of finding out virtually everything about anything at any time one chooses to do so. From using Google to research any topic, issue, or person to downloading books, articles, documents, and other materials, the world has opened up to anybody with access to a computer or smartphone. While for the most part this is a positive development, the downside is that a lot of material online is inflammatory and can inspire to take action those who may otherwise have never thought to do so. A blog or a webpage does not have to be controlled by extremists to have a catalyzing effect on volatile individuals.

Furthermore, even legitimate sources of information accessed on the Internet can propel individuals into violent action, whereas years ago such people may not have even thought about current affairs or any other issue. No longer do people have to go to a library, buy a newspaper, visit a bookstore, or attend a lecture to learn about the world around them. The Internet provides them with sufficient information to formulate views on any topic or issue they choose. For some potential lone wolves, this may be all that is needed to fuel hidden passions that can lead them to violence.

Another often-overlooked aspect of the technological and Internet age we are living in is that an individual can be "connected" to people, things, and ideas while at the same time being isolated, anonymous, and very alone. Individuals can hide behind screen names and yet share details about their lives with others while never having to meet face-to-face. People can walk down the street and be oblivious to all that is around them while they are tuned into their smartphone, iPod, or any other device providing them with music, conversation, or other information. We are living in a society where eye contact and interpersonal relations can be replaced by e-mails, texting, and tweets. All this plays into the hands of lone wolves, who can remain "alone," if they choose to do so, while still connecting with the world around them.

LEADERLESS TERRORISM

The growth of lone wolf terrorism can also be viewed as part of a trend in terrorism that began in the 1990s and has been described as "leaderless resistance." The main proponent of this form of terrorism was Louis Beam, a white supremacist who, in 1992, wrote an influential article, "Leaderless Resistance," that was published in his own journal, the *Seditionist.* Beam called for the creation of small, autonomous, underground groups that would be driven by ideology and shared beliefs rather than the direction of leaders and members of organizations. In his article, Beam credited the origins of the concept of "leaderless resistance" to a retired US Air Force colonel, Ulius Amoss, who several decades earlier had proposed the strategy as a defense against a Communist takeover of the United States. For Beam, the strategy now was needed "to defeat state tyranny." The advantage of leaderless resistance over other strategies was that only those participating in an attack or any other type of action would know of the plans, therefore reducing the chance of leaks or infiltration. As Beam wrote, "All individuals and groups operate independently of each other and never report to a central headquarters or single leader for direction or instruction. . . . Participants in a program of Leaderless Resistance through phantom cell or individual action must know exactly what they are doing, and exactly how to do it."[25]

It is not just white supremacists who have followed the strategy of leaderless resistance. So too have environmental extremist groups such as the Animal Liberation Front and the Earth Liberation Front, which are not actually groups but rather small autonomous cells with no central leadership. The same is true for antiabortion militant movements such as the Army of God. Many Islamic extremists have also followed a form of "leaderless resistance," which terrorism scholar Marc Sageman aptly describes as "leaderless jihad." These are Islamic militants who do not rely on direction or orders from al Qaeda or any other terrorist organization. As Sageman notes, these extremists "form fluid, informal networks that are self-financed and self-trained. They have no physical headquarters or sanctuary, but the tolerant virtual environment of the Internet offers them a semblance of unity and purpose. Theirs is a scattered, decentralized social structure—a leaderless jihad."[26]

There have been numerous cases of leaderless jihadist attacks in recent years. This does not mean, however, that in all cases "face-to-face radicalization has been replaced by online radicalization."[27] Islamic militants can still form leaderless jihadist links with each other in "real life," such as through meetings at mosques, coffee shops, schools, and so forth. But Sageman is correct in viewing the Islamic extremist threat as coming more from informal networks of small numbers of militants rather than from large-scale, hierarchal organizations. With so many different types of terrorists adopting a "leaderless" philosophy but not all fitting into a "resistance" category (hence Sageman's *leaderless jihad* phrase), it would seem that a better term to use would be *leaderless terrorists*. This would, of course, include the multitude of lone wolves with varied causes who operate either entirely alone or with minimal assistance from others.

The idea that the world of terrorism is being populated by individuals not formally linked to an organization or central command is a difficult concept for many people to accept. The history of terrorism has been characterized by many well-known, organized groups such as the Palestine Liberation Organization, the Irish Republican

Army, the Baader-Meinhof Gang, and hundreds of others active in previous decades. There is also an assumption held by many that terrorist operations are complex endeavors that require detailed planning, resources, training, and leadership directed by large-scale organizations. That is not always the case, and as we have seen in recent years, the number of terrorist incidents and plots involving terrorists not affiliated with any group has increased. This adds to the challenges in combating terrorism. While centralized and even decentralized groups provide governments and others dedicated to fighting terrorism with a concrete object on which to focus their policies, the leaderless terrorists are more problematic. They are difficult to identify, track, and arrest. It is also difficult to proclaim a "war on terrorism" or any other catchy phrase when the threat emanates from leaderless terrorists.

Government, law-enforcement, and intelligence agencies from around the world have taken notice of the leaderless terrorist and lone wolf threat. The Canadian government's Integrated Threat Assessment Centre warned in 2007 that "lone wolves motivated by Islamist extremism are a recent development. Islamist terrorist strategies are now advocating that Muslims take action at a grassroots level, without waiting for instructions."[28] An Australian government white paper stated that, in terms of al Qaeda and Islamic extremism, "'lone-wolf' attackers with no group affiliation but motivated by the same ideology can emerge at any time."[29] And it is not just the lone wolf seduced by jihadism that worries officials. The European Law Enforcement Agency (Europol) noted in 2010 that, in terms of right-wing terrorism in Britain, "individuals motivated by extreme right-wing views, acting alone, pose far more of a threat than the current [right-wing] networks or groups."[30] Meanwhile, a 2009 US Department of Homeland Security report stated that "lone wolves and small terrorist cells embracing rightwing extremist ideology are the most dangerous domestic terrorism threat in the United States."[31]

THE DEFINITIONAL DILEMMA

Any book on terrorism raises the question of how exactly does the author define *terrorism*. The problem with most definitions is that they are either too narrow and thereby exclude many significant cases of terrorist activity or are so broad as to be quite useless in understanding the terrorist phenomenon. There are also obvious biases and contradictions in many definitions, since they are usually based on ideological and political perceptions of the terrorist threat as well as the bureaucratic interests of various government agencies and departments around the world. The more disagreements there are on defining terrorism, the more terrorists can benefit by the added confusion on the issue.

The difficulty in defining terrorism has given rise to the famous slogan, "One person's terrorist is another person's freedom fighter." Communities that support various groups in their violent acts do not necessarily see them as "terrorists." Since the essence of terrorism is the effect that violent acts can have on various targets and audiences, it would make more sense to talk about terrorist-type *tactics*— which can be utilized by extremist groups, guerrillas, governments, and lone wolves—than to attempt to determine who exactly qualifies as a "terrorist." The blowing up of planes, whether done by lone wolves or organized groups, is terrorism. The same is true for hijackings, assassinations, bombings, product contaminations, and other violent acts. Several decades of futile efforts to reach a consensus on defining terrorism should be a clear enough signal to move on to other aspects of the terrorist threat.[32]

However, more than twenty-five years of being involved in terrorism research and analysis has convinced me that readers and others expect some type of definition to be offered. This volume's appendix provides a detailed discussion of the key elements needed for a practical definition of terrorism, in general, and lone wolf terrorism, in particular. For now, though, we can think of lone wolf terrorism as the use or threat of violence or nonviolent sabotage (including cyber attacks) by an individual acting alone, or with minimal support from one or two other people, to further a political, social, religious, financial, or other related goal, or, when not having such an objective, nevertheless has the same effect upon government and society in terms of creating fear and/or disrupting daily life and/or causing government and society to react with heightened security and/or other responses.

We need, however, to go beyond the issue of definitions of terrorism in order to fully understand the motivations of lone wolf terrorists. Why exactly do lone wolves do the things they do? Is it for the same reasons that terrorist groups and cells perpetrate their violence, or are there some unique characteristics that propel the individual terrorist into action? Addressing this issue is an important part of understanding the lone wolf phenomenon.

CHAPTER 2

WHO ARE THE LONE WOLVES?

Trying to understand what makes terrorists tick has perplexed academics, policymakers, and the public for centuries. The once-popular notion that terrorists must be irrational because they kill innocent people has long been discarded as political, religious, territorial, and other objectives have been linked to various terrorist activities. For those terrorists with consciences, the French anarchist Émile Henry's proclamation in 1894 that "there are no innocent bourgeois"[1] created the template that helps soothe the pangs of guilt that terrorsts of any ideological stripe might feel as a result of the deaths of children and other "innocents." The only justification, however, that most terrorists have needed throughout history for their violence was a belief that the ends justified the means. If those ends were winning a homeland or an autonomous region, then even if innocent civilians were killed, that was the price that had to be paid for the "cause." The same was true if the objective was the overthrow of a government, a global revolution, or any other cause.

Lone wolves, however, usually do not even have to consider whether the ends justify the means. Since they are beholden to nobody but themselves, they alone can determine the course of action they will take. While some, like many terrorist groups, will make rational decisions based on the costs and benefits of various attacks, others will simply act without much thought being given to the consequences. But, like all terrorists, lone wolves have to decide whether the tactics and targets they choose will achieve their objectives. Understanding those tactics, targets, and objectives can help unlock some of the mysteries concerning who the lone wolves really are.

LONE WOLF TACTICS, TARGETS, MOTIVATIONS, AND OBJECTIVES

Throughout the history of terrorism, there have been a surprisingly small number of different tactics employed by terrorists, whether they are lone wolves or members of a terrorist organization. Just ten basic tactics have characterized terrorist behavior over time: bombings, hijackings, assassinations, kidnappings, armed assaults (machine-gun, rocket, or other violent attacks against people or buildings), barricade-hostage incidents (seizures of embassies or other government or business structures), product contamination, release of chemical or biological agents, cyberterrorism, and suicide attacks. The latter category often overlaps with several of the other types of tactics, such as bombings and armed assaults, in which the perpetrator willingly dies in the attack. And there can be, of course, combinations of tactics, such as the hijacking-suicide attacks of September 11, 2001, in New York City; Washington, DC; and Shanksville, Pennsylvania.

While lone wolves can do many of the same things that terrorist groups do, such as hijack an airplane, assassinate a government leader, or shoot up a gathering of people, there are some operations that are better suited for larger groups or cells. For example, a kidnapping usually requires several people to abduct the targeted individual, transport him or her to a safe house, keep guard, and so forth. And lone wolves obviously cannot commit simultaneous attacks, unless they use timing devices and place bombs in several locations. They can, however, commit dual attacks where there is a short time period between incidents. This occurred in Norway in July 2011 when Anders Breivik set off a bomb in Oslo and then two hours later massacred youths at a political summer camp. Lone wolves, for the most part, have at their disposal the same array of tactics that other terrorists have.

The targets of lone wolves are also not that significantly different from those of terrorist groups or cells. Lone wolves have attacked government, business, military, and civilian targets, and they have conducted both indiscriminate and selective killings. Among the indiscriminate murders by lone wolves were those of Timothy McVeigh, who was responsible for the 1995 bombing of the federal building in Oklahoma City that killed 168 people, including several children. Among the more infamous selective attacks by lone wolves were those of Theodore Kaczynski, the Unabomber, who sent package bombs to specific individuals over a seventeen-year period.

It is when we look at motivations and objectives that we begin to see some of the discrepancies between terrorist groups and lone wolves. A terrorist organization is comprised of individuals who join the group for a variety of reasons, ranging from agreement with the group's overall objectives, such as the overthrow of a government or attaining a separate state or territory, to personal needs, such as the desire to belong to a group, rebellion against authority figures, revenge, and so forth. But once in the group, these individuals have to conform to the group's overall objectives. Otherwise, there could be dissension and potential compromise of a mission. As one observer noted, al Qaeda members "pledge their personal loyalty to [Osama] bin Laden, thus declaring their membership in the family of global jihad and willingness to sacrifice their lives for the goal as defined by the group's leader. This personal declaration of loyalty obligated organization members to carry out bin Laden's orders with strict obedience."[2] It can be assumed that Ayman al-Zawahri, who took over the leadership of al Qaeda in the aftermath of bin Laden's killing in May 2011, will try to become the new focal point for pledges of loyalty by members of the group, although al Qaeda has become a more decentralized organization in recent years.

The lone wolf, however, doesn't have to make any pledges to a leader or make his or her desires align with that of a group. While lone wolves often perpetrate their violence for political, religious, ethnic-nationalist, and other "traditional" terrorist-group objectives, some of them also have a personal, psychological, criminal, or idio-syncratic motive for their violence. According to noted terrorism scholar Jessica Stern, "Lone wolves often come up with their own ideologies that combine personal vendettas with religious or polit-ical grievances."[3] Because lone wolves have their own agendas, they sometimes tend to be perceived as too dangerous and unstable for membership in a terrorist or similar type of group. Once rejected, the lone wolves can be motivated to take action by themselves. For example, McVeigh began plotting the bombing of the federal building in Oklahoma City after a Michigan militia group distanced itself from him because, according to the FBI, "it became apparent that his views were too radical."[4]

We have to be careful, however, in explaining lone wolf behavior as being driven by personal or psychological needs for which the lone wolf then simply attaches an ideology to justify his or her actions. That detracts from the dedication that many lone wolves have to the cause they adopt. Until we have data on the motivations of *all* members of every terrorist group, we cannot say with certainty that some members of a terrorist group do not have similar personal and psychological factors that are part of their motivations for violence.

In fact, some leaders of terrorist groups have been portrayed as having similar personalities to those of lone wolf terrorists. In an article published shortly after the September 11, 2001, suicide attacks in the United States, a noted political scientist, Ehud Sprinzak, wrote about certain terrorists being "self-anointed individuals with larger-than-life callings." Sprinzak labeled these individuals "megaloma-niacal hyperterrorists" and included a lone wolf such as Timothy McVeigh in the category. But Sprinzak also put in this category Osama bin Laden (the leader of al Qaeda), Ramzi Yousef (the mastermind of the 1993 bombing of the World Trade Center), and Shoko Asahara (the leader of the Aum Shinrikyo cult and key figure in the 1995 sarin nerve gas attack in the Tokyo subway system). "Megalomaniacal hyperterrorists operate according to an altogether different logic," Sprinzak wrote.[5] "While often working with the support of large terror groups and organizations, they tend to be loners. They think big, seeking to go beyond 'conventional' terrorism and, unlike most terrorists, could be willing to use weapons of mass destruction. They perceive themselves in historical terms and dream of individually devastating the hated system." Sprinzak also placed Yigal Amir, a young Israeli man who assassinated Prime Minister Yitzhak Rabin in November 1995, in the "megalomaniacal hyperterrorist" category, since, even though he was not involved in mass-casualty terrorism, "the impact of his act on the Israeli people could not have been more catastrophic." Sprinzak notes that Amir, who was a right-wing loner, believed that "God wanted him to personally save the nation."[6]

The role of the lone wolf as an assassin has, of course, been well documented.[7] The list of lone wolf assassins, both those who succeeded in killing their target(s) and those who did not, is long, with motivations ranging from political, religious, and ethnic-nationalist causes to personal and pathological reasons.[8]

THE FIVE BASIC CATEGORIES OF LONE WOLF TERRORISM

In order to better understand who the lone wolves are and what makes them tick, it would be useful to design a simple typology that can account for the basic differences among lone wolves as well as for the differences between lone wolves and terrorist organizations. Any categorization scheme is, of course, open to debate. One may not agree with the choice of categories, their definitions, or the placement of various lone wolves into specific categories. But a typology can nevertheless help organize and clarify our thoughts and assumptions regarding lone wolf behavior.

There are five basic types of lone wolf terrorists. Three of these categories are similar to the categories for terrorist organizations, while two are unique to lone wolves. The first type is the secular lone wolf who, like secular terrorist groups, is committing violent attacks for political, ethnic-nationalist, or separatist causes. This is the most diverse category of lone wolf terrorism, since it covers a wide range of issues, such as terrorism related to protests against government policies or attacks due to desires for a homeland, separate state, and so forth. While secular lone wolves may have personality and psychological issues that affect their decision to commit terrorist attacks (just like members of a terrorist group could have personality and psychological issues that led them to join the group in the first place), their main motivation is the same as that of secular terrorist organizations—namely, to further a political or ethnic-nationalist cause. Secular lone wolves can also use the Internet to learn about various secular extremist movements and subsequently become committed to their ideologies and objectives.

The second type of lone wolf terrorist is the religious lone wolf. Just like a terrorist group, this type of individual perpetrates terrorist attacks in the name of some religion, whether Islam, Christianity, Judaism, or another religious belief system. Islamic extremists and white supremacists have been among the most active religious lone wolves in recent years. White supremacists and neo-Nazis can be classified as religious terrorists because many are adherents to, or are at least influenced by, the Christian Identity movement and use its racist and anti-Semitic ideology as a religious justification for their violence.[9] Just like secular lone wolves, religious lone wolves can also find inspiration for their violence on the Internet, through various chat rooms, websites, and Facebook pages of religious extremist movements.

The third type of lone wolf terrorist is the single-issue lone wolf, who perpetrates attacks in the name of specific issues, such as abortion, animal rights, or the environment. These lone wolves also resemble their counterparts in single-issue terrorist groups. In fact, the Earth Liberation Front (ELF) and Animal Liberation Front (ALF) are basically loose affiliations of individual militants without leaders or formal organizational structures. One of the FBI's most wanted terrorists is an individual with ties to animal rights extremist groups. Daniel Andreas is wanted for involvement in the 2003 bombings of two office buildings in northern California.

While secular, religious, and single-issue lone wolves have, in many ways, the same objectives and motivations as their counterparts who are members of terrorist organizations, the fourth type of lone wolf is more unique. The criminal lone wolf is motivated mainly by the desire for financial gain. While some terrorist groups may also have money in mind when they commit a particular attack, their main motivation is not financial. The secular or religious (or on rare occasions, the single-issue) terrorist group that kidnaps or takes hostage an individual for ransom is still driven by the ultimate goal of a change in government policy, a revolution, a separate state, and so forth. Not so for the criminal lone wolf, who has no political, social, religious, or ethnic-nationalist goal in mind. As noted earlier (and in the appendix), I consider acts of violence committed by criminals to be terrorism when the tactics used and the effects upon government and society are the same as if the act(s) had been committed by a "terrorist."

The fifth type of lone wolf terrorist is the idiosyncratic lone wolf. This category of lone wolves is also unique, since, with the exception of cults that commit terrorist acts, there are really no idiosyncratic terrorist groups in operation. Although the idiosyncratic lone wolf may commit attacks in the name of some cause, it is the severe personality and psychological problems that mainly drive these individuals to violence. Their causes are usually irrational, and they are often diagnosed as paranoid schizophrenics.

As with any typology, there is some overlap among the categories described above. For example, special-interest lone wolves such as antiabortion militants have a religious theme connected to their violence (i.e., the belief that human life begins at conception), while animal rights and environmental terrorists have a left-wing, antibusiness, and antigovernment theme attached to their attacks. White supremacists and neo-Nazis, while placed in the religious category above due to their adherence to the Christian Identity movement, tend to hold extreme right-wing, antigovernment views. But even though the category boundaries are not ironclad, a typology can still be useful for providing insight into the lone wolf phenomenon. Further insight can be gained by examining in detail some of the more intriguing cases of secular, religious, single-issue, criminal, and idiosyncratic lone wolf terrorism.

SECULAR LONE WOLVES: TIMOTHY McVEIGH AND ANDERS BREIVIK

One individual perpetrated an act of terrorism that claimed more lives than any other terrorist event on US soil, with the exception of the September 11, 2001, al Qaeda attacks. The fact that he was a homegrown terrorist surprised and shocked most people. Another homegrown terrorist committed the worst mass shooting in Norway's history. Both cases illustrate the impact that a secular, antigovernment extremist can have upon a nation.

Timothy McVeigh

For most Americans, the first image of Timothy McVeigh on television and in newspapers was shocking. Clad in an orange prison-issue jumpsuit as he was taken into federal custody two days after the April 19, 1995, bombing of the Alfred P. Murrah Federal Building in Oklahoma City that killed 168 people, including fifteen children, people saw an all-American boy with a crew cut. This was not the portrait of a terrorist most Americans had come to expect. With the 1993 World Trade Center bombing still fresh in the public's memory, Islamic extremists were the poster boys for terrorism, not clean-cut American youths. Yet McVeigh demonstrated how a secular lone wolf with fervent antigovernment sentiments could inflict horrific damage upon a community and, by extension, the country as a whole.

On the morning of April 19, McVeigh parked a rental truck packed with almost five thousand pounds of explosives in front of the federal building and then left the scene before the bomb exploded. He had some help from Terry Nichols, who assisted McVeigh in mixing a deadly combination of ammonium-nitrate fertilizer, diesel fuel, and other explosives used in the bombing. Nichols was convicted of his crime in December 1997 and later sentenced to life in prison without the possibility of parole, while McVeigh was found guilty in June 1997 and executed for his crime in June 2001.

The Oklahoma City bombing caused more casualties than any other act of terrorism in the United States until the 9/11 attacks. It led to a focus on right-wing militias as the new terrorist threat in the country, since McVeigh (and Nichols) had attended meetings of a militia group in Michigan. McVeigh was upset with the 1993 government raid on the Branch Davidian cult's compound in Waco, Texas, in which more than eighty cult members died when the compound burst into flames during the raid, which took place after a fifty-one-day standoff. Federal authorities had claimed that the cult members possessed large numbers of illegal weapons. The Oklahoma City bombing occurred on the second anniversary of the government's raid.

For McVeigh, like others who belonged to or were sympathetic to the militia movement, the raid symbolized the government's intent to confiscate all citizens' weapons, thereby abrogating the Second Amendment's guarantee of the right of all citizens to keep and bear arms. "Waco started this war, hopefully Oklahoma would end it," McVeigh said in an interview in prison. "The only way they're going to feel something, the only way they're going to get the message is quote, with a body count."[10] McVeigh further explained his kinship with the victims of the Waco raid: "You feel a bond with this community. The bond is that they're fellow gun owners and believe in gun rights and survivalists and freedom lovers."[11] McVeigh's sister recalled his anger over Waco as they watched a documentary together about the government raid on the compound. "He was very angry," Jennifer McVeigh testified during her brother's trial. "I think he thought the government murdered the people there, basically gassed and burned them." She also said that McVeigh felt that "somebody should be held accountable" for the deaths of the people inside the compound.[12]

Two other events contributed to McVeigh's path to becoming a terrorist. One was the 1992 government siege at white separatist Randy Weaver's cabin in Ruby Ridge, Idaho. Weaver had failed to appear in court on weapons charges, and when FBI agents came to arrest him, an eleven-day siege ensued. Weaver's wife and son and a deputy marshal were killed before Weaver and an associate surrendered. McVeigh, like many others in the militia movement, felt that the government had been intrusive and used excessive force. "What the U.S. government did at Waco and Ruby Ridge was dirty," McVeigh said. "And I gave dirty back to them in Oklahoma City."[13] McVeigh's experience as a solider in Iraq during the Persian Gulf War in 1991 also shaped his fervent antigovernment feelings. He believed that the US government made him kill innocent people. "My overall experience in the Gulf War taught me that these people were just that—they were people, human beings. Then I had to reconcile that with the fact that I killed them."[14]

McVeigh had originally considered other targets, including assassinating elected officials, but chose to bomb the federal building instead because a bombing would have a better visual impact for the television cameras. There would also be several federal agents inside the building.[15] The fact that he originally considered assassination as a tactic reveals that, at one point in his planning for a terrorist operation, large numbers of casualties were not necessarily a prime objective. He even claimed that he did not know there was a daycare center inside the building, and had he known, "it might have given me pause to switch targets. That's a large amount of collateral damage."[16] That assertion, however, was dismissed by the lead FBI investigator, Danny Defenbaugh, who said there was enough evidence just by glancing at the building from the outside that there was a daycare center inside, including "little [paper] cut-out hands, all the little apples and flowers showing that there's a kindergarten there, that there are children in that building."[17]

The Oklahoma City bombing had a profound effect on the United States. Americans discovered that homegrown terrorists could be just as lethal as those who come from foreign shores. McVeigh had single-handedly changed the perception of the terrorist threat in this country away from Islamic militants and toward right-wing, antigovernment extremists. The bombing led to renewed efforts to combat terrorism in the United States, including heightened security measures across the country, the creation of a Domestic Counterterrorism Center headed by the FBI, and the hiring of a thousand new federal officials by the administration of President Bill Clinton to deal with terrorism. McVeigh demonstrated how a lone wolf extremist could be as deadly and effective as larger terrorist groups. Until the 9/11 attacks occurred more than six years later, Oklahoma City remained the tragic symbol of America's vulnerability to terrorism. As McVeigh said, "The truth is, I blew up the Murrah Building. And isn't it kind of scary that one man could reap this kind of hell?"[18]

Anders Breivik

The same could be said for Anders Breivik, a thirty-two-year-old Norwegian man, who, in a couple of hours of violence, put his country through a "kind of hell" people there never imagined could happen. Norway, for the most part, had been spared the endless terrorism that for decades plagued many other countries around the world. Between 1970 and 2010, there were only fifteen terrorist attacks in Norway, with only one person killed and thirteen wounded in those incidents.[19] Yet on July 22, 2011, Breivik launched a twin terrorist assault that resulted in seventy-seven deaths and changed his country forever. "I think what we have seen," said Prime Minister Jens Stoltenberg, "is that there is going to be one Norway before and one Norway after July 22."[20]

After setting off a car bomb that killed eight people in Oslo near government offices (including the prime minister's), Breivik traveled by boat to Utoya Island, approximately twenty miles to the northwest, where a summer camp attended by the youth wing of the ruling Labor Party was in its third day. Wearing a policeman's uniform,

Breivik told camp officials he was there to protect the campers, who had already heard the news about the Oslo bombing. Breivik then walked to the area where the campers' tents were located and began shooting whoever he could find. Some of the campers fled to the shore and jumped into the water in an attempt to swim away, but Breivik began shooting them, too. At one point during the massacre, four campers ran toward Breivik, thinking he was a real policeman who could protect them from the gunman on the island. Breivik shot all four dead. When Norwegian police finally arrived—they were delayed for more than an hour due to several problems, including a stalled engine on the first boat they tried to use to reach the island— Breivik surrendered. He had killed sixty-nine people, mostly youths, during the rampage.[21]

Breivik was not in the Norwegian police's database of right-wing extremists.[22] "He just came out of nowhere," a police official said after the carnage was over.[23] Indeed, one of the advantages lone wolves have over terrorist groups is that they are often not on anybody's radar, as they quietly plot their attacks with minimal or no communication with others. Breivik was, however, put on a Norwegian security-service watch list in March 2011, after buying large amounts of ammonium nitrate fertilizer from an online store in Poland. The fertilizer was used to construct the car bomb that Breivik set off in Oslo. He was soon taken off the list because Norwegian authorities decided that the purchases were for use on a farm that Breivik had rented.[24] Breivik was careful not to raise any alarm bells as he planned his attacks. Janne Kristianse, the director of the Norwegian Police Security Service, said that Breivik "had been extremely law-abiding" and that there were "no warning lights" that he was a terrorist. "He has also deliberately failed to be violent in statements online, not been a part of any extremist network and had registered guns, but was a member of a gun club," the director said.[25]

Breivik, though, advocated violence in passages he wrote in a fifteen-hundred-page manifesto that he posted online shortly before the attacks. "Once you decide to strike," he wrote, "it is better to kill too many than not enough, or you risk reducing the desired ideological impact of the strike."[26] Breivik called for an end to "the Islamic colonisation and Islamisation of Western Europe" and the "rise of cultural Marxism/multiculturalism," blaming Norwegian politicians for allowing that to happen.[27] The Labor Party had long been in favor of immigration.[28] More than 12 percent of Norway's population of five million consists of immigrants or children of immigrants, with half coming from Asia, Africa, or Latin America.[29] Breivik wrote the following chilling warning in the manifesto:

> We, the free indigenous peoples of Europe, hereby declare a pre-emptive war on all cultural Marxism/multiculturalist elites of Western Europe. . . . We know who you are, where you live and we are coming for you. We are in the process of flagging every single multiculturalist traitor in Western Europe. You will be punished for your treasonous acts.[30]

Breivik's path to violence does not appear to stem from his upbringing. Although his parents divorced when he was one year old and he eventually became estranged from his father, he wrote that he had a happy childhood. He attended an elite high school, where he joined the youth wing of the Progressive Party, which had an anti-immigration platform. He soon became angered by reports that immigrant gangs were attacking ethnic Norwegians. He was also incensed by the NATO bombing of Serbia in 1999, which he perceived as an attack on Christians for the sake of Muslims.[31]

Although Breivik was described after the attacks by some observers as a religious extremist—the *New York Times* carried a headline portraying Breivik as a "Christian extremist"[32]—he fits more into the category of a secular lone wolf terrorist than a religious one. He attacked symbols of the ruling Labor Party—government offices and a government-run youth camp—during his rampage, rather than mosques or other Muslim targets. He even tried to spare one person, whom he thought was not a leftist, when he began his shooting rampage at the camp. "Certain people look more leftist than others,"

Breivik said during his trial in April 2012. "This person . . . appeared right-wing, that was his appearance. That's the reason I didn't fire any shots at him."[33] In his manifesto, which he said took three years to complete, Breivik warned against targeting Muslims, since it would likely elicit sympathy for them.[34] He also wrote, "As for the Church and science, it is essential that science takes an undisputed precedence over biblical teachings."[35] Religious extremists, whether Christian, Muslim, or Jewish, are likely to view their religion's holy books as the guiding force in their lives.

Breivik wrote that the attacks, which were several years in the making, were aimed at drawing global attention to his manifesto. He certainly accomplished that, for soon after the attacks, the manifesto, titled "2083: A European Declaration of Independence," was studied, assessed, and debated by scholars, journalists, policymakers, pundits, and many others throughout the world. It led to accusations that Breivik had been influenced by some of the anti-Islamic blogs and other Internet materials that were prevalent in the United States and Europe. In his manifesto, Breivik quoted Robert Spencer numerous times. Spencer runs a "jihad watch" website. Breivik also cited other Western writers who argued that Muslim immigration posed a threat to Western culture.[36] Furthermore, Breivik included, without citing them, several passages from the manifesto of Theodore Kaczynski, the Unabomber. Breivik substituted the words "multiculturalists" or "cultural Marxists" for Kaczynski's diatribe against "leftists" and others.[37]

In addition to igniting a debate over the effects that anti-Islamic writings on the Internet may have had on Breivik, there was also criticism lodged against some right-wing politicians in Europe who had advocated anti-Islamic and anti-immigration policies in inflammatory speeches.[38] One view held that "a trend toward xenophobia and nationalism in the region had fostered the attacks in Norway."[39] The right-wing, antigovernment nature of Breivik's attacks drew comparisons to Timothy McVeigh's bombing of the federal building in Oklahoma City. In both cases, the prevailing terrorism threat before the attacks was seen as emanating from Islamic extremists and not from right-wing, homegrown terrorists. A Norwegian Police Security Service report released in early 2011 stated that "the far-right and far-left extremist communities will not represent a serious threat to Norwegian society."[40] That it wasn't a far-right or far-left "community" that wreaked havoc on Norway, but rather an individual extremist, illustrates the dangers of lone wolf terrorism. Although Breivik tried to portray himself as being part of a larger movement, warning that there were other cells planning future attacks throughout Europe, authorities were not able to uncover any evidence to support those claims.

A panel of five judges at Oslo's district court declared Breivik sane and therefore legally responsible for the murder of seventy-seven people in August 2012.[41] The verdict most likely pleased Breivik "who had hoped to avoid what he called the humilaiton of being dismissed as a madman."[42] He was sentenced to twenty-one years in prison, the maximum term allowed under Norwegian law. He will probably, however, spend the rest of his life in prison, since the sentence could be extended, potentially indefinitely, if he is still considered dangerous to society.[43]

Anders Breivik is clearly an angry young man who, according to his manifesto, began thinking as early as 2002 about taking action to defend the "free indigenous peoples of Europe."[44] As one observer noted: "For at least nine years he carried anger towards the changes occurring in Norwegian society. He did not accept the multicultural country that was emerging. It threatened his identity and he felt alienated from it."[45] Rather than channel that anger and alienation into nonviolent actions, Breivik chose to lash back in one of the worst lone wolf attacks in history. Nobody saw it coming, which is what many lone wolf terrorists count on.

RELIGIOUS LONE WOLVES: NIDAL MALIK HASAN AND JAMES von BRUNN

Anger and alienation can also be found among some of the religious lone wolves. Two cases illustrate the lengths to which an individual will go when he or she is convinced that the policies and actions of governments and societies are contrary to his or her religious beliefs. In both cases, the lone wolf intended to kill as many people as possible in a mass shooting. That one of the cases involved an Islamic extremist while the other involved a white supremacist illustrates the diversity that is to be found in the belief systems of religious lone wolf terrorists.

Nidal Malik Hasan

The threat of religious extremist violence has been at the forefront since the 9/11 attacks. While the concern has primarily been with al Qaeda and other Islamic extremist groups, religious lone wolf terrorists have also made their presence known. There was enough concern about potential religious lone wolf attacks in the aftermath of the May 2011 killing of Osama bin Laden that the FBI and Department of Homeland Security issued threat advisories to law-enforcement agencies throughout the United States to be on the alert for retaliatory lone wolf attacks.[46] There was good reason for that concern. Less than two years earlier (as noted in chapter 1), a US Army major, who was partly influenced via the Internet by an Islamic extremist cleric living overseas, opened fire at Fort Hood in Texas, killing thirteen people and injuring thirty-two others in the worst terrorist attack ever to take place at a US domestic military installation. The case of Maj. Nidal Malik Hasan is revealing for how life experiences, technology, and government policies can converge to create a religious lone wolf terrorist.

Early in the afternoon on November 5, 2009, Hasan entered the Soldier Readiness Processing Center at Fort Hood, where soldiers obtain medical checkups before being deployed or after returning from overseas. After shouting "God is great" in Arabic, Hasan began shooting at random before he was wounded by return fire and taken into custody. Hasan did not expect to survive the attack, as he had given away all of his possessions to a neighbor before he embarked upon his mission. Hasan, who was scheduled to be court-martialed in 2012, faced the death penalty if convicted.

Hasan's path to becoming a terrorist was an unusual one. The son of Palestinian immigrants from a small town near Jerusalem, Hasan was born and grew up in Virginia. His parents became American citizens and ran businesses in Virginia, including restaurants and a store. Hasan was patriotic and joined the army after graduating college. His parents objected, but he told them, "I was born and raised here. I'm going to do my duty to the country."[47] In that sense, he didn't fit the profile of some of the Islamic extremists in Britain and other European countries, who were the children of immigrants but found discrimination and unhappy lives as they grew up in their parents' new country. For Hasan, the discrimination would come later, after 9/11, when he claimed that he faced hostility within the military because he was a Muslim.[48]

While in the army, Hasan attended medical school at the Uniformed Services University of Health Sciences in Bethesda, Maryland. Upon graduation in 2003, he did his internship and residency in psychiatry at Walter Reed Army Medical Center in Washington, DC. Hasan raised eyebrows at Walter Reed when, instead of delivering a presentation on a medical topic as part of the final requirement of his residency, he spoke on the topic, "The Koranic World View as It Relates to Muslims in the U.S. Military." Among his comments were: "It's getting harder and harder for Muslims in the service to morally justify being in a military that seems constantly engaged against fellow Muslims."[49] He continued making controversial statements after he arrived at Fort Hood, where he told his supervisor that, as an infidel, she would be "ripped to shreds" and "burn in hell."[50]

Both at Fort Hood and at Walter Reed, Hasan treated soldiers who were returning from the wars in Iraq and Afghanistan with post-traumatic stress disorder and other psychological problems. Hasan was reportedly anxious himself about possibly being deployed to a war zone. He expressed his opposition to the wars in Iraq and Afghanistan to colleagues and others and made no secret of his support for Islamic extremists. A US Senate investigation report on the Fort Hood shooting stated the following:

> Evidence of Hasan's radicalization to violent Islamist extremism was on full display to his superiors and colleagues during his military medical training. An instructor and a colleague each referred to Hasan as a "ticking time bomb." Not only was no action taken to discipline or discharge him, but also his Officer Evaluation Reports sanitized his obsession with violent Islamist extremism into praiseworthy research on counterterrorism.[51]

Hasan's journey toward radicalization was aided by numerous e-mails he exchanged with Anwar al-Awlaki, a radical American-born Islamic cleric who was living in Yemen. Al-Awlaki was a leading figure of a Yemen-based branch of al Qaeda (al Qaeda in the Arabian Peninsula) and had been linked to Umar Farouk Abdulmutallab, who attempted to blow up a plane over Detroit, Michigan, in December 2009. He had also been connected to Faisal Shahzad, who attempted to set off a car bomb in Times Square in May 2010. (Al-Awlaki was killed in a US drone attack in Yemen in 2011). In one of the e-mails Hasan exchanged with al-Awlaki, Hasan asked al-Awlaki when jihad is appropriate and whether it is permissible if there are innocents killed in a suicide attack. Al-Awlaki had also been Hasan's spiritual leader at a mosque in the United States before al-Awlaki fled to Yemen. After the Fort Hood massacre, al-Awlaki stated that he may have influenced Hasan's radicalization and praised Hasan, referring to him as a "hero" who "did the right thing" in killing the soldiers.[52]

While some lone wolves cannot be stopped before they act because they fly under the radar and their intentions are not known to others, this was clearly not the case with Hasan. There were enough prior indications that he was committed to Islamic extremist ideology. As the US Senate investigation report noted, one of the lessons of the Fort Hood shootings was the need for the military "to identify radicalization [among soldiers] to violent Islamist extremism and to distinguish this ideology from the peaceful practice of Islam."[53]

James von Brunn

Another religious lone wolf for whom there were plenty of signs of potential violent behavior was James von Brunn. He holds the dubious record for being one of the oldest terrorists in history. At the age of eighty-eight, he walked into the lobby of the US Holocaust Memorial Museum in Washington, DC, on June 10, 2009, with a rifle by his side, intending to kill as many people as possible. However, after fatally shooting the security guard who opened the door for him, Von Brunn was wounded in return fire from other guards. Von Brunn had planned to die in his assault, having finalized his funeral plans and put his finances in order for relatives. He survived, though, and was indicted by a federal grand jury on charges of first-degree murder, committing a hate crime, and gun violations. Before he could stand trial, however, he died in January 2010 at a hospital near the federal prison in North Carolina where he was being held.[54]

Von Brunn can be considered a religious lone wolf because his terrorism was directed at a target associated with the Jewish religion and he had long espoused neo-Nazi and white-supremacist views. He symbolized the ideology of the Christian Identity movement, which is "a racist and anti-Semitic religious sect whose adherents believe that white people of European descent are the descendants of the 'Lost Tribes' of ancient Israel. . . . Despite its small size, Christian Identity influences virtually all white supremacist and extreme anti-government movements."[55] Von Brunn self-published a book titled *Kill the Best Gentiles!* Its main thesis is that Jews are on a mission of "destruction of all Gentile nations through miscegenation and wars." He viewed his book as "the racialist guide for the preservation and nature of the white gene pool."[56]

Two themes that Von Brunn continually discussed in his book, as well as in other essays and writings posted on his website, were that Jewish bankers controlled the Federal Reserve Board and that the Holocaust never occurred.[57] In addition to his terrorist attack on the Holocaust Memorial Museum, Von Brunn also attacked the

Federal Reserve Board headquarters years earlier in Washington, DC. In December 1981, Von Brunn walked into the building with a bag slung over his shoulders, telling the security guards he was a photographer who wanted to take pictures of the boardroom. When he was told to wait, he ran up the stairs to where the board was meeting. He was captured and found to be carrying a pistol, a shotgun, a knife, and a mock bomb. He told police that he wanted to take board members hostage to garner media attention regarding the board's responsibility for high interest rates and the country's economic problems. He was convicted in 1983 and served six and a half years in prison on attempted kidnapping, second-degree burglary, assault, and weapons charges.[58]

Despite the fact that he had a criminal record and was posting anti-Semitic and racist writings for years on the Internet, Von Brunn was still able to double-park his car outside the Holocaust Memorial Museum on the day of the shooting and walk up undetected to the entrance while carrying a rifle. Perhaps it was because he was an aging white supremacist that the authorities did not regard him as a high risk to commit a violent act. There were plenty of signs, though, that Von Brunn would one day strike again. In 2004, he wrote to an Australian Holocaust denial website that it was "time to FLUSH all 'Holocaust' Memorials."[59] He also foreshadowed his attack on the museum in e-mails he sent to John de Nugent, another white supremacist. After the shootings, de Nugent stated that, in the weeks before the attack, Von Brunn "had been sending a lot of e-mails with violent content."[60] According to de Nugent, Von Brunn was depressed over having his monthly Social Security check cut in half and blamed it on somebody in the federal government reading his website and punishing him for his views.[61]

That Von Brunn went many years between attacks demonstrates the patience some lone wolves possess in plotting their operations. A terrorist group would have had to continue to attack or risk losing support among its members and those in the community who sympathize with the cause. Failure to launch continual attacks would also portray an image of the terrorist group as losing in its battle against its perceived enemies. Lone wolves do not have those concerns. Time is on their side, as the Von Brunn case illustrates. It is likely that, during the long period between his attacks, Von Brunn took comfort with the thought that he was contributing to the cause with his white supremacist postings on the Internet. But, in the end, even for a man in his eighties, that was not enough. The lure of going out in a blaze of glory with a major terrorist attack in the nation's capital was too much for Von Brunn to resist.

SINGLE-ISSUE LONE WOLVES: ERIC RUDOLPH AND VOLKERT van der GRAAF

Abortion, animal rights, and the environment have long been specific issues motivating both groups and individuals to violence. These types of extremists are consumed with their particular issue and are not trying to bring about widespread political change or revolution. Still, they can have a significant impact on government and society with their actions. In one case, a lone wolf opposed to abortion set off a bomb during the 1996 Olympics Games in the United States and raised fears concerning a new wave of domestic terrorism. That he was also able to elude capture for many years made him a folk hero to some people. In the other case, a lone wolf committed a political assassination in the Netherlands in the name of animal rights and touched a nerve in a country not used to such events.

Eric Rudolph

Every two years, when the Summer or Winter Olympic Games approach, the media and government officials raise the specter of an increased terrorist threat. This is understandable, since terrorists like to strike high-profile targets and garner maximum media exposure. The fear of terrorism during the Olympics is also fueled by the fact that, during the 1972 Summer Games in Munich, Palestinian terrorists took Israeli athletes hostage, resulting in what became known as the "Munich Massacre." The terrorists killed the hostages as German police launched a failed hostage rescue mission.

The irony, however, is that the Olympics are usually the safest place to be in terms of being protected against a terrorist attack. When authorities can put in place a tremendous amount of security around a specific area (i.e., the Olympic venues) for a limited amount of time, such as the approximately two weeks it takes to stage the Olympics, it deters most terrorists from attempting an attack. The reason that terrorists were able to perpetrate one during the 1972 Games was because it caught everybody by surprise. It was the first time there had been a terrorist incident at the Olympics. There was very little security at the 1972 Games, with the terrorists only having to climb over a fence to get into the Olympic Village. Since then, with one exception, all subsequent Olympics have been devoid of terrorist attacks.

That one exception occurred at the 1996 Summer Olympic Games in Atlanta, Georgia. Eric Rudolph, an antiabortion militant, decided that the Olympics would be the perfect place to violently protest his opposition to abortion. He set off a bomb during a rock concert in Centennial Olympic Park, which didn't have as much security as the Olympic sports events. The bomb killed one person and injured more than a hundred others. A Turkish cameraman also died from a heart attack as he ran to cover the incident. Rudolph would eventually explain his motivation for the bombing in a statement he made after pleading guilty to that attack as well as to three other attacks in subsequent years. The goal was "to confound, anger and embarrass the Washington government in the eyes of the world for its abominable sanctioning of abortion on demand."[62]

Rudolph had originally intended to sabotage the power grid in Atlanta and thus force the cancellation of the Games or "at least create a state of insecurity to empty the streets around the venues and thereby eat into the vast amounts of money invested."[63] He abandoned that plan when he could not acquire the necessary high explosives to do the job. Instead, he set off a pipe bomb hidden in a knapsack he placed near the concert stage. An alert security guard, Richard Jewel, noticed the unattended knapsack and began clearing people away. He was later falsely accused of placing the bomb himself at the concert in order to be a hero. The July 27, 1996, terrorist attack at the Olympics, coming just a little more than one year after the Oklahoma City bombing, raised new fears about domestic terrorism in the United States.

Rudolph continued his violent campaign over the next two years, with bombings at an abortion clinic in an Atlanta suburb in January 1997 that injured six people; a bombing at a gay nightclub in Atlanta one month later, in which five people were wounded; and a third bombing, at an abortion clinic in Birmingham, Alabama, in January 1998, which killed one person and injured another. Rudolph planted second bombs at both the gay nightclub and the Atlanta suburb abortion clinic, set to go off after police and emergency-services personnel had arrived at the scene in response to the first explosions. Police discovered the second bomb at the gay nightclub and defused it, but the second bomb at the suburban Atlanta abortion clinic went off, injuring several people, including police officers. Rudolph later explained his motives for targeting law enforcement and emergency-services personnel:

> Because this government is committed to the policy of maintaining the policy of abortion and protecting it, the agents of this government are the agents of mass murder, whether knowingly or unknowingly. And whether these agents of the government are armed or otherwise they are legitimate targets in the war to end this holocaust, especially those agents who carry arms in defense of this regime and the enforcement of its laws. This is the reason and the only reason for the targeting of so-called law enforcement personnel.[64]

It was after the Birmingham bombing that Rudolph took to the woods of North Carolina to hide from the authorities, having learned that his truck had been seen near the explosion site and that it had been traced to him. Despite a massive manhunt by the FBI and other law-enforcement agencies, Rudolph was able to avoid capture for more than five years. He most likely learned survivalist skills while serving with the US Army's 101st Airborne Division in the late 1980s. His ability to survive in the woods and thumb his nose at the authorities for so long gained him a folk-hero status among some people in Murphy, North Carolina, his last residence before he went on the run. T-shirts appeared that exclaimed, "Run, Rudolph, Run," and "Eric Rudolph—Hide and Seek Champion of the World."[65] Rudolph was finally arrested in May 2003 after a rookie policeman on routine patrol spotted him behind a grocery store around four o'clock in the morning. Thinking that a burglary was in progress, the policeman arrested Rudolph, who gave the officer a false name. Another officer, however, later recognized him to be Rudolph.[66]

In April 2005, Rudolph pled guilty to the Olympic bombing and the three other bombings in order to avoid the death penalty. He was eventually sentenced to multiple consecutive life sentences without the possibility of parole. As part of his plea agreement, Rudolph provided authorities with the location of more than 250 pounds of dynamite that he had buried in the North Carolina woods. FBI and other federal agents recovered the explosives at three different sites and destroyed them. In the statement released at his plea-bargain hearing, Rudolph explained his motivation for the bombing of the gay nightclub in Atlanta:

> Along with abortion, another assault upon the integrity of American society is the concerted effort to legitimize the practice of homosexuality. . . . Practiced by consenting adults within the confines of their own private lives, homosexuality is not a threat to society. . . . But when the attempt is made to drag this practice out of the closet and into the public square . . . every effort should be made, including force if necessary, to halt this effort.[67]

Yet it was the abortion issue more than anything else that drove Rudolph to violence. He made it clear that his terrorism against the government was not part of any sweeping ideological motivation. "I am not an anarchist," he said. "I have nothing against government or law enforcement in general. It is solely for the reason that this government has legalized the murder of children that I have no allegiance to nor do I recognize the legitimacy of this particular government in Washington."[68] At his sentencing hearing in August 2005, Rudolph expressed remorse only for the bombing at the Olympics. "I cannot begin to truly understand the pain that I have inflicted upon these innocent people," Rudolph said. "I would do anything to take back that night."[69] He did not apologize for the bombings of the abortion clinics and gay nightclub.

Rudolph also denied that he was part of the Christian Identity movement. He issued a postscript to his plea-bargain statement in protest of the book *Hunting Eric Rudolph*, which claims that he was indeed a Christian Identity supporter.[70] In the postscript, Rudolph wrote, "I would like to clear up some misconceptions about me which are based upon the false information, innuendos and lies disseminated by some unscrupulous individuals." Rudolph claimed that "I am not now nor have I ever been an Identity believing Christian. I was born a Catholic, and with forgiveness I hope to die one." He admitted to attending an Identity church for approximately six months in the early 1980s but claimed that was because the father of a woman he was dating went there. "While attending this church," Rudolph wrote, "I never bought into the convoluted Identity argument of racial determinism."[71]

Eric Rudolph therefore felt the need to once again convince everyone that he was a true lone wolf extremist, devoted to a single issue and not part of any other movement or ideology. He expressed some ambivalence, however, about resorting to violence in his fight against abortion in a letter that he sent to his mother while in prison. After telling her that perhaps he "should have found a peaceful outlet" for what he wanted to accomplish, he still voiced a rationale expressed by those terrorists who later in life may have doubts about what they did. "However wrongheaded my tactical decision to resort to violence may have been," he wrote, "morally speaking my actions were justified."[72]

Volkert van der Graaf

On May 6, 2002, animal rights activist Volkert van der Graaf walked past Pim Fortuyn, a controversial politician and potential prime ministerial candidate, and shot him five times from behind in the parking lot of the Dutch National Broadcasting Center as Fortuyn was leaving a radio interview. The assassination represented the first political murder in the Netherlands since it became a kingdom in 1813.[73] For a country that felt immune to the terrorist assassinations common in many parts of the world, the Fortuyn killing sent shockwaves throughout the nation. "Things like this don't happen in Holland," said one resident of an Amsterdam suburb. "It's like the 11th of September for us. Everybody thought this couldn't be, but we see that it is possible. I feel very insecure."[74] Dutch prime minister Wim Kok said that the political assassination was "deeply tragic for our democracy"[75] and that "a dark shadow has fallen over the Netherlands that has given way to deep emotions."[76] Belgian prime minister Guy Verhofstadt said he believed something like this was "impossible in this day and age, in the European Union, in the 21st Century."[77]

The shooting came just nine days before national elections in which Fortuyn's party, List Pim Fortuyn (LPF), was expected to do well. Despite the assassination, the elections were still held as scheduled, with LPF winning 17 percent of the vote and thereby becoming the second-largest party in parliament. A coalition government of LPF, Liberals, and Christian Democrats was formed, but it collapsed just six months later. By the next elections, the LPF had lost most of its support and was no longer a force in Dutch politics. Fortuyn had been a lightning rod for controversy with his anti-environmental, anti-immigrant, and anti-Islamic views. He had stated that he was in favor of legalizing mink farming, complained about "the problems of multicultural society," and called Islam a "backward religion."[78] Fortuyn also told an environmental group, "The whole environmental policy in the Netherlands has no substance any more. And I'm sick to death of your environmental movement."[79]

Comments like those did not sit well with Van der Graaf. A lifelong advocate for animal rights, he had fought most of his battles in the courtroom. In 1992, he cofounded the Association Environmental Offensive (VMO) with a friend. The organization, through the court system, systematically challenged permits that had been awarded to fur and cattle farmers. Their goal was to force those businesses to shut down.[80] Also, Van der Graaf believed it was his duty to stand up for animal rights. "People think it normal that you eat animals and that you let fish suffocate in nets when you catch them," he once wrote. "But inside me arose a sense of justice—such things shouldn't be happening in a civilized country, I thought, but there is no one to stand up for them."[81]

Prior to the event, Van der Graaf did not let anyone know about his intention to kill Fortuyn. The assassination, however, did not surprise people who knew him. "In my opinion, Volkert devoted all his time in doing stuff for VMO and animals," one of his friends said. "His life was all about that. Whenever a person like Fortuyn comes along and says fur animals can be bred again, I can imagine Volkert losing his temper. Volkert is a rational person, who thinks always carefully over the purpose of his actions and consequences."[82]

As his friend suggested, Van der Graaf meticulously planned his attack on Fortuyn. On May 5, 2002, he searched the Internet for information on Fortuyn's daily schedule. When he learned that the politician would be having a radio interview the next day at the 3FM building at the Media Park in Hilversum, a town thirty kilometers southeast of Amsterdam, he decided that would be a good opportunity to implement his plan. He went there with a map of Media Park and the 3FM building that he obtained from the Internet and waited until Fortuyn exited the building. He claimed he did want to injure anybody else, so that is why he decided to shoot Fortuyn from behind:

I had figured out that if I would approach Fortuyn from the front, he might be able to see the attack coming. Shooting Fortuyn from behind would be least problematic. In that case he would not be able to duck away, which could cause danger for the others present at the scene. Next to that, I did not wanted [*sic*] Fortuyn to suffer more than necessary. Shooting from behind would make it possible to deadly wound him immediately.[83]

After the shooting, Van der Graaf ran from the scene but was captured a short time later. He did not talk about his motives for several months. He then claimed in a confession that he killed Fortuyn in order to stand up for the "weaker and vulnerable members" of Dutch society. He compared Fortuyn's rise in politics to that of Adolph Hitler and stated that he killed him as a favor to the Muslim minority in the Netherlands as well as other vulnerable segments of society.[84] He described Fortuyn as a dangerous man "who abused democracy by picking on vulnerable groups" and who had terrible ideas "about immigrants, asylum seekers, Muslims, animals, and the environment."[85]

With the exception of animal rights, and to some extent the environment, Van der Graaf's friends and relatives were shocked at his claiming his actions were done in the name of all the other causes that he mentioned above. They did not remember him as being politically engaged in those issues.[86] Under Dutch law, even though Van der Graaf confessed to the murder, prosecutors still had to prove their case in court. In April 2003, Van der Graaf was convicted and sentenced to eighteen years in prison. He told the court that he regretted the killing and that he still "wrestled" with the question of whether he was right in murdering Fortuyn. "Every day I see it before me. I see myself shoot and Fortuyn fall," he said in court.[87]

The Fortuyn assassination was a watershed in the Dutch experience with terrorism. As noted above, it sent shockwaves throughout the country. Several spontaneous shrines were created in the days after the shooting, with thousands of people leaving messages and thousands more paying their respects.[88] It was not only the fact that a political assassination had taken place that shocked the Netherlands, a country with a nonviolent and pacifist heritage, but that a powerful new voice in Dutch politics had been silenced. Although he was controversial, Fortuyn and his party had challenged the establishment and won many supporters. He "represented a political voice in which a substantial, but regularly ignored, part of the lower and middle classes of the nation heard their views and feelings reflected."[89]

The assassination also led to an investigation concerning whether the government was negligent in not protecting Fortuyn, since he was a controversial figure who had received many death threats in the past. An independent commission concluded that, while the assassination of Fortuyn was "a serious attack on the democratic constitutional state,"[90] the government could not be blamed for his murder. The commission emphasized that, even with protection, the complete safety of a politician cannot be guaranteed. As one government official noted, with the lone wolf assassination of Fortuyn, "the Netherlands had lost its innocence."[91]

CRIMINAL LONE WOLVES: JOHN GILBERT GRAHAM AND PANOS KOUPPARIS

A unique category of lone wolves consists of those who perpetrate their violence for purely personal or financial gain. I discuss in the appendix why I believe these types of individuals should be considered terrorists; even though their motives are different from those extremists with political, religious, or ethnic-nationalist objectives, the impact of their actions upon society and government can be just as profound as that of more-traditional terrorists. Two cases illustrate this point. One involves an individual who carried out the first major midair plane bombing in US history in order to collect an insurance policy. The other deals with an individual working with a few family members in order to extort millions of dollars from the government of Cyprus.

John Gilbert Graham

Acting the role of a loving, devoted son, twenty-three-year-old John Gilbert Graham drove his mother to Stapleton Airport in Denver on November 1, 1955, carried her luggage inside the terminal, and kissed her good-bye before she departed on her United Airlines flight to Portland. From there she planned to continue on to Anchorage to visit her daughter. Daisie King must have thought that all was well with her son, who had previously been in trouble with the law. What she didn't know was that hidden in one of her suitcases were twenty-five sticks of dynamite, a timer, two dynamite caps, and a dry-cell battery.

Graham waited at an airport coffee shop until he heard word that the plane had crashed shortly after takeoff. He later telephoned the airline's office to find out if his mother was killed in the crash. When a sympathetic airline official informed him that it was very likely she was among the forty-four dead, Graham simply replied, "Well, that's the way it goes." His motive for the bombing was greed: a $37,500 insurance policy on his mother's life that he bought from an airport vending machine shortly before she boarded the plane. He was also in line to share in his mother's $150,000 estate. What he collected, however, was execution in the gas chamber at the Colorado State Penitentiary a little more than two years later.[92]

Since this was the first major midair plane bombing in the United States, the FBI had no prior experience in investigating such acts of terrorism. It was, therefore, a pathbreaking effort on their part in reconstructing the aircraft to determine that explosives were the cause of the crash. Their investigation set standards for future scientific analyses of airplane bombings. The investigation of the Denver crash marked the first time that residues from parts of a plane were examined in a scientific manner to determine the exact cause of an explosion. Parts of the wreckage were sent to the FBI laboratory in Washington, DC, for analysis, where it was discovered that sodium carbonate was on some of the parts of the aircraft. That led the FBI to conclude that the plane was brought down by a dynamite explosion.[93]

Meanwhile, in Denver, FBI agents studied the passenger list to see if there was anybody on board the doomed plane who might have been the target of a murder plot by someone who knew how to use explosives. Extensive background checks on all the passengers and their relatives led the FBI to Graham, who had a prior arrest record for forgery and knew how to use explosives, having worked for construction and logging companies that used dynamite. The insurance policy was another piece of the puzzle that led the authorities to Graham, who confessed but later recanted his confession. Ironically, even if Graham had never been caught, he might not have been able to cash the insurance policy because his mother never countersigned it.

Graham was arrested in November 1955, convicted of first-degree murder, and sentenced to death in May 1956. He was executed in January 1957. His execution occurred under Colorado law, since there was no federal law to cover his offense at that time. The bombing led Congress to pass a bill in 1956 that established the death penalty for anyone convicted of causing loss of life by damaging an airplane, bus, or commercial vehicle. An existing statute covered the sabotage of trains.[94]

The Graham bombing shocked the nation, including President Dwight Eisenhower, who was outraged by this new form of violence, along with most Americans. The bombing also led the FBI and the Civil Aviation Administration to conduct studies on measures that might be taken to detect explosives in luggage. However, sophisticated technology was not yet available to aid in designing effective and speedy airport security systems. As one observer noted shortly after the bombing, "The rigmarole involved in merely running the detector over every suitcase and hat box going aboard a plane would make present baggage routine, a frequent annoyance, seem like the essence of convenience. So, if the airlines continue current policy, the suitcase with the bomb inside is unlikely to be detected."[95]

The United States had never before experienced an incident like the Graham bombing—a midair plane bombing over Chesterton, Indiana, in 1933 (see note 4 from the introduction) did not receive the media exposure or reaction across the country that the Graham bombing did. People were perplexed not only by the fact that individuals were capable of blowing up planes in midair, but also by the fact that the person responsible was motivated by the desire to kill his mother for money. An editorial in a local newspaper best captured the bewilderment of people over Graham's crime:

> In Denver County Jail sits the greatest criminal enigma in Denver history and possibly the greatest in the reprehensible annals of American crime. . . . What kind of mind could grind out in minute and exacting detail the steps that John Gilbert Graham's mind did in piecing together his horrendous jigsaw of death. . . . What kind of heart could block out those compelling and instinctive bonds that exist between mother and son? . . . [And] what kind of a being could block out entirely 43 other lives in plotting for greed or hatred or convenience the death of one other person? . . . There seems to be no logical explanation.[96]

There was, however, a logical explanation. It was rooted in a troubled young man's personality and behavior, which gave plenty of warning signs that he was capable of this horrendous deed. Graham, who showed no remorse throughout his trial, had fought many times with his mother, despite her continual efforts to help him out of bad situations. He was convicted in November 1951 on forgery charges, having stolen several blank checks from a manufacturing firm he worked for as a payroll clerk the previous March. He signed the name of the company's owner on the checks and cashed them for $4,200. He bought a late-model convertible with the money and left Denver.

Graham was arrested the following September in Lubbock, Texas, on a different charge—bootlegging—after he tried to run a roadblock and was shot at by the police, who found a gun in Graham's car. He served a sixty-day sentence in the county jail and was then released to Denver authorities. He received a suspended sentence for the check-forgery charges and was placed on probation for a period of five years. His mother paid $2,500 toward restitution on the $4,200 in forged checks, with Graham paying the rest in monthly installments of $40 per month. He regularly made those payments and had only $105 left to pay at the time of the plane bombing.[97]

Graham's mother also helped her son by hiring him to be the manager of a drive-in restaurant she owned in Denver. She was reported to be "downright proud" of him and how he had gotten his life together since his forgery conviction.[98] However, Graham's probation report described her as someone who "appears to be a type that has over-protected her son."[99] She either turned a blind eye to his transgressions or just simply wouldn't believe her son meant to do anything wrong. This despite the fact that, when Graham confessed to the FBI regarding the plane bombing, he also admitted both to causing an explosion at the drive-in restaurant and to leaving his car on a railroad track and allowing it to be hit by an oncoming train in order to collect insurance on the car. His half sister reported that Graham had a violent temper and that, on one occasion, he knocked her down and kneed her in the chest. On another occasion, he hit her with a hammer. She also told the FBI that she and her mother had once witnessed him strike his wife for no apparent reason, scaring his mother, who was afraid her son might also hit her.[100]

Graham didn't seem too concerned about tipping his plans concerning the bombing of the plane his mother would be on. A credit manger testified at his trial that Graham once told him he had observed the way luggage was handled at Denver's Stapleton Airport and that it would be easy for someone to place a bomb on a plane.[101] After his arrest, psychiatrists who met with him were curious as to his feelings about being responsible for the deaths of forty-four people, including his mother. He stated that he "realized that there were about 50 or 60 people carried on a DCB [DC-6B plane]." But, he continued, "the number of people to be killed made no difference to me; it could have been a thousand. When their time comes, there is nothing they can do about it."[102]

With the Graham bombing, America was introduced to a form of terrorism that unfortunately would become all too familiar in subsequent decades. Increased security measures would gradually be introduced at airports as the public came to understand the need for metal detectors, x-rays, and other measures designed to ensure its safety. No longer would the public only fear the possibility of an accidental plane crash. Now they had to also fear midair plane bombings. A wayward youth with a troubled past had ushered America into a new age of terrorism.

Panos Koupparis

One of the more unusual terrorist threats in recent history took place in Cyprus in March 1987, when a thirteen-page letter was sent to the president, Spiros Kiprianou. The letter was signed by a man calling himself "Commander Nemo of Force Majerus."[103] Commander Nemo was actually Panos Koupparis, a thirty-six-year-old British citizen of Cypriot origin. He threatened to disperse dioxin, a toxic chemical, over the Troodos Mountains south of Nicosia unless he was paid $15 million.

Koupparis claimed that the dioxin would be released by radio-controlled devices already in place and would be carried by wind over populated areas. He argued that Cyprus would not have the medical facilities and resources to deal with the human casualties of a dioxin attack. He further pointed out that the economy of Cyprus was dependent on agriculture and therefore could not afford the damage that would be caused by the release of the dioxin. He even suggested that the government try an experiment. He told them to burn a large number of tires and watch as the black smoke drifted across populated areas. He warned them that a dioxin attack would be a thousand times worse.

In his letter, Koupparis also cited the disaster at Seveso, Italy, to emphasize the danger of a dioxin attack. An explosion at a chemical factory in Seveso in 1976 caused dioxin to escape. Several people near the plant suffered burns and sores on their skin, and large numbers of people complained of nervousness, fatigue, and loss of appetite. Many animals were killed, and Italian authorities were forced to slaughter more than eighty thousand domestic animals as a protective measure. He also mentioned the explosion at a chemical factory in Bhopal, India, in 1984 and the nuclear reactor disaster at Chernobyl in the former Soviet Union in 1986. Koupparis warned that his attack would be much worse, since Cyprus is a small island.

Because the letter was written in fluent English, Cypriot officials suspected it originated in London. (Cyprus gained independence from Britain in 1960.) The blackmail letter was extremely detailed, including data on the ingredients Koupparis claimed he used to make the dioxin. The threat was taken seriously by the Cypriot government, which consulted with British scientists. The British scientists analyzed the blackmail letter and concluded that Koupparis could not make dioxin from the ingredients he listed. However, the letter was couched in enough scientific jargon that the scientists had to spend some time analyzing its contents before dismissing the threat.

Koupparis continued to contact the government of Cyprus after his initial letter and was finally apprehended by Scotland Yard detectives when he went to the Cyprus High Commission office in London, posing as the "scientific advisor" to Commander Nemo, to collect a passport and some money. Also arrested in London were his wife and two brothers, one of whom was a chemistry student at London's Polytechnic Institute. (Koupparis's sister-in-law was arrested in Cyprus but ordered released by a judge for lack of evidence.) According to police, weapons were found in Koupparis's Cyprus apartment (he had been staying in Cyprus after setting up an offshore company there) along with documents showing that he had planned a series of bombings on the island to convince the government that his dioxin threat was real.

Due to the potential for panic among the Cypriot public, the entire matter was kept secret until after the arrests in London. The incident led to a political crisis for the Cypriot government. The public reaction to the dioxin hoax was one of fear and concern about weapons of mass destruction. The government was criticized by some people for keeping the whole affair secret when lives were potentially at stake, while others criticized it for taking the hoax too seriously. The government defended its actions, stating through a spokesman that "the content of the threat and the nature of the blackmail were such that it would be an act of lack of responsibility for the Government and the police to underestimate the affair, the more so that first assessments by British experts spoke of a realizable threat if the blackmailers had the necessary means."[104] The government and police also stated that steps had been taken to protect lives in case the threat was real but did not disclose what those steps were.

Koupparis was found guilty in July 1989 and sentenced to five years in prison. The dioxin hoax was a very clever scheme by an individual criminal who, working with just a few family members, was able to hatch a plan that caused two governments to consult in secrecy and bring in top-level scientists to assess the threat. It also led to a crisis for the Cypriot government in explaining its handling of the affair. Had the scientific data been more credible and Koupparis's intentions more believable, the crisis could have been much worse for the government. Public revelations by Koupparis before he was caught, through communications to newspapers or radio and television stations, might well have caused great alarm and panic in Cyprus. Even though his motive was purely financial gain, the effect of his actions was the same as if he had threatened to release dioxin in order to protest a government policy or further a religious or political cause. The Koupparis case, along with the Graham case, clearly demonstrates why we can't ignore the terrorist threat of criminal lone wolves simply because they don't fit the traditional definitions of who a terrorist is.

IDIOSYNCRATIC LONE WOLVES: THEODORE KACZYNSKI AND MUHAREM KURBEGOVIC

Another type of lone wolf for whom political or religious objectives are not the driving force for their violence is the idiosyncratic lone wolf. As noted earlier, while these individuals may adopt some cause as the raison d'être for their terrorist attacks, it is really their severe personality and psychological issues that explain their actions. The causes they adopt are also far-fetched and usually irrational. One of the more infamous cases of an idiosyncratic lone wolf involved an individual who became known as the "Unabomber." This man avoided identification and capture for over seventeen years as he sent package bombs to various individuals throughout the United States. Another case involves an individual who became known as the "Alphabet Bomber." This man terrorized a community with an airport bombing and threats to unleash nerve gas over populated areas.

Theodore Kaczynski

For a long period of time, Americans lived in fear of packages they received in the mail. They were warned by the United States Postal Service (USPS) and the FBI to be on the lookout for packages sent to them from people or businesses they were not familiar with and packages that had excessive postage, handwritten addresses, and/or oily stains on the outside. New regulations were issued requiring people to bring packages weighing more than thirteen ounces and bearing only postage stamps to a post office employee rather than dropping them off in a mailbox. All this was due to a terror campaign waged by a brilliant yet eccentric and mentally ill individual who just never quite fit into society.

Theodore Kaczynski had a promising career as a mathematics professor at the University of California at Berkeley in the late 1960s, when he abruptly resigned from his position for no apparent reason. He eventually moved to Montana, where he lived the life of a recluse. He began his campaign of violence in May 1978, when he left a package in a parking lot at the University of Illinois in Chicago with a return address from Northwestern University in Evanston. The package was taken to Northwestern, where it exploded when it was opened, injuring a security guard. Over the course of the next seventeen years, Kaczynski perpetrated several more bombings. He was responsible for a total of sixteen bombings, which together resulted in the deaths of three people and injuries to twenty-three others. Kaczynski either sent his victims a package bomb through the USPS or left the package bomb at the scene of the attack.

The violence occurred in all regions of the country. In one incident in 1979, a bomb exploded in a 727 jetliner's cargo hold during an American Airlines flight, forcing an emergency landing at Dulles International Airport near Washington, DC. Nobody was killed in that attack, although several people suffered smoke inhalation. In another incident, Kaczynski sent a package bomb to an advertising executive in 1994, killing the man as he opened the package. And in a letter he sent to a newspaper one week before the Fourth of July holiday in 1995, Kaczynski threatened to place a bomb on an airliner flying out of Los Angeles International Airport. Although the airline bomb turned out to be a hoax, it nevertheless increased public anxiety over terrorism; disrupted the USPS, as a temporary ban was placed on all airmail packages sent from California weighing more than twelve ounces; forced authorities to increase security measures at California airports, which in turn led to major delays for travelers; and even caused the Secretary of Transportation, Frederico Pena, to fly to Los Angeles to explain how the government intended to handle the crisis.[105]

Kaczynski was the target of one of the largest and most frustrating FBI manhunts in history. The FBI gave the code name "Unabomb" to its investigation (which eventually became popularly known in the media as "Unabomber"), since Kaczynski's early targets were primarily people associated with universities and airlines ("UN" for universities, "A" for airlines). Over the course of seventeen years, the FBI task force assigned to the Unabomber case acquired 3,600 volumes of information, 175 computer databases, 82 million records, 12,000 event documents, and 9,000 evidence photographs.[106] Yet no matter how hard FBI investigators tried, they could not capture the Unabomber or even discover his true identity for nearly two decades.

Kaczynski demonstrated the advantage that lone wolves have in eluding the authorities. As noted earlier, since these individuals work alone and do not communicate with others regarding plans and operations, intelligence and law-enforcement agencies have little to go on when trying to capture this type of terrorist. In the case of the Unabomber, all the authorities had in terms of a physical description of Kaczynski was a composite sketch made in 1987 by a forensic artist, which was based on a witness's description of a man she saw place a bomb behind a computer store in Salt Lake City. Kaczynski was wearing a hooded sweatshirt and sunglasses. He looked like many other people, and despite publicly distributing the sketch, the FBI did not receive any worthwhile leads.

But in the end, it was Kaczynski's need to communicate and be heard that led to his capture. He threatened to continue to send package bombs to people unless the *New York Times* or the *Washington Post* published a thirty-five-thousand-word manifesto that he sent to them (as well as to *Penthouse* magazine) in June 1995. The manifesto called for a revolution against the industrial-technological society. This was not the first time a terrorist had demanded a manifesto be published in a newspaper. Croatian extremists made similar demands during a 1976 hijacking, and their manifesto was indeed published in several newspapers.[107] The *Washington Post*—with the *New York Times* sharing the printing costs—published the Unabomber's manifesto in September 1995. Kaczynski's brother, David, later discovered writings by Kaczynski that resembled the published manifesto, and he contacted the FBI, leading to Kaczynski's arrest at his remote Montana cabin in April 1996.[108] Kaczynski pled guilty in January 1998 and received a sentence a few months later of life in prison without the possibility of parole.

Kaczynski's manifesto revealed a political viewpoint that had elements of anarchism and Luddism. He wrote that the "Industrial Revolution and its consequences have been a disaster for the human race" and that "in order to get our message before the public with some chance of making a lasting impression, we had to kill people." He claimed that the industrial-technological society "cannot be reformed in such a way as to prevent it from progressively narrowing the sphere of human freedom." He also criticized "leftism" as "anti-individualistic" and "pro-collectivist" and praised anarchy, which he argued would allow people "to control the circumstances of their own lives."[109]

It is in the psychiatric evaluation of Kaczynski to determine if he was competent to stand trial that we get insight into how he became a lone wolf terrorist. Based on interviews with Kaczynski and a review of his journals, an unpublished autobiography, and other writings and letters, the court-appointed psychiatrist, Dr. Sally Johnson, diagnosed him as a provisional paranoid schizophrenic. She qualified her diagnosis due to the limited number of sessions she had with Kaczynski. Nevertheless, she found that he was preoccupied with two delusional beliefs. One was that he was controlled by modern technology. The other was that his inability to establish a relationship with a female was the result of extreme psychological verbal abuse by his parents. Johnson wrote in her report that Kaczynski "is resentful and angry, and fantasizes and actually does resort to violence against those individuals and organizations that he believes are hurting him."[110] Kaczynski was mistrustful of other children when he was growing up, and in high school, he was an outsider. "By the time I left high school," he stated, "I was definitely regarded as a freak by a large segment of the student body." He also told Johnson that he built a small pipe bomb in chemistry class that gained him some notoriety and attention.[111] Despite the diagnosis that Kaczynski was mentally ill, he was still deemed competent to stand trial, since he was able to understand the nature and consequences of the proceedings against him.

Kaczynski's terror campaign left emotional scars in addition to the physical pain he caused his victims and their families. Charles Epstein was a geneticist at the University of California at San Francisco when, on June 22, 1993, he opened a package that was sent to his home. The package exploded, and he lost several fingers and suffered permanent hearing loss. He went to court and witnessed Kaczynski plead guilty to his crimes. He told reporters that Kaczynski is "the personification of evil" and that, while he is glad the case is over, he does not expect to heal emotionally anytime soon. "There's never closure," he said. "I mean, every time I look at my hand [the effect of the bombing] is still there, every time I have to ask someone to speak up, it's still there." Epstein also addressed the issue of Kaczynski's mental illness. "I distinguish between being mentally ill and being evil," he said. "There are plenty of paranoid schizophrenics in the world who don't spend their time meticulously plotting to kill people, and then taking glee in the effects of what they have done."[112]

Idiosyncratic lone wolves like Kaczynski are particularly dangerous when they combine a high degree of intelligence, which allows them to design clever plots and strategies, with a total lack of guilt or remorse for their actions. As Johnson, the court-appointed psychiatrist, noted, Kaczynski "has demonstrated a reckless regard for the safety of others. He demonstrates a lack of remorse as indicated in his writings by being indifferent to having hurt, mistreated, or stolen from others."[113]

Muharem Kurbegovic

Another mentally ill yet highly functional lone wolf terrorist was Muharem Kurbegovic.[114] Known as the "Alphabet Bomber," Kurbegovic, who committed his criminal acts in the United States in the 1970s, can be considered a terrorist ahead of his time. He was one of the first to threaten to release nerve agents in populated areas, to acquire sodium cyanide, and to use the media in a systematic way to communicate his message and spread fear among the public. His actions received attention from the highest levels of government.

The violence began on August 6, 1974, when a bomb exploded in a locker at the overseas passenger terminal lobby of Pan American World Airways at Los Angeles International Airport. The eleven-pound bomb created a ten-by-fifteen-foot hole in a wall and devastated a hundred-foot area in the lobby, sending bodies, metal, glass, and debris flying through the air. The blast killed three people—two died at the scene and one later in a hospital—and injured thirty-five others, including one man who had to have his leg amputated. It was one of the deadliest incidents of random violence in Los Angeles history. Late that night, a man telephoned the city editor of the *Los Angeles Herald-Examiner* and claimed credit for the bombing. He correctly gave the publicly undisclosed locker number, T-225, where the bomb had exploded. He said that his name was Isaiak Rasim, "Chief Military Officer of Aliens of America," and that the bombing had been committed by this new terrorist group.

Rasim was actually Kurbegovic, who acted alone in the bombing. He telephoned the CBS television station in Los Angeles three days later and told them that a tape cassette about the bombing could be found in a trash bin outside a local bank. When police recovered the tape, they found with it the key to the airport locker that had contained the bomb. "This first bomb was marked with the letter 'A,' which stands for Airport," Kurbegovic said on the tape. "The second bomb will be associated with the letter 'L,' the third with the letter 'I,' etc., until our name has been written on the face of this nation in blood."[115] Kurbegovic had indeed stamped the words "Aliens of America" on the lip of the canister of the airport bomb.

Kurbegovic subsequently placed a bomb in a locker (letter "L") at a downtown Los Angeles Greyhound bus station but decided to alert police to its location. The bomb was safely defused. He indicated that he was pleased with the media coverage his acts and threats of violence were receiving, and that is why he decided not to detonate the bus-station bomb. "The letter 'L' in our name stands for 'locker,' and it also stands for 'life,'" Kurbegovic said on a tape he left with the *Herald-Examiner.* "We have decided because our cause is getting publicity that it is momentarily not necessary to continue to horrify the population of this land, and we can afford the luxury of revealing the location of such a bomb and let it stand for the word 'life!' Nothing could make us happier than if we could conclude that we can reveal the location of bomb 'I,' which is already planted."[116]

There was no "I" bomb, but Kurbegovic threatened to unleash

"two tons of sarin" nerve gas over Washington, DC. "Imagine what will happen if we are lucky and the wind blows from Supreme Court to Capitol Hill to White House to Pentagon," Kurbegovic stated in one of his communiqués. He also claimed that he had acquired the plans for the air-conditioning systems of thirty skyscrapers in Los Angeles and was researching ways to release chemical agents in those buildings. The fear of terrorism gripped Los Angeles, as people were afraid to venture outside due to the possibility of another bombing. Among the newspaper headlines were "L.A. Bomber Pledges Gas Attack" and "Race against Time to Find Third Bomb." A Watts Summer Festival concert at the Los Angeles Coliseum that was expected to attract seventy thousand people drew only thirty-five hundred.

Kurbegovic stated that he was committing his acts of violence to protest unfair treatment of immigrants and other various causes. Among his demands were that all immigration, naturalization, and sex laws be declared unconstitutional. Even before his bombing at Los Angeles International Airport, he had left a tape with the media, issuing an ultimatum to all governments of the world to surrender to "Aliens of America." He stated that his objective was to bring about a society free of nationalism, religion, fascism, racism, and communism. He also claimed in that tape to have sent to all the US Supreme Court justices postcards that had toxic material placed in metal disks underneath the stamps. Postal authorities intercepted the cards when they became caught in the canceling machine in a Palm Springs post office, but no toxic material was found in the metal disks.

The effort to catch Kurbegovic involved the US Secret Service and other federal law-enforcement agencies. During his campaign of violence in 1974 and his subsequent years in prison, Kurbegovic threatened the life of every US president. A special office in the basement of the White House was set up to aid in his capture. The CIA provided sophisticated audio equipment to analyze the cassette tapes, and linguists worked to identify Kurbegovic's accent, which was Yugoslavian. That information, combined with Kurbegovic's having mentioned in his tapes the names of several individuals against whom he had personal grudges, eventually led investigators to identify him as the Alphabet Bomber. Kurbegovic was finally arrested on August 20, 1974.

Kurbegovic, who had been born in Yugoslavia, was an engineer who developed an extensive knowledge of chemicals by reading books and other documents. He had been denied a permit to open a dance hall in Los Angeles because of a prior arrest, and he felt that the justice system was persecuting him and other immigrants. When police searched his apartment after his arrest, they found pipe bombs, explosive materials, books and manuals on germ and chemical warfare, gas masks, catalogues for purchasing chemicals and laboratory equipment, and maps of Washington, DC, and London's Heathrow Airport. In subsequent searches of his apartment, police found twenty-five pounds of sodium cyanide, which is a precursor chemical for the manufacture of the nerve agent tabun. It can also be used to generate toxic hydrogen cyanide gas. Interestingly, Kurbegovic learned about chemical warfare agents by checking out books from a public library and obtaining declassified government documents. What took him a few months of research in the 1970s to learn would probably take a person today only a few hours of searching the Internet.

Kurbegovic's trial did not begin until February 1980. The delay of more than five-and-a-half years from the time of his arrest resulted from legal questions concerning his mental competency to stand trial. Even though he was diagnosed as a paranoid schizophrenic, he was still ruled competent (like Theodore Kaczynski) to stand trial. He was found guilty eight months later of twenty-five counts of murder, arson, attempted murder, possession of explosive material, and exploding a bomb. He was sentenced to life in prison. Upon hearing the sentence, Kurbegovic complained to the judge that a life sentence was too vague. He asked her to change it to one thousand years in prison "so I can have something to look forward to."[117]

The Kurbegovic case illustrates how a disturbed but highly intelligent lone wolf can think up a variety of terrorist tactics and act upon them, since he is accountable only to himself. In one of his tapes, Kurbegovic stated, "We do not ask American people to support us; in fact, we don't give a damn whether they like what we have to offer or not."[118] He also didn't mind shocking people with his statements, as was evident in court when, acting as his own attorney, he asked a pastor who had lost his leg in the airport bombing, "So where was your God when this bomb went off?"[119] Kurbegovic also asked Judge Nancy Watson to declare him the Messiah. His behavior during the trial took its toll on Watson. "I really felt beaten down after a while," she recalled. "I mean it was just unending with him." She told Kurbegovic during the sentencing that she considered him to be "the most dangerous person in custody that I know of." She said that Kurbegovic had an "enormous capacity for feelings of vengeance and anti-social acts" and that he had intended to "kill as many people as he could" with his bombs.[120] Kurbegovic, though, had the last word, as he held up a sign while being led from the courtroom. The sign read, "I shall return!"

OBSERVATIONS FROM THE CASES EXAMINED

This brief analysis of ten cases of lone wolf terrorism reveals some interesting observations regarding the different types of lone wolves. First, there was little difference among the lone wolves in terms of the tactics they chose to use. Bombings were committed by secular (Timothy McVeigh), single-issue (Eric Rudolph), criminal (John Gilbert Graham), and idiosyncratic (Theodore Kaczynski and Muharem Kurbegovic) lone wolves; while shootings were chosen as the means of attack by religious (Nidal Malik Hasan and James von Brunn) and single-issue (Volkert van der Graaf) lone wolves. A secular lone wolf (Anders Breivik) committed both a bombing and a mass shooting, while a criminal lone wolf (Panos Koupparis) attempted an elaborate hoax in order to extort money from the Cypriot government.

There was some difference in terms of the targets chosen, with secular lone wolves (McVeigh and Breivik) attacking government buildings (with Breivik also attacking civilians, although the civilians were youths who were political activists for the ruling Norwegian government party), a religious lone wolf (Hasan) attacking military personnel, and another religious lone wolf (Von Brunn) attacking civilians at the Holocaust Memorial Museum. Civilian targets were also chosen by the criminal lone wolves (Graham and Koupparis; in the case of Koupparis, the threat was to harm the Cypriot population), the idiosyncratic lone wolves (Kaczynski and Kurbegovic), and a single-issue lone wolf (Rudolph), while the other single-issue lone wolf (Van der Graaf) chose a politician to attack.

All the lone wolves who were active in the first decade of the twenty-first century, when online activity was already pervasive throughout the world, used the Internet in various ways. This included Breivik (secular), Hasan and Von Brunn (religious), and Van der Graaf (single-issue). Criminal lone wolves Graham and Koupparis, as well as idiosyncratic lone wolf Kurbegovic, did not have the Internet available to them when they were committing their crimes. The Internet was in its early stages of development when McVeigh (secular), Rudolph (single-issue), and Kaczynski (idiosyncratic) were active.

The major differences, however, among the lone wolves discussed above can be seen in their motivations, level of creativity and innovation, and degree of guilt or remorse for their actions. Secular lone wolves McVeigh and Breivik were motivated in part by a hatred of government, and their violence was due to the desire to take revenge for a government raid at the Branch Davidian cult's compound in Waco, Texas, in the case of McVeigh, and for the Norwegian government allowing Muslim immigration into Norway, in the case of Breivik. (Related to that was Breivik's desire for an end to "multiculturalism" and the "Islamization" of Western Europe). Religious lone wolves Hasan and Von Brunn were motivated respectively by Islamic extremist views, in the case of Hasan, and neo-Nazi, white-supremacist ideology, in the case of Von Brunn. The single-issue lone wolves we examined perpetrated their violence in the name of specific issues, such as abortion, in the case of Rudolph, and animal rights, in the case of Van der Graaf. Criminal lone wolves Graham and Koupparis were motivated by financial gain, while idiosyncratic lone wolves Kaczynski and Kurbegovic had irrational objectives (an end to the industrial-technological society, in the case of Kaczynski, and an end to nationalism, religion, fascism, racism, and communism, in the case of Kurbegovic) that motivated their violence and were due to severe personality and psychological problems.

The lone wolves we examined also exhibited different levels of creativity and innovation in their terrorist attacks or threats. As noted earlier, lone wolves in general tend to be more creative than organized terrorist groups, since there is no group decision-making process that they have to go through in order to get approval for their plans. Therefore, they are free to think up any scenario they want and then implement it. However, in the cases examined above, it was the criminal and idiosyncratic lone wolves who proved to be the most innovative in their plans. Graham thought up and implemented the first major midair plane bombing in US history, while Koupparis designed an elaborate hoax involving a chemical agent. Kurbegovic was among the first terrorists to threaten to use nerve agents over populated areas and was also creative in using the media to gain publicity and reaction to his terror campaign, particularly in the use of the alphabet to spell out the name of his fictitious group. While Kaczynski's sending of package bombs was not unique (it had been done by terrorists in the past), he did demonstrate a level of creativity in handcrafting his bombs with wooden parts and in targeting a diverse array of individuals living in different parts of the United States. This prevented federal authorities from discerning a clear pattern that could lead to his arrest.

The lure of money in the cases of criminal lone wolves and the effect of severe psychological issues in the cases of idiosyncratic lone wolves apparently free these types of individuals to think up the most creative and innovative ways to meet their objectives, even more so than the other types of lone wolves. Two other cases of innovative terrorist attacks that were not discussed in detail above also involved idiosyncratic lone wolves. The first case of product tampering in the United States is suspected to be the work of a mentally ill individual who laced Tylenol capsules with cyanide in 1982, while the first case of successfully sending anthrax spores through the mail to kill people was the work of a mentally ill microbiologist.

There was also a difference among the lone wolves who did not die in their attacks regarding how they viewed their actions after they were arrested. Secular and single-issue lone wolves expressed some degree of guilt or "apology" for their violence, while the criminal and idiosyncratic lone wolves remained unapologetic. McVeigh claimed that he was not aware that there was a daycare center in the Alfred P. Murrah Federal Building in Oklahoma City and that, had he known, he might have chosen a different target. While Breivik did not feel remorse for his twin terror attacks in Norway, he did acknowledge to his lawyer that what he did was indeed "atrocious." Rudolph expressed remorse over the bombing at the 1996 Summer Olympics in Atlanta and even some doubts about the bombings of abortion clinics and other targets in a letter he sent to his mother while he was in prison. In court, Van der Graaf stated that he still "wrestled" with the question of whether he was justified in killing Dutch politician Pim Fortuyn.

There was no remorse, however, shown by Graham, the criminal lone wolf, after he was arrested for blowing up a plane carrying his mother and forty-three other people in order to cash an insurance policy. Likewise, Koupparis showed no remorse for his dioxin plot in Cyprus. Idiosyncratic lone wolves Kaczynski and Kurbegovic also never expressed any regrets for their violence. In terms of the religious lone wolf cases we examined, Hasan, as of November 2012, has yet to speak about the shootings at Fort Hood, while Von Brunn was killed in his attack at the Holocaust Memorial Museum. It is unlikely, however, that religious lone wolves would express any doubts or guilt over their actions, since that would make them question their religion or at least their interpretation of what their religion teaches them, which could be a very painful experience.

We have seen in this chapter how lone wolf terrorism is a diverse phenomenon that can have as much, and sometimes even more, impact on governments and societies than violence committed by larger and more organized terrorist groups. We now turn to a discussion of why lone wolves can be so dangerous and why they are prime candidates to use weapons of mass destruction.

CHAPTER 3

WHY LONE WOLVES ARE SO DANGEROUS

One of the unique characteristics that separates terrorism from all other types of conflicts is the ability of a single incident to throw an entire nation into crisis and create repercussions far beyond the original event. The taking of American hostages at the US embassy in Tehran in November 1979, for example, led to a more than fourteen-month-long crisis that virtually paralyzed the administration of President Jimmy Carter and may have led to his defeat in the 1980 presidential election. The September 11, 2001, hijacking-suicide attacks in the United States changed the course of US domestic and foreign policy for years afterward. For many Americans, it was the first time they seriously thought about the threat of terrorism. And the November 2008 terrorist attacks in Mumbai, India, led to deteriorating relations between India and Pakistan. India accused Pakistan of being involved in the shootings that left more than 160 people dead. Many other countries have also seen a terrorist incident affect government and society long after the event is over.

Yet for all the crises and repercussions that terrorism has caused in the past, the potential for a major, successful terrorist attack involving a weapon of mass destruction is the most troubling. The fatality level would likely be higher than any previous terrorist incident, with one estimate running as high as between one and three million people killed if there were an anthrax attack over Washington, DC.[1] Such an event would also create a medical, political, and social crisis unparalleled in our history. How real, then, are the prospects for such an attack, and how likely are lone wolves to be among the perpetrators?

TERRORISTS AND WEAPONS OF MASS DESTRUCTION

When I first began writing about the potential of terrorists using weapons of mass destruction (commonly referred to as "WMD") in the late 1980s,[2] there were two main criticisms leveled at anybody dealing with this topic. The first was that you might be giving new ideas to terrorists, who were busy at the time setting off car bombs, hijacking planes, kidnapping individuals, and doing other types of conventional terrorist attacks throughout the world. The assumption then was that terrorists did not know much about these weapons, so the less said or written about the subject, the better. The days of WMD terrorism being a taboo topic, however, are long gone. Today, there are countless books, articles, Internet websites, television commentaries, and government reports devoted to this issue.

The second criticism was that terrorists did not have the capabilities to effectively acquire and use WMDs, and, therefore, any publications that warned about the threat would needlessly alarm the public. That criticism can still be heard today. The example that is often pointed to is the failure of the Japanese cult Aum Shinrikyo to launch a successful WMD attack despite a multiyear research effort to acquire and use such weapons and virtually unlimited funds and personnel to support that effort. Their 1995 sarin nerve gas attack in the Tokyo subway did not cause maximum casualties (twelve people died), mainly because the cult had not manufactured a potent-enough batch of the nerve agent. Even if they had, the group still chose a poor delivery method to disperse the sarin; they simply left several punctured containers on the floor of the five subway trains they attacked. Aum also failed in its efforts to produce biological agents.[3]

The thinking is that if Aum could not perpetrate an effective attack with a weapon of mass destruction, then why should we worry about this threat? There are, however, plenty of reasons to worry. First, Aum's large size (approximately fifty thousand members) may have actually worked against the cult's efforts to launch a major, successful chemical or biological terrorist attack. Bureaucratic politics, factions, divisions in the group, and lack of focus and coordination all can add to the problems that large groups sometimes face in planning and implementing a terrorist operation. Furthermore, Aum's members were constantly striving to please their leader and guru, Shoko Asahara, and were basically on a "fishing expedition" to find the most effective weapon, including conventional weapons, for an attack.[4] The ineptitude shown in the cult's efforts to devise an effective delivery system for the sarin nerve gas indicates that the group had not researched thoroughly or correctly understood the dispersal method regarding chemical and biological agents.[5]

The technological revolutionary age that we are now living in, however, should aid future terrorists in overcoming the challenges in properly dispersing WMDs, including dealing with issues such as wind direction, sunlight, and temperature when releasing biological agents. As more information becomes available on the Internet and from other sources, we can expect to see more groups and individual terrorists experimenting with dispersal techniques. As analysts at Sandia National Laboratories point out, "The ever increasing technological sophistication of society continually lowers the barriers, resulting in a low but increasing probability of a high consequence bioterrorism event."[6]

Not all terrorists, though, would be interested in acquiring and using weapons of mass destruction. One of the major factors that could inhibit a group from using these weapons is concern that an attack would create a backlash among the organization's supporters. Many terrorist groups, such as the Provisional Irish Republican Army when it was active in Northern Ireland, depend upon the support—political, logistical, and financial—of significant segments of the population. While its "constituency" may not necessarily approve of the group's violent acts, they nevertheless support the group's political objectives. That support could be eroded if such a group were to use weapons of mass destruction. Supporters may condone certain killings as necessary to further the cause, but it is quite another thing to justify killing thousands of people.

It is not just the reaction from their supporters that would inhibit many terrorist groups from launching an attack with a weapon of mass destruction. There would also be concern that such an attack would unleash too strong a response from the government that is the target of the attack. While eliciting a repressive response that curtails civil liberties is sometimes the goal of terrorist groups, since such a response could turn the population against the government, a WMD attack would likely result in the enthusiastic support of the public to crush the group responsible by eliminating it through arrests and other acts.

Many terrorists might also be concerned about the personal risks involved in using WMDs. Terrorists tend to work with what they are familiar with. Conventional explosives, automatic weapons, and rocket-propelled grenades are among the weapons in the comfort zone of most terrorists. The fear of being infected with a biological agent or being exposed to radiation when working with a nuclear weapon could scare away many terrorists. Further, if the terrorists believe that conventional attacks, such as car bombings, hijackings, armed assaults, are meeting their objectives, there would be little incentive to launch a chemical, biological, or nuclear attack.

What type of terrorists, then, would be interested in using weapons of mass destruction? It would likely be those who exhibit the following characteristics: a general, undefined constituency whose possible reaction to a WMD attack does not concern the terrorists; a perception that conventional terrorist attacks (car bombings, hijackings, assassinations) are no longer effective and that a higher form of violence or a new technique is needed; and a willingness to take risks by experimenting with and using unfamiliar weapons.[7] Among the groups that could be described as meeting these criteria are doomsday religious or millenarian cults and neo-Nazi and white-supremacist groups.[8] These types of terrorist groups have amorphous constituencies whose concern about a public backlash is unlikely to deter the use of nuclear, chemical, or biological weapons. Furthermore, they are likely to view conventional terrorist tactics as insufficient for gaining the attention and reaction they seek. They might, therefore, be willing to experiment with unfamiliar weapons.

For example, among the reasons cited for Aum Shinrikyo's sarin attack on Tokyo's subway system was the goal of setting in motion a sequence of events that would eventually lead to Armageddon, a prediction that had been made by the cult's leader, Shoko Asahara. Another reported reason for the attack was to create a crisis in Japan that would preoccupy or topple the Japanese government and thereby prevent an anticipated raid by Japanese authorities on the cult's headquarters. Conventional weapons were likely viewed by the cult as inadequate to bring about either of these objectives. White supremacists and neo-Nazis have also been attracted to weapons of mass destruction, due to the potential of killing large numbers of people. In one incident, a white-supremacist group, known as The

Covenant, the Sword, and the Arm of the Lord, intended to poison the water supplies of major US cities in the mid-1980s with potassium chloride. When federal agents raided the group's compound in Arkansas, they discovered a large cache of weapons, including thirty gallons of potassium cyanide.[9]

Religious militants are also potential users of WMDs. If terrorists believe that acts of violence are not only politically but also morally justified, there is a powerful incentive for any type of attack. The belief that one is rewarded in the afterlife for violence perpetrated on earth encourages the undertaking of high-risk and high-casualty attacks. One of the biggest worries after the 9/11 attacks was whether al Qaeda was going to drop the other shoe with a major WMD attack. Although they did not, the group was certainly thinking about it. Documents and equipment discovered in Afghanistan in 2002 indicated that al Qaeda was considering the use of biological weapons and had constructed a laboratory near Kandahar in southern Afghanistan to develop anthrax.[10] In addition, al Qaeda was interested in nuclear weapons. A twenty-five-page essay titled "Superbomb" was discovered in 2002 in the Kabul home of Abu Khabab, a senior al Qaeda official. That document included information on different types of nuclear weapons, the properties of nuclear materials, and the physics and effects of nuclear explosions.[11]

Groups that have the sponsorship of a foreign government may also be potential candidates to use weapons of mass destruction. Due to such sponsorship, they could easily be provided with the necessary training, resources, and weapons, particularly in the case of chemical and biological agents. The risk, however, for any government supplying terrorists with these weapons is the possibility of the terrorists turning them against that government itself one day. State sponsors of terrorism also have to be convinced that any attack with a weapon of mass destruction by a group they are supporting cannot be traced back to that government. Otherwise, they may face a massive retaliatory strike by the country that was targeted.

Retaliation, of course, is not a concern for lone wolf terrorists. In fact, they have very little to worry about in terms of the reactions of government or society should they use a WMD. They have no supporters or financial and political backers who might be alienated by a WMD attack and no headquarters or training camps that could be hit in retaliatory raids. A lone wolf might also believe that committing a conventional terrorist attack similar to those occurring regularly around the world would not yield as much publicity and notoriety as an attack with a chemical, biological, or nuclear weapon.

One of the biggest reasons why lone wolves are likely to use a weapon of mass destruction is that these individuals have proven time after time that they can "think outside the box." They are not afraid to try new things. We have seen how a lone wolf, Mario Buda, committed the first vehicle bombing in the United States in 1920. Although not a WMD, Buda's vehicle bomb nevertheless demonstrated the creative nature of lone wolves, a characteristic necessary for those terrorists who might use WMDs. Buda had no idea if his plan would work; there had not been any standoff attacks like that attempted in the United States. The idea to put explosives in a horse-drawn wagon, park it near his targets on Wall Street, and then walk away after setting a timer was novel for those times. There had been an attempt in France in 1800 to assassinate First Consul Napoleon Bonaparte (before he became emperor) with a bomb that had been built into a barrel on a horse-drawn cart. That attempt failed, and the bomb exploded after Napoleon's carriage had passed the spot in the street where the horse and cart were parked. Approximately fifty-two people were either killed or injured in the blast. It is doubtful that Buda was aware of this novel use of a horse and cart for a terrorist attack, since it happened more than a hundred years before he sprang into action on Wall Street.[12]

THE STRANGE CASE OF DR. IVINS

Another example of a lone wolf thinking outside the box—and this time using a weapon of mass destruction—is the case of Bruce Ivins. Ivins was responsible for the 2001 anthrax letter attacks in the United States, which represented the first time anthrax was sent through the mail with the intent to infect people who opened the letters. His story is revealing for how dangerous lone wolves can be.

When the bestselling novel *The Hot Zone* was written by Richard Preston in the 1990s, it made famous a little-known military research facility located just an hour's drive from Washington, DC. The US Army Medical Research Institute of Infectious Diseases (USAMRIID), located at Fort Detrick in Frederick, Maryland, is the military's premier research laboratory for developing medical defenses against biological warfare threats. In 1989, USAMRIID personnel helped contain an outbreak of an Ebola virus among primates in a commercial laboratory animal-holding facility in Reston, Virginia. Had the virus spread to humans, it would have been a national medical catastrophe. Preston's book described the incident and rightly portrayed the USAMRIID scientists as national heroes.[13]

Ivins, however, who began working at USAMRIID in 1980, was definitely not a national hero. He was a very troubled man who turned his brilliant mind against his own country. His path to becoming the first person to successfully send "live" anthrax through the mail is one filled with obsession, revenge, fear, and mental illness.

When Ivins first came to USAMRIID in 1980, he was assigned to work on developing a new and more effective anthrax vaccine. This was a high priority for the US defense community, since, only one year earlier, there had been an accidental anthrax outbreak at a secret Soviet military microbiology plant in Sverdlovsk that killed at least sixty-six people. That incident proved that the Soviets were producing anthrax to be used as a biological weapon. Ivins, who had a doctorate in microbiology, thus began his lifelong research on anthrax. By the time of his death by suicide in 2008, Ivins had become one of the world's leading authorities on growing anthrax spores. He not only provided spores to his colleagues at USAMRIID for their own research, but many other anthrax researchers around the world also relied on his work.[14]

Ivins was a family man who volunteered at the local Red Cross and attended church regularly. He led what his friends called a "hippie mass" in church, playing keyboards and acoustic guitar. He was known as an eccentric, showing up for work in clothes that were a few sizes too small and working out at the gym in dark socks and heavy boots. When he became flustered over something, he would stammer and flap his arms, trying to make his point. His colleagues liked him, finding him to be both smart and generous.[15]

Ivins, however, hid a dark side from everyone. He was obsessed with the Kappa Kappa Gamma (KKG) sorority, driving three hours or more to visit KKG chapter houses on various campuses, look at the house for approximately ten minutes, and then drive home for another three hours. He broke into the houses on two occasions, once to steal the sorority's cipher, which was a decoding device for the sorority's secret rituals, and another time to steal the actual ritual book.[16] He also showed an excessive interest in a former University of North Carolina (where Ivins did postdoctoral work) graduate student when he learned that she had been an advisor to the sorority. He vandalized the property where she lived.[17] Later in the anthrax investigation, when FBI agents asked Ivins about his interest in KKG, he stated, "Oh, it's not an interest. It's an obsession."[18] What, then, could have caused Ivins to focus so much energy on the sorority and want to take revenge against it? All it took was a Kappa Kappa Gamma co-ed turning him down for a date when he was a student at the University of Cincinnati.[19]

Ivins did not have a happy childhood. He had a dominating mother who was physically abusive to his father. She struck her husband on different occasions with a broom, a skillet, and a fork.[20] Ivins felt that his family treated him as an "unwanted outsider" and that his father ignored him.[21] He was a loner as a teenager and had difficulty communicating with females.[22] Nevertheless, Ivins eventually married and raised a family. However, although he was a renowned microbiologist, he became very worried by the summer of 2001 that funding for his anthrax-vaccine research at Fort Detrick would be drastically cut or even eliminated. Ivins was working on two different types of anthrax vaccines. One was a military anthrax vaccine, known as AVA, which had come under intense scrutiny and criticism by many military personnel who had been given the vaccine. They complained about its side effects, which included painfully swollen muscles and joints, headaches, and serious immune-system disorders. There were also questions raised about whether the vaccine would remain effective after up to three years in storage. Ivins was working with a private company to solve these problems, but the company was having trouble in its efforts to produce a better AVA vaccine. Meanwhile, Ivins was also working on another type of anthrax vaccine, called rPA (recombinant Protective Antigen). This was a genetically engineered vaccine, also known as the "Next Generation Vaccine," that Ivins believed would solve all the problems associated with the AVA vaccine. Ivins was coinventor of that new vaccine and was set to collect patent royalties if the vaccine ever came to market.[23]

This was unlikely, though, as Pentagon officials were telling managers at USAMRIID to shift personnel and resources away from research on anthrax vaccines and into the research and development of products that could be used against other biological agents, such as glanders, tularemia, and plague. When USAMRIID management approached Ivins in the summer of 2001 about working on glanders (a bacterium that kills both livestock and humans), Ivins replied angrily, "I am an anthrax researcher. This is what I do."[24] The fear of not being allowed to work on anthrax vaccines was cited by the US government as a motive for his anthrax letter attacks.

According to the Department of Justice's official report on the incident, "Dr. Ivins' life's work appeared destined for failure, absent an unexpected event."[25] That event would, of course, be an anthrax attack that created demand for anthrax vaccines. And that is exactly what happened following the September and October 2001 anthrax letter attacks, when the Food and Drug Administration fast-tracked approval of the AVA vaccine, putting Ivins back to work on anthrax vaccines.[26] Ivins may also have had a financial motive for the attacks, since, as noted above, he had a patent for the rPA vaccine. The more concern there was throughout the country about the threat of anthrax, the higher the probability that Ivins's rPA vaccine might someday make it to market.

In addition to worries over not being able to work on anthrax vaccines, Ivins was also under severe emotional distress in the period leading up to the anthrax letter attacks. He wrote several alarming e-mails to a former female colleague, Mara Linscott, who used to work with him at Fort Detrick. In one e-mail, sent in October 1999, he wrote: "It's getting to be lately that I've felt there's nobody in the world I can confide in. You're gone now, and one of the reasons I was so sorry to see you go was a very selfish one—I could talk to you openly and honestly, and that was in itself a great lifter of my spirits."[27] He confided in her that he was seeing a psychiatrist and going to group therapy sessions but that it wasn't helping. In a June 2000 e-mail, he wrote: "Even with the Celexa [an antidepressant drug] and the counseling, the depression episodes still come and go. That's unpleasant enough. What is REALLY scary is the paranoia. . . . Depression, as long as I can somewhat control it with medication and some counseling, I can handle. Psychosis or schizophrenia—that's a whole different story. . . . Ominously, a lot of the feelings of isolation—and desolation—that I went through before college are returning. I don't want to relive those years again."[28] In an earlier e-mail, in April 2000, he wrote that, at times, "it's like I'm not only sitting at my desk doing work, I'm also a few feet away watching me do it. There's nothing like living in both the first person singular AND the third person singular!"[29] In yet another e-mail sent to Linscott, in August 2000, Ivins wrote: "I wish I could control the thoughts in my mind. It's hard enough sometimes controlling my behavior. When I'm being eaten alive inside, I always try to put on a good front here at work and at home, so I don't spread the pestilence. . . . I get incredible paranoid, delusional thoughts at times, and there's nothing I can do until they go away, either by themselves or with drugs."[30]

Ivins was fixated on Linscott, who was twenty-nine years younger than him. He told one of his therapists that he had intended to kill Linscott (at one point he had been angry with her) by driving to upstate New York in 2000 to watch her play in a soccer game and offering her a glass of wine afterward from a jug of wine that he had spiked with poison. Linscott, however, was injured during the game, and Ivins changed his mind. The therapist told Ivins that she would have to report this to the authorities and had him sign a statement pledging to contact her immediately if he had any further homicidal thoughts.[31]

Despite his deteriorating mental health, nobody stopped Ivins from continuing to work with anthrax spores at Fort Detrick. A report in later years (March 2011) by a panel of behavioral analysts stated that Ivins's history of mental problems should have disqualified him from obtaining a security clearance and that he should not have been allowed by the army to work with dangerous biological agents.[32]

But work he did, and in the weeks leading up to the first wave of anthrax letters in September 2001 and the second wave in October 2001, Ivins spent unusually long hours alone at night in his lab, a behavior that investigators later argued was evidence he was preparing the deadly anthrax spores for the letter attacks. There was even stronger circumstantial evidence pointing to Ivins as the anthrax letter culprit, including the finding by the FBI that an anthrax spore-batch (from the Ames anthrax strain) known as RMR-1029 was the parent material for the anthrax letter attacks and that Ivins had created and maintained this spore-batch in his laboratory at USAMRIID. Ivins was also among the few anthrax researchers in the country who had the ability to produce the highly purified spores that were used in the mailings.[33]

Additional circumstantial evidence identifying Ivins as the perpetrator was the fact that the anthrax letters were sent from a mailbox outside the Princeton University offices of the Kappa Kappa Gamma sorority, the same sorority with which Ivins later admitted he was obsessed. Even though Princeton, New Jersey, was an approximately three-hour drive from Frederick, Maryland, where USAMRIID is located, as noted earlier, Ivins often took three-hour or even longer drives to visit various KKG sorority chapter houses in different states.[34] Investigators also learned that Ivins had taken unauthorized environmental samplings (by taking swabs) for anthrax contamination after the attacks in the Fort Detrick building where he worked. When he found anthrax contamination only in the area where he himself worked and realized that it would point to him as a suspect in the attacks, he decontaminated his office and lab and failed to report it.[35] He also submitted questionable samples of RMR-1029 when asked to do so by the FBI, a move viewed by investigators as a way to deceive them into thinking that he never had the same batch of anthrax spores that were used in the attacks.[36]

The anthrax letter attacks occurred in two waves. First, two letters postmarked on September 18, 2001, were sent to television news anchor Tom Brokaw at NBC News and to "Editor" at the *New York Post*, both located in New York City. Then, two more letters, postmarked on October 9, 2001, were mailed to the Washington, DC, offices of Senators Tom Daschle and Patrick Leahy. Another envelope filled with anthrax spores that was never recovered was believed to have been sent to the American Media, Inc., building in Boca Raton, Florida. Five people died from inhaling the *Bacillus anthracis* spores, and seventeen others were infected, some by inhaling the spores and others by absorbing the spores through the skin, which is known as cutaneous anthrax. Ten thousand more people believed to have been exposed to the anthrax spores underwent antibiotic prophylaxis. Several postal facilities and mailrooms were contaminated, as were buildings and offices on Capitol Hill. The Environmental Protection Agency spent $27 million from its superfund program to decontaminate the Capitol Hill facilities.[37]

The anthrax attacks, coming on the heels of the 9/11 suicide attacks, spread fear throughout the country that al Qaeda had struck again. There was also concern that the United States would now experience bioterrorism in addition to the usual conventional terrorist attacks such as hijackings, bombings, assassinations, and so forth. Meanwhile, the investigation by the FBI would last nearly seven years and become one of the largest and most complex in the agency's history. The Amerithrax Task Force, as the investigative effort was called, involved twenty-five to thirty full-time investigators from the FBI, the US Postal Inspection Service, and other law-enforcement agencies, as well as federal prosecutors from the District of Columbia and the Justice Department's Counterterrorism Section. More than ten thousand witness interviews were conducted on six different continents, as were eighty searches. More than six thousand items of potential evidence were recovered. The case also involved the issuance of more than 5,750 grand jury subpoenas and the collection of 5,730 environmental samples from sixty site locations.[38]

It took many years before the FBI was able to connect all the dots and identify Ivins as the prime suspect. Along the way, the agency wrongly suggested that a physician who used to work at Fort Detrick, Steven Hatfill, might be the anthrax attacker. Hatfill sued the government and won a $5.8 million settlement from the Department of Justice, which also issued an official letter exonerating him.[39] When the FBI finally started questioning Ivins in 2007 about his role in the anthrax attacks, the troubled scientist began to unravel. He never admitted to the attacks, but there were many inconsistencies in his interviews with investigators, including telling them that he really wasn't an expert on anthrax.[40] His mental health, which was always fragile, further deteriorated during this period. In a group therapy session on July 9, 2008, he told the participants that he had access to a .22-caliber rifle, a Glock handgun, and body armor and planned to kill all his coworkers and everybody else who had wronged him in his life. The therapist called the police the next day. Instead of arresting him, though, the police took Ivins to Frederick Memorial Hospital for evaluation. He was released two weeks later. Soon afterward, he committed suicide by taking an overdose of Tylenol PM.[41]

Because of the missteps in the FBI investigation, including initially suggesting that Hatfill was the anthrax letter attacker, and the lack of a "smoking gun" to implicate Ivins, many people believed that Ivins was innocent. The FBI, however, announced shortly after his suicide that charges were about to be brought against Ivins for the anthrax letter attacks. Then, in February 2010, the Justice Department, FBI, and the US Postal Inspection Service formally concluded their investigation into the attacks and issued a report that presented the circumstantial case against Ivins.[42] In January 2011, a National Academy of Sciences panel concluded that while the genetic analysis of the anthrax used in the attacks "did not definitively demonstrate" that they were grown from a sample taken from his laboratory, the evidence was "consistent with and supports an association" between Ivins's flask and the anthrax used in the attacks.[43] Additionally, the panel of behavioral analysts that faulted the army for not taking earlier action against Ivins in view of his serious psychological problems also stated that the government's case against Ivins was persuasive. They wrote: "Dr. Ivins was psychologically disposed to undertake the mailings; his behavioral history demonstrated his potential for carrying them out; and he had the motivation and the means."[44] The panel also found that Ivins committed the attacks in order to get revenge against an array of imagined enemies, including the news media, and also "to elevate his own significance" and thereby rescue his anthrax vaccines research, the funding for which was being threatened in 2001.[45]

The tragic case of Bruce Ivins demonstrates what can happen when you take a brilliant but very troubled man and give him access to some of the deadliest germs in the world. Although he served his country well for most of his life, dedicating his career to finding the best vaccine to protect Americans from anthrax infection, he ultimately could not fight the demons in his mind that drove him to become the most infamous lone wolf bioterrorist in US history. Part ego, part greed, and a lot of paranoia, Ivins could not resist the temptation to use the very germs he dedicated his life to fight against as a weapon in his nefarious plans for glory, revenge, and possible financial reward. That an entire nation was held at bay by the acts of a solitary individual illustrates the impact of the lone wolf terrorist.

WHEN INNOVATION AND CREATIVITY BECOME DANGEROUS

In most fields, we applaud individuals and organizations that are innovative and creative. From art, music, and theater to science, technology, and business, those who dare to be different and think outside the box can be rewarded with financial and professional success. But when terrorists become innovative and creative, they can be quite dangerous. Their innovations can become new ways to inflict fear and bloodshed upon the world. Earlier, I described some of the reasons why lone wolves are innovative, including the lack of any group decision-making process that could stifle creativity. Lone wolves are also not afraid of failing, unlike many terrorist groups that carefully calculate the costs and benefits of any planned attack. How, then, do some lone wolves use their creativity and innovation for terrorist operations?

First, several lone wolves have combined knowledge of a particular field with creativity in designing an attack. For example, Bruce Ivins was one of the world's foremost authorities on anthrax and was able to use that expertise in preparing anthrax spores for the letter attacks. Other individuals or groups may have thought up a similar scenario but felt it was beyond their capability to produce spores that would survive being sent through the mail. Ivins, although depressed and suffering most of his life from mental illness, was still confident enough in his own abilities as a scientist to believe he could do something nobody before had ever attempted. He was aware, like most people, that the Postal Service had been used in the past for terrorist attacks, such as the sending of letter and package bombs in the United States and other countries. Why not try something different, he most likely thought, such as sending a biological agent through the mail?

Mario Buda, another lone wolf we discussed earlier, combined expertise with creative thinking as the likely perpetrator of the 1920 Wall Street bombing. Buda was quite knowledgeable about dynamite, having been involved in prior attacks that used that type of explosive. When he was active with an Italian anarchist group, the Galleanists, Buda was a major player in constructing dynamite bombs that were used in a national mail-bomb plot and then in another series of attacks in which the Galleanists simply left bombs in the middle of the night in front of the homes of prominent officials, including the home of Attorney General A. Mitchell Palmer. When Buda, who was hiding in New Hampshire, decided in September 1920 to strike one last time in retaliation for the recent indictment of his friends and fellow Galleanists, Nicola Sacco and Bartolomeo Vanzetti, he had to come up with a new mode of attack. He probably knew that the authorities would be on the lookout for attacks similar to those that Galleanists had tried before. That would eliminate the use of package bombs or placing bombs at the doorsteps of targets. A standoff attack, in which a powerful bomb would be far enough away from the target not to arouse suspicion but still near enough to cause damage, would seem to be the best option. Since there had not been any major automobile or horse-and-cart bombings by terrorists in the United States in the past, Buda likely felt confident that police and security guards would not be suspicious of a horse-drawn wagon parked close to the J. P. Morgan building and other targets on Wall Street.[46] Buda was thus able to implement the first vehicle bombing in US history. He traveled to New York, where he constructed the bomb with a timer and placed it in a horse-drawn wagon that he rode to Wall Street.[47] He then fled the scene of his carnage, never to be heard from again.

Another area where a lone wolf can combine expertise in a field with imaginative thinking is cyberterrorism. This involves using the Internet and other communication and information systems that are linked by computers to cause disruptions and chaos in government, businesses, and everyday life. Among the worst-case scenarios would be terrorists sabotaging air traffic control systems and thereby causing airplane crashes; sabotaging electric power systems, thereby causing power blackouts; or sending computer viruses around the world that cause disruption or even collapse of international financial and banking systems. Most cyberterrorist attacks thus far, however, have been relatively low-level incidents, including distributed denial of service (DDoS) attacks, which are "attempts to render computers unavailable to users through a variety of means, including saturating the target computers or networks with external communication requests, thereby denying service to legitimate users."[48] Although no cyberterrorist attack has yet to approach the worst-case scenarios, the history of terrorism has taught us to never underestimate the ability of individuals or groups to defy expectations. What makes cyberterrorism so attractive to lone wolves is that they can launch an attack in the privacy of their own home. The targets could be a government or business located anywhere in the world. Just as the Internet is growing with breathtaking speed, so too are the computer skills of individuals everywhere. It would be naïve and dangerous to assume that a sophisticated cyberterrorist attack is beyond the capabilities of the knowledgeable and skilled lone wolf computer geek.

Having a particular skill, however, is not a prerequisite for a lone wolf to think up and implement an innovative attack. Lone wolves can get up to speed regarding weapons, tactics, and other aspects of a terrorist operation through individual research via the Internet or, in pre-Internet days, through acquiring books, articles, and other materials from libraries and other sources. For example, Muharem Kurbegovic, the Alphabet Bomber, who was among the first terrorists to threaten to use chemical warfare agents, learned how to make chemical weapons in the mid-1970s by reading such books as *Guide to Chemical and Gas Warfare, The Book of Poison,* and *Unconventional Warfare Devices and Techniques.* These books were found in his apartment after his arrest.[49] In today's Internet world, there is really nothing holding a creative terrorist back. Once an individual thinks up a new or different type of terrorist scenario, he or she can begin reading webpages, blogs, online publications, and other information to learn enough about the target, tactic, and/or weapon required for the planned attack.

Lone wolves can also use their creativity and innovation to catch counterterrorist planners off guard. Protecting against terrorism in the past has been more of a reactive than anticipatory strategy. Airport security, for example, adapts rather than anticipates what terrorists may do. Once terrorists began sneaking knives and other weapons onboard for hijackings in the early 1960s, airports screened passengers with metal detectors. When terrorists began blowing up planes in midair with bombs hidden in luggage in the late 1960s, x-ray machines were put in place at airports in an effort to discover these bombs. Following an attempt by Richard Reid, a British citizen with ties to al Qaeda, to bring down an American Airlines flight from Paris to Miami on December 22, 2001, with explosives hidden in his shoes, airports began requiring passengers to take off their shoes for inspection before boarding planes. The tendency by security officials to wait until something happens and then take measures to try to prevent similar attacks plays into the hands of the creative terrorist, who, by thinking up something clever and new, is able to stay one step ahead of those dedicated to combating this threat.

When lone wolves suffer from mental illness, their creativity and innovation present even greater challenges for counterterrorist officials. No longer can any sense of rationality be expected from these types of terrorists. While all lone wolves, as noted earlier, have an advantage over terrorist groups in not having to worry about alienating their supporters with a misguided attack or having their group wiped out in a government or law-enforcement crackdown following a major incident, there is still an element of rationality for most lone wolves in their decision making. Not so for those lone wolves who are emotionally disturbed. That makes it more difficult for authorities to anticipate the actions of these types of terrorists.

The creative and innovative nature of lone wolves also makes them capable of launching "black swan" types of attacks. These are unique, novel terrorist incidents that nobody had previously thought possible. The term "black swan" was originally a metaphor for things that were believed impossible to exist. This was due to the fact that, for centuries, people in Europe had only seen white swans in nature. However, after the discovery of Australia and the sightings of black swans in the late-seventeenth century, the meaning of the term changed to refer to things and events that were perceived to be impossible but could actually occur. According to Nassim Nicholas Taleb, author of the bestselling book *The Black Swan: The Impact of the Highly Improbable,* a black swan has three main attributes. First, it is an event that is an outlier, since it lies beyond the realm of normal expectations. Second, it has an extreme impact. And third, even though we never expect such an event to occur, we tend to come up with explanations for it after its occurrence, which then makes the black swan seem to be explainable and predictable.[50] While terrorist groups may also be capable of perpetrating black-swan attacks, the boundless nature of lone wolves and their total freedom to think up anything they want and then try to act on it makes them more likely than a terrorist group to commit an attack off everyone's radar.[51]

GAS, GERMS, OR NUKES: WHICH IS MORE LIKELY FOR A LONE WOLF WMD ATTACK?

I discussed earlier why I believe lone wolves are prime candidates for using weapons of mass destruction. These reasons range from a lack of any self-constraints concerning casualties or reactions as lone wolves decide upon an attack to the ability to think outside the box and design creative, innovative, and dangerous attacks. However, since WMDs include chemical, biological, and nuclear weapons, it is important to determine which of these is more likely to be used by the individual terrorist.

Of the three different, basic types of WMDs, chemical weapons are the easiest for a lone wolf with a background in chemistry to produce. Chemical agents are "poisons that incapacitate, injure, or kill through their toxic effects on the skin, eyes, lungs, blood, nerves, or other organs."[52] The precursor chemicals for the production of many chemical warfare agents are readily available from commercial chemical suppliers, and several chemical weapons, such as sarin, tabun, and VX gas, can be made either at home or in a small laboratory. As is true for terrorist groups, a lone wolf still has obstacles to overcome in terms of dispersing chemical agents. If not done properly, as in the case of Aum Shinrikyo, the attack is compromised. Yet, with information on how to effectively disperse chemical agents available from the Internet and other sources, this is not an insurmountable obstacle for a lone wolf.

Acquiring, producing, and dispersing biological agents is somewhat more difficult, but it's still within the ability of those lone wolves with scientific backgrounds. While Bruce Ivins had the expertise to produce the particular strain of anthrax that he sent through the mail to his various targets, not every lone wolf who chooses to use bioweapons needs to be a Fort Detrick microbiologist. As with chemical weapons, there is enough publicly available information on the Internet and in other sources to help the lone wolf who wants to launch a bioterrorist attack. One of the major differences between chemical and biological weapons is that chemical weapons are primarily manmade (such as sarin nerve gas), while biological weapons are comprised of living organisms such as bacteria and viruses as well as toxins derived from plants or animals. Biological warfare agents involve "the deliberate use of disease and natural poisons to incapacitate or kill people."[53] Among the biological agents that could be used by lone wolves are bacterial agents such as anthrax, viral agents such as smallpox, and toxin agents such as ricin. An important distinction to make regarding biological agents is that some, such as anthrax, cause infectious but not contagious diseases, while others, such as smallpox, cause infectious and contagious diseases. People exposed to anthrax, therefore, do not have to be quarantined, but those exposed to smallpox will have to be isolated from others. Contagious diseases can also spread around the world as one person passes the disease to another. The mass-killing potential of biological agents makes these attractive weapons for lone wolves.

There is, however, a great deal of uncertainty regarding how exactly a bioterrorist attack will unfold. Bioterrorism is characterized by much more uncertainty regarding tactics, targets, weapons, and scenarios than is the case for conventional terrorism, the terrorism that we are all more familiar with because it has happened so many times before. Conventional terrorism includes tactics such as hijackings, bombings, shootings, kidnappings, barricade/hostage incidents, suicide airplane attacks, and the like. The targets of conventional terrorist attacks include governments, militaries, businesses, and society, while the weapons used by conventional terrorists are, among other things, explosives, guns, knives, and rocket-propelled grenades. And with many different types of conventional terrorist attacks occurring over the years, ranging from simultaneous car and truck bombings to assassinations and hijackings, we know of thousands of different scenarios that may occur.

But it is an entirely different story when we look at the world of bioterrorism. Since there has never been a bioterrorist attack with large numbers of casualties, perpetrated either by a lone wolf or a terrorist group, there is no substantial track record of previous major bioterrorist incidents to guide us in planning for this threat. We really don't know what tactics, targets, weapons, or scenarios will be associated with current and future bioterrorists. In terms of tactics, lone wolves could disperse anthrax spores from a low-flying airplane or crop duster, or they might release a biological agent from the ground in an aerosol device such as a spray can. They could place ricin in the heating, ventilation, air-conditioning (HVAC) system of a building, or they could infect somebody with smallpox and watch it spread around the world. The targets could be the usual suspects, such as governments, militaries, businesses, and the general public, or it could be the economy. A viable target could be agriculture, for example, in the form of destroying crops and livestock. The weapons for a lone wolf bioterrorist attack could be any one biological agent or a combination of several different biological agents, including anthrax, smallpox, botulinum toxin, ricin, and/or new, novel agents that are genetically engineered. And when it comes to scenarios, we are confronted with basically a blank slate. We know of the anthrax letter attacks, but almost everything else when assessing what terrorists are likely to do with bioweapons is pure speculation, since we just do not have a database or history of major incidents to analyze. All this works to the advantage of the lone wolf perpetrating a bioterrorist attack. Furthermore, since biological agents are invisible, odorless, and tasteless, and symptoms of a biological-agent attack may not appear for hours or even days, a lone wolf could thus unleash these agents without raising suspicions at the scene of the attack.

The technological barriers for a lone wolf interested in producing and disseminating a biological agent are not insurmountable. As one microbiologist writes:

> Today, anyone with a high school education can use widely available protocols and prepackaged kits to modify the sequence of a gene or replace genes within a microorganism; one can also purchase small, disposable, self-contained bioreactors for propagating viruses and microorganisms. Such advances continue to lower the barriers to biologic-weapons development.[54]

Former secretary of the navy Richard Danzig agrees, noting:

Compared to working with nuclear materials, the challenges of developing the requisite know-how and obtaining the required equipment for bioterrorism are modest. The hurdles that impede obtaining an effective biological weapon will vary from pathogen to pathogen, according to the mode of distribution and the efficiency desired by an attacker. But all these hurdles are being lowered by the dissemination of knowledge, techniques, and equipment.[55]

The most difficult, and therefore least probable, of the weapons of mass destruction that could be used by a lone wolf is a nuclear weapon. The appeal of such a weapon to a terrorist lies in its killing potential. Nuclear weapons "can be more than a million times more powerful than the same weight of conventional explosives, create shock waves, high pressures, flying debris, and extreme heat—the same mechanisms by which conventional explosives injure and kill, albeit at vastly increased scale."[56] Nuclear explosions also create radiation, which can kill or injure exposed people at the instant of detonation. There is also the risk of fallout, which can spread over an area much greater than that affected by the bomb's immediate radius. Fallout can also lead to long-term, delayed medical problems, including cancer and genetic abnormalities.[57]

Yet the technological, logistical, and financial obstacles involved in acquiring or building and using nuclear weapons would seem to be too much for a lone wolf to overcome. Nuclear weapons are much more expensive to produce than chemical or biological weapons, and the technology needed to devise such weapons is not widely available. It is also much more difficult for a lone wolf to transport a nuclear device to a target site without being discovered through radiation detectors and other security devices than it would be for a lone wolf to transport a chemical or biological weapon. While a lone wolf could attempt to attack a nuclear power plant with a conventional explosive, the tight security in place at most nuclear plants would be difficult for a lone wolf to penetrate. Furthermore, a conventional explosive is unlikely to do much damage to nuclear-reactor plants because they are built to resist damage by explosives and even the impact of commercial aircraft.[58]

There has been much discussion in policy and academic circles regarding terrorists building a crude nuclear device or stealing a nuclear weapon. Distinguished political scientist Graham Allison observed that "nuclear terrorists are most likely to use a small weapon stolen from the arsenal of one of the nuclear states."[59] However, one of the world's leading terrorism experts, Brian Michael Jenkins, disputes this argument, noting, "While the possibility that some talented team of terrorists conceivably might someday design and build a crude nuclear device cannot be entirely dismissed, no terrorist group, not even those with potential access to poorly guarded nuclear sites like Russia's Chechens or those with hundreds of millions of dollars to spend like al Qaeda, has come close."[60] Both Allison and Jenkins were referring to groups or cells of terrorists and not to lone wolf operatives, for which obtaining and using a nuclear weapon would be even more difficult. Lone wolves are, however, capable of setting off a "dirty bomb," which is not a nuclear bomb but rather a conventional explosive filled with radioactive material. While such an attack would not kill large numbers of people, except for those killed by the initial blast, it would still cause widespread panic and health problems related to airborne radiation.

Given how dangerous lone wolves can be, their creativity and innovation make them difficult to ignore. Yet there is a missing link in the story of lone wolf terrorism. Unlike many terrorist groups that have female members or even female leaders, the majority of lone wolves have been male. Why, then, have we not had many female lone wolves, and should we expect this to change in the coming years?

CHAPTER 4

WHERE ARE THE WOMEN?

When it comes to explaining lone wolf terrorism, the absence of women is one of the more perplexing issues. After all, women have played significant roles in terrorist groups throughout history, and a few have ascended to leadership positions. Terrorists as diverse as the Russian revolutionary group Narodnaya Volya, the German leftist Baader-Meinhof Gang, the separatist Liberation Tigers of Tamil Eelam, the Revolutionary Armed Forces of Colombia, and the Palestinian al-Aqsa Martyrs Brigade, to name just a few, have all had women in their ranks. Women have been used in various roles within terrorist organizations, including providing logistical support, joining their male comrades in violent attacks, and even becoming suicide bombers themselves. Women have been involved in virtually every type of terrorist tactic used by a group, ranging from hijackings and midair plane bombings to armed assaults and kidnappings.

Yet with only a few exceptions, all lone wolf terrorists have been male. It is not as though women are excluded from becoming lone wolves. This form of terrorism is an equal-opportunity employer. No barriers would seem to exist in preventing a woman from venturing out on her own to blow up a building, hijack a plane, or initiate a mass shooting. Why, then, has lone wolf terrorism been a male-dominated activity? In order to answer this question, we have to first examine the role of women in various terrorist groups both today and in earlier periods for any clues as to why women have not acted as lone wolf terrorists.

FEMALE PARTICIPATION IN TERRORIST GROUPS

When women began embarking on suicide operations in recent years as members of various terrorist movements, people were understandably shocked. The public had grown accustomed to male suicide bombers, but the idea that a woman would also blow herself up in order to kill innocent victims was mind-boggling. The concept of a female terrorist was still something most people had a hard time grasping, despite the fact that women had participated in terrorist groups for a long time. Beginning with the Russian terrorists in the late-nineteenth century and continuing today with both Islamic and non-Islamic militant groups, women have consistently been integral players in the world of terrorism.

Terrorism was rampant in Russia in the 1880s, as the first modern terrorist group, Narodnaya Volya ("The People's Will"), waged a relentless campaign of dynamite bombings against government officials, culminating in the assassination of Tsar Alexander II in 1881. Dynamite, which was invented in 1867 by Swedish chemist Alfred Nobel, was a godsend for anarchists and other militants, since it was a powerful weapon that was easy to conceal. Nobel was so dismayed to see his invention used for violent purposes—he had intended it to be used for peaceful endeavors such as construction—that he left millions of dollars in his will to establish the annual Nobel Prizes, including the Nobel Peace Prize. The Russian terrorists embraced dynamite because, in addition to its wide availability and easy use, it had an important symbolic value. Since the assailant was usually killed along with the targeted person, it separated the terrorists from common criminals, who would be afraid to use such a weapon.[1] It also inspired admiration among some segments of the public, since the perpetrators were basically sacrificing their lives in the attacks.

Women were quite prominent in Narodnaya Volya. There were ten females among the twenty-nine members of the original executive committee.[2] Throughout the 1880s, women participated directly in the group's operations.[3] Nearly a quarter of all Russian terrorists during this period were women.[4] It was a woman, in fact, who inspired the Russian terrorist movement. As I noted in chapter 1, Vera Zasulich's proclamation that she was a "terrorist, not a killer" after shooting a police commander in 1878 made her a heroine throughout Russia. Narodnaya Volya was eventually crushed by the new regime of Tsar Alexander III, after the assassination of his father, Tsar Alexander II. This led to a reduction in terrorist attacks. Terrorism, however, was revived in Russia in the early 1900s by the Socialist Revolutionary Party, with women once again being very active. In fact, from 1905 to 1908, there were eleven terrorist attacks committed by Socialist Revolutionary women.[5]

It would be several decades, however, before women once again became prominent in terrorist activities. The late 1960s and early 1970s witnessed a surge in terrorism around the world, with many spectacular incidents captivating public attention. Palestinian militants were at the forefront of this violence. In July 1968, the Popular Front for the Liberation of Palestine (PFLP) hijacked an Israeli El Al plane on a flight from Rome to Tel Aviv and diverted it to Algeria. Later that same year, the PFLP attacked an El Al plane at the Athens airport, killing one passenger. There were more attacks on El Al airliners in 1969, including a hijacking in August, in which two PFLP terrorists seized the plane on a flight from Rome to Athens and diverted it to Damascus. After allowing the passengers and crew to disembark, the two terrorists blew up the plane's cockpit. One of the terrorists was a woman, and she quickly gained notoriety and, in some places around the world, admiration. Leila Khaled instantly became the most famous female terrorist of her time. People were mesmerized by the concept of women seizing and blowing up planes or doing other dangerous things thought to be the sole province of men.

It didn't hurt that Leila Khaled was beautiful, smart, and daring. As one observer noted, "She became a sex symbol for her violence; she shattered a million and one taboos overnight; and she revolutionized the thinking of hundreds of other angry young women around the world."[6] Her value to the PFLP was so high that when she was captured during another hijacking less than a year later, the PFLP went all out to gain her release. Khaled and another PFLP member hijacked an El Al plane bound for New York on September 6, 1970. (The PFLP also hijacked three other planes [from Pan American World Airways, Trans World Airlines, and Swissair] bound for New York from European cities on that same day, making it the most spectacular hijacking in terrorism history until the 9/11 hijacking-suicide attacks in the United States.) Israeli security guards on the plane were able to kill Khaled's fellow hijacker and capture her while the plane was still airborne. The plane then landed in London, where British authorities arrested Khaled. The PFLP wanted her released but didn't feel that the British hostages they were holding from the three other hijacked planes would be enough to use as bargaining chips. They wanted something more important, so they came up with a simple solution—hijack a British plane! They did that a few days later and then used the hostages from the British Overseas Airlines Corporation airliner to eventually win Khaled's release.[7]

Another female hijacker who gained publicity around the world was Julienne Busic, who, along with her husband, Zvonko, and three other Croatian extremists, seized a Trans World Airlines plane flying from New York to Chicago in September 1976. They demanded that a manifesto promoting the cause of Croatian independence from the Serbian-dominated Yugoslav federation be published in several newspapers and that pro-Croatian independence leaflets they had carried with them be dropped by helicopters flying over cities across the United States and Europe. To demonstrate their willingness to kill passengers if their demands weren't met, they told the authorities that they had a bomb aboard the plane and that another explosive device, as well as the manifesto that they wanted published, could be found in a locker across the street from Grand Central Station in New York City. The police located the bomb and took it to a demolition area, where they attempted to trigger it by remote control. When nothing happened after fifteen minutes, the bomb experts approached the device without wearing protective gear, and it exploded, killing one officer and injuring three others.

Meanwhile, the hijacked plane embarked on a long odyssey that included stops in Montreal, Gander, Newfoundland, Reykjavík, and finally Paris, where French authorities shot out the tires from the plane so it could not take off again. Before the ordeal was over, the Croatian independence manifesto was published in the *New York Times*, the *Washington Post*, the *Chicago Tribune*, and the *Los Angeles Times*. Leaflets were also dropped over North American cities as well as London and Paris. The hijackers surrendered in Paris and were sent back to the United States. The most remarkable aspect of the hijacking was that the terrorists had no weapons onboard. The "bombs" they claimed they had turned out to be fake, some of them made from clay.[8]

Just like Leila Khaled after her first hijacking, Julienne Busic, who was born in the United States, was viewed as a heroine by many people in Croatia and other parts of the world. This was yet another example of the famous slogan: "One person's terrorist is another person's freedom fighter." Busic had poets write to her, and Croatian television, newspapers, and magazines interviewed her after her release from prison.[9] Interestingly, both she and Khaled did not consider themselves to be terrorists. Khaled told an interviewer, "My work as a freedom fighter has given me happiness; you identify yourself with the struggle. It is the difference between a freedom fighter and an ordinary person. As a Palestinian I wouldn't be happy with myself unless I was a freedom fighter. I am glad I have done so much."[10] Busic said, "I could never consider myself a terrorist. I'm just not a terrorist. I'm not a criminal, I mean in so far as I have no criminal nature, no criminal mind."[11]

There is another similarity between these two female hijackers who had very different backgrounds and causes for which they were fighting. Both Khaled and Busic fell victim to a variation of the "Stockholm Syndrome." The term originated with a bank robbery and hostage incident in Stockholm, Sweden, in August 1973. The hostage episode lasted five days, with the hostages gradually viewing their captors as their protectors, fearing that a police rescue attempt might result in their deaths. When the gunmen finally surrendered, the hostages were afraid that the police might shoot the gunmen, so the hostages formed a protective shield around them as they all came out of the bank. Some of the hostages said later that they felt no hatred toward their captors. They felt that their captors, by not killing them, had given them their lives back. And one of the hostages actually wound up marrying one of the gunmen while he was serving his prison sentence. Therefore, whenever there is a hostage situation and the hostages, after the ordeal is over, do not condemn their captors, they are described by the media and other observers as having fallen victim to the Stockholm Syndrome. However, this syndrome can affect both the hostages *and* the hostage takers. The three basic phases of the Stockholm Syndrome are positive feelings of the hostages toward their captors, negative feelings of the hostages toward the police or other government authorities, and the reciprocation of the positive feelings by the captors.[12]

Julienne Busic had positive feelings for those she was holding captive on the plane. "I felt like I was experiencing sort of a reverse Stockholm Syndrome," she recalled years later. "It was like I identified with the passengers, too, to the extent that I believed that we were all on the same side." One former hostage told reporters that Busic "acted almost like a stewardess walking up and down the aisle talking politely to people and calming them."[13] After she was arrested and was in the airport control tower in Paris, she realized that she had in her possession her husband Zvonko's address book. She did not want the authorities to discover this, but she didn't know how to dispose of it. When she saw the released passengers and crew walk by her in the tower, she came up with an idea. "I go up to the steward . . . and I said, 'Listen, you've got to hide this for me! Because this is Zvonko's address book!' And he looked at me like I was crazy. And I was so upset. Because you know we had gone through all this and we were all one big happy family. And now he wouldn't do that."[14]

Khaled also identified with her captives. Before she hijacked her first plane in 1969, she was waiting in the lounge to board the aircraft when she saw a little girl playing with her sister. "For the first time I realized that I would be endangering her life," Khaled said. "If the plane blew up during our hijack, or if it was shot down by Israeli anti-aircraft fire, then those innocent children would die."[15] Khaled was also troubled by a conversation she had with a Greek man before she boarded the plane. He told her that he lived in the United States and was returning to Greece for the first time in many years to visit his mother. This reminded her of separations in her own family when she was growing up. "I knew very well what it meant to be away from home, from your mother and sisters, and I was thinking about this while this man talked to me." After the hijacking was over, she saw him sitting and crying. She told him, "Now you are OK. We will send your mother a telegram, and she can meet you."[16]

The experiences of Khaled and Busic illustrate the emotional effects that a hijacking or other type of hostage episode can have on a female member of a terrorist group. It may well be that some male hijackers have similar experiences, but perhaps there is a "softer" side of the female psyche that may have played a factor, in addition to the Stockholm Syndrome, in these two women identifying with their captives. However, female terrorists can at times be as tough, if not tougher, than their male colleagues. There have been some instances reported in which male terrorists, when faced with a confrontation with police or other counterterrorist forces, hesitated for a moment before they fired their weapons, whereas the female terrorists shot at once. Advice, therefore, reportedly given to European counterterrorist forces by the International Criminal Police Organization (Interpol) was to "shoot the women first."[17]

Another example of the emotional effects a terrorist operation can have on a female extremist can be seen in the case of Susan Albrecht, who was a member of the German Red Army Faction (RAF), which was originally known as the Baader-Meinhof Gang. Her godfather was Jurgen Ponto, the chairman of Dresdner Bank and the target of a planned RAF kidnapping in 1977. The RAF wanted to take advantage of Albrecht's personal relationship with Ponto in order to gain access to his house. Their objective was to kidnap Ponto and then demand the release of RAF members in prison.

Albrecht, however, refused to help. She told the group that she felt close to her godfather and wouldn't want to harm him in any way. The RAF then applied enormous psychological pressure on Albrecht to get her to participate. As one RAF member pointed out, because she refused to take part in the operation based on emotional reasons, the group accused her of having no political identity and no loyalty to her imprisoned comrades, who would supposedly be freed in return for the release of the kidnapped Ponto. Since the RAF was a small group, isolated from society, it was difficult for Albrecht to continue to voice her opposition to participating in the kidnapping plan. The group was basically her life, her main frame of reference for the entire world.

Psychological pressure was applied over the course of several days, with different RAF members taking turns challenging Albrecht's reasons for not wanting to help in the plot. Finally, the group pressure was too much, and Albrecht agreed to take part in the kidnapping along with two other RAF members. But it all went terribly wrong. One of the RAF members killed Ponto when the group tried to kidnap him at his house. In the aftermath of the killing, Albrecht had a nervous breakdown. She was extremely depressed and no longer capable of performing any functions for the terrorist organization. As one of the RAF members stated, "For days on end, she was shaken by incessant crying spells. She had no strength left. She had broken down completely and should, under normal circumstances, have been hospitalized." The RAF arranged for her transfer to East Germany, where she assumed a new name, Ingrid Jaeger, got married, and had a child. She was finally arrested in East Berlin in 1990 after the collapse of the Communist regime.[18]

The RAF was among the terrorist groups of that period that were very female friendly, with a woman, Ulrike Meinhof, having cofounded the group in 1970 (along with Andreas Baader). Meinhof was a left-wing journalist before she helped form the terrorist group. Her name "became associated with the whole era of anti-imperialist protest turned to violence."[19] The RAF was involved in hijackings, kidnappings, assassinations, and other widely publicized terrorist acts. Women were believed at one point to constitute approximately 50 percent of the RAF membership and about 80 percent of the group's supporters.[20] One scholar, however, argues that, for the most part, women only served in support roles in the RAF, despite the fact that its cofounder was a woman.[21]

During its existence, the RAF demonstrated a remarkable ability to adapt to changing circumstances in order to survive and remain relevant. The group's initial targets were capitalists and other symbols of the industrialized states, with the goal being to bring about a Marxist-Maoist revolution. In the early 1980s, the group switched its main focus away from business targets that represented capitalism to those representing the US military and NATO. The placement of intermediate-range nuclear missiles in Europe in the early 1980s was highly unpopular among the public, and it led to large-scale, nonviolent protests in many countries. The RAF, therefore, decided to take advantage of this situation by targeting NATO and US military personnel and facilities for terrorist attacks. This did not, however, result in any significant increase in the number of new recruits to the group or in a rallying among the masses to its cause. Therefore, when the Cold War began to wind down in the late 1980s, the RAF had to find a new strategy. As a result, it basically returned to its original cause, focusing once again on capitalist symbols. In 1989, the RAF assassinated Alfred Herrhausen, the chairman of Deutsche Bank, and in 1991, it assassinated Detlev Rohweder, a German government official who was responsible for economic reforms that led to the loss of thousands of jobs.[22]

By 1998, however, the RAF announced that it was officially disbanding, ending more than two decades of terrorist activities. Its leadership stated in a seven-thousand-word communiqué that they had made a strategic error in not building up a political organization alongside the armed one, and as a result, "the urban guerrilla in the form of the RAF is now history." It was a remarkable statement, because not many terrorist groups issue official declarations announcing an end to their activity due to their own mistakes in strategy and ideology. As the group acknowledged, "The lack of a political-social organization was a decisive mistake by the RAF. It wasn't the only mistake, but it's one important reason why the RAF could not become a stronger liberation project." The influence of women in the RAF could also be seen in one of the passages from the final communiqué: "The marketing of people and the violence in the home and on the streets, these are the violence of suppression, the social coldness against others, the violence against women—all of these are expressions of patriarchal and racist conditions."[23]

Women were prominent in other terrorist groups in the 1960s and 1970s, including the Red Brigades in Italy and the Weather Underground in the United States. The latter was originally known as the "Weathermen," but the name was changed to avoid alienating feminist supporters.[24] In one shocking episode during that period, Patty Hearst, the granddaughter of newspaper magnate William Randolph Hearst, was kidnapped and then joined the leftist Symbionese Liberation Army in the United States in 1974.

By the 1980s, however, the terrorism of the leftist revolutionary groups was replaced by the emergence of a seemingly more frightening wave of terrorism—namely, religious extremists bent on changing governments and societies to their own fundamentalist beliefs.[25] Whereas secular terrorists usually have self-imposed constraints on the level of violence they perpetrate (since they are concerned with not alienating their supporters in the general population and do not want to create an overwhelming response by the targeted country that could result in the elimination of the group), religious extremists march to a different beat. Believing that God is on one's side and that one will be rewarded in the afterlife for committing horrendous crimes on earth is a powerful incentive to keep on fighting, no matter what the consequences.[26]

The emergence of religious terrorists, particularly Islamic extremists, coincided with the growth in suicide terrorist attacks. Hezbollah, a pro-Iranian Shiite militant group, burst onto the scene in Lebanon in 1983 with a series of suicide bombings, including bombings that targeted the US embassy and US Marine barracks in Beirut.[27] But, while many people today still equate suicide attacks with religious extremists, it was actually a secular group in Sri Lanka, the Tamil Tigers of Tamil Eelam (LTTE), that was responsible for the most suicide attacks in the 1980s and 1990s. By the time the group was defeated by the Sri Lankan army in 2009, after more than twenty-five years of violence, it had committed approximately two hundred suicide attacks. The hostilities pitted the minority Tamils, who are Hindu, against the ruling majority Sinhalese, who are Buddhist. The conflict was a secular one, however, with LTTE's goal being to create a separate, nonreligious Tamil state in the north and east of Sri Lanka. LTTE had no religious or cultural restrictions on using females for their militancy. Women, therefore, committed between 30 and 40 percent of the suicide attacks that LTTE was responsible for. The group was so dedicated to the use of suicide bombings that it formed a special squad for these individuals, known as the "Black Tigers," and had an annual ceremony to celebrate the squad's accomplishments. The dedication of the group to women's participation could also be seen in LTTE's website, which had separate sections extolling the virtues of the female comrades. Female members of the Black Tigers were responsible for some of LTTE's most high-profile attacks, including the assassination in 1991 of former Indian prime minister Rajiv Gandhi.

Another secular group that used women as suicide terrorists was the Kurdistan Worker's Party (PKK), an organization that was very active in the 1990s. Between 1996 and 1999 alone, the PKK, which is comprised of Turkish Kurds fighting to establish an independent Kurdish state in southeastern Turkey, carried out twenty-one suicide attacks or attempted suicide attacks, with women being the suicide terrorists in eleven out of the fifteen successful attacks and in three out of six attacks that were intercepted by Turkish authorities.[28]

Other terrorist groups that included women in their suicide

attacks were the Palestinian al-Aqsa Martyrs Brigade, the Syrian Socialist Nationalist Party, and the Chechen rebel movement. All these groups were secular and therefore did not have any religious proscriptions against using women for terrorist activities. The emergence of female Chechen suicide terrorists gave rise to the term "black widows." Two deadly wars in Chechnya in the 1990s (Chechens were fighting for independence from Russia) left tens of thousands of casualties. Many Chechen women lost their husbands or other relatives in the wars, so once these women began taking part in suicide attacks in Russia, sometimes dressed head-to-toe in black, the popular notion was that they were doing so to exact revenge. Among the female suicide attacks were bombings of planes, a subway system, and a music festival. In addition, women were part of Chechen teams that seized a Moscow theater in 2002 and a Beslan school in 2004, resulting in hundreds of casualties.

Religious extremist groups had long prohibited women from participating in their violent activities in the past. The waging of "jihad," or holy war, was historically seen as the purview of men. As one terrorism scholar notes, "Given the strict gender demarcation of the public and private sphere in Islam, the resort to violence by women and girls, rather than constituting a restorative act, amounted to a sign of cultural fragmentation."[29] The success of female terrorists in other movements, however, eventually led fundamentalist religious extremist groups, such as Hamas (Islamic Resistance Movement), to change their practices. The spiritual head of Hamas, Sheikh Ahmed Yassin, who was killed in an Israeli air strike in 2004, stated in an interview with an Arab journalist in London in August 2001 that "Palestinian women do not need a religious ruling in order to perpetrate a suicide attack." He claimed that, under certain circumstances, "Islam permits it." A senior Hamas activist, Abdel Aziz Rantisi, also supported the use of women in suicide operations, stating, "There is no reason that the perpetration of suicide attacks should be monopolized by men."[30]

In some cases, though, religious women who are recruited to par-

ticipate in a suicide mission have problems with shedding their religious appearance in order to not look suspicious when infiltrating
the target area prior to carrying out the attack. One such case is that
of a would-be female Palestinian suicide terrorist, twenty-six-year-old
Thawiya Hamour, who provides us with insight into the thinking of
some of these religious female terrorists. Her mission was to set off
explosives in a densely populated area in West Jerusalem. She was
fitted with an explosive belt and underwent a briefing on how to
detonate it.

Hamour, however, was arrested before she could commit the
attack, and she revealed in interviews that she had many problems
psychologically in carrying out the mission. She stated that her com-
manders directed her to dress like a Western woman—wearing
her hair down, putting on heavy makeup, and wearing tight pants.
During media interviews, Hamour stated, "I wasn't afraid. I'm not
afraid to die. I went for personal reasons. However, I did not want to
arrive 'upstairs' (in Paradise) for impure reasons. I did not want to
dress that way, because it is against my religion."[31] Another dispute
between the would-be suicide terrorist and her handlers was their
demand that she detonate the bomb even if she did not reach the
target site, such as if there were a chance she had aroused suspicion
and would get caught. "To blow myself up for nothing, what for?" she
asked. "To die just so that my operators can brag about carrying out
a terrorist attack?"[32]

Female suicide terrorists were also prevalent during the 2003–
2011 war in Iraq and US occupation of the country, where it was
believed that some women were motivated by the loss of their husbands or other loved ones, just as in the case of the Chechen "black
widows." Specifically, al Qaeda in Iraq, a home-grown Sunni insur-
gent group that was believed to be led by foreigners, recruited many
of these women.[33]

The widespread use of female suicide bombers in different
countries reflects the tactical advantages that women provide for
terrorist organizations. First, women are less suspicious than men

and are therefore less likely to attract the attention of security personnel. Second, in many of the conservative societies of the Middle East, South Asia, and elsewhere, there is a hesitation to body-search a woman. And third, a woman can wear a suicide device beneath her clothes, appear to be pregnant, and thus easily bypass security while approaching her target.[34] However, with the rise in female suicide attacks around the world in recent years, security personnel are becoming more aware of this form of terrorism, thereby eliminating the element of surprise for the female terrorist.

By the second decade of the twenty-first century, the role of women in terrorist organizations has changed from the heyday of female terrorism of the 1960s and 1970s. Whereas women had ascended to leadership and other important positions in the leftist revolutionary groups of that time, the new female terrorists of the twenty-first century are different. In many groups, they have simply been used as cannon fodder, another body to throw at the enemy in a suicide mission. No modern-day group has featured women in leadership roles, and there have been no female terrorists in recent history espousing ideology or gaining the type of worldwide publicity that Leila Khaled and Ulrike Meinhof were able to accomplish during their years of violence.

There have been many different opinions offered for why women join terrorist groups in general and become suicide bombers in particular. Some of these explanations point to a desire to achieve a level of status and respect in a society that is normally precluded for them. Others point to the exploitation and manipulation of these women by male leaders and recruiters of the terrorist organizations. Still others argue that women join for the same reasons men join—namely, to overthrow a government, establish a homeland, promote global revolution, and so forth. Meanwhile, studies have found that female suicide bombers tend to be mostly young, usually between the ages of seventeen and twenty-four, although there have been some who were as young as fifteen and others who were as old as sixty-four. These women come from various educational, religious, social, and personal backgrounds, with the more educated among them, including lawyers, paramedics, and students, accounting for the highest percentage of suicide attacks by women. It has also been found that most of the female suicide terrorists have average economic status and that they are rarely impoverished. Some, however, may have been "dishonored" through sexual activity or are unable to have children. Finally, some, as noted above, are motivated by revenge or grief from losing loved ones, including their husbands or children.[35] One terrorism expert succinctly describes the motivations for women as the "four Rs": revenge, redemption, relationship, and respect.[36]

We therefore have many different reasons offered for why women become involved with various terrorist movements. The common thread, however, is that all of their activity is conducted with some form of control by a terrorist group or at least by their recruiters and handlers. The female terrorist, whether voluntarily joining a movement or being manipulated or coerced into participating, is part of a group setting. Even if the time between being recruited or manipulated and then embarking upon a violent mission is just a few days, as has been the case for some female suicide bombers, there is still a sense of "belonging" to a group or movement. There will be interaction with others, perhaps in some cases only with the handlers, but, nevertheless, there is some human interaction, a characteristic that appears to be valued more by women than by men. This may offer us a clue as to why we haven't seen many female lone wolf terrorists. Like many things in life, the explanation has a lot to do with the social, emotional, and psychological differences between men and women.

WHY THERE ARE SO FEW FEMALE LONE WOLVES

While there is no consensus on how many lone wolf attacks have occurred throughout history, most observers agree that the total is quite small. Part of the problem in gaining a consensus stems from that old nemesis, the definitional dilemma. Disagreements abound about whether a lone wolf has to be an individual acting entirely alone or whether he or she can have some help from others, whether there has to be a political or religious motive, and so forth.[37] Furthermore, some terrorism databases do not even include lone wolf attacks, since their definitions of terrorism require that the violent act be committed by two or more people. However, in one chronology that has been published, it was found that, between 1940 and 2007, there were only thirty-two cases of lone wolf terrorism in the United States and only forty-two between 1968 and 2007 for a sample of other countries around the world. In comparison, there were 5,646 terrorist incidents for the same sample of countries (including the United States) between 1968 and 2007. In terms of the lone wolf attacks, a woman committed just one of them.[38]

The lack of female lone wolf activity can be attributed to several factors. These include women being less likely than men to take risks, women placing higher value on social interactions and belonging to a group than men, the lower probability of women developing antisocial personality disorders than men, the lower likelihood that women will kill a stranger, and the tendency for women to kill more on impulse and emotion than on premeditation.

Women Are More Risk-Averse Than Men

Lone wolf activity is a risky endeavor. This is true for both the lone wolf animal and the lone wolf terrorist. For the animal, going it alone increases the chance of death. Since wolves travel in packs to ensure their survival in the wilderness, including the ability to bring down large prey and ward off predators, it is rare when one wolf breaks away to venture out on its own. This can occur when a subordinate wolf in the pecking order of the pack is not getting enough food to eat (because that wolf must wait until the higher-ranking wolves have eaten and may only get scraps or even nothing at all) or is facing increased aggression from the pack's dominant wolves. It can also occur when a wolf wants to find a mate and is prohibited from doing so within the pack. Once the subordinate wolf leaves the pack, however, more difficulties can ensue, including the dangers of trespassing into lands belonging to other packs, the need to search hundreds of miles to safely find food, and other hardships. Sometimes, lone wolves may find mates and form new packs, but more often, they are likely to die, since they do not have the support of the original pack. When a wolf decides to leave the pack, then, it is taking a lot of risks. Lone wolves are estimated to comprise less than 15 percent of the world's wolf population.[39]

Similarly, lone wolf terrorists have to make choices about taking risks before venturing out on their own to commit a terrorist attack. An individual has to have enough confidence in his or her ability to hatch up a scheme, acquire the necessary weapons or explosives, reach the target, commit the attack, escape from the scene, and so on. There might at times be one or two other people to provide minimal assistance, but for the most part, the lone wolf terrorist is on his or her own. It is not an activity for those who are risk-averse. While joining a terrorist group and embarking on group missions is also filled with risks (i.e., death, capture, etc.), there is still the security of knowing that one is part of a group endeavor and that there will be others around to provide different levels of support, whether that be logistical, financial, or emotional. Decisions on taking risks are left to the leaders of the group or cell and not to the individual terrorist.

Being part of a group also provides protection against the risk of self-doubt and guilt over the killing of innocent people. Alison Jamieson, an expert on the Italian Red Brigades, pointed out the difficulty some Red Brigade (RB) prisoners had once they lost faith in their group while in prison: "As long as he feels his actions are group actions, performed on the basis of collective decision, he can avoid the sensation of personal responsibility. But if the group identity falls away he is forced to assume his individuality, see himself as a murderer, and is left alone with his guilt. The immediate reaction of many of the RB prisoners was to see suicide as a realistic and even attractive way out."[40]

To be a lone wolf terrorist, therefore, involves many different types of risks. And here is where gender differences become relevant. Research has found that women are less likely than men to take risks.[41] Among some of the explanations offered are that women view risky behavior as resulting in unfavorable outcomes more so than do men, and they believe that they will become emotionally upset or harmed by the negative outcomes, should these occur.[42] Another explanation proposed is that women are not as overconfident as men (where that could be a negative trait for men) and therefore not as likely to take risks.[43] Still another reason cited is that as primary caregivers (in the role of mother), women avoid risks that could harm that situation.[44] And yet another explanation links risk aversion to lower levels of testosterone in women.[45]

The relative lack of risk taking in women as compared to men appears, therefore, to be one reason for the scarcity of female lone wolf terrorists. We do not know whether, when contemplating a lone wolf mission, a man looks upon it as an adventure and throws caution to the wind while a woman is likely to be more cautious and calculate the numerous risks involved in going it alone. However, it would not be surprising if this were indeed the case.

Women Desire Interactions and Human Connections More So Than Do Men

Another important difference between the sexes that is relevant to understanding the dearth of female lone wolf terrorists is that women value human interactions and connections more so than do men. This is due to the different socialization processes that men and women experience throughout their lives. According to some experts, "Women are socialized to be interdependent and attuned to relationships, whereas men are socialized to be autonomous, independent, and self-reliant."[46] It has also been argued that "a women's primary motivation . . . is to build a sense of connection with others. Women develop a sense of self and self-worth when their actions arise out of, and lead back into, connections with others. Connection, not separation, is the guiding principle of growth for women."[47] Being and acting alone are not comfortable situations for women. As one observer noted, "Women perceive loneliness and social isolation as dangerous and threatening situations."[48]

Since lone wolf terrorism is an isolated activity, it is not surprising that we haven't seen many women engage in this type of violence. It is not an attractive option for those individuals who desire human interactions, even if those individuals have an interest in committing a violent act. Lone wolf terrorists choose to be separated and isolated from others when planning an attack. They may sometimes see this as an advantage, since it could increase their chances for a successful mission (no communications with others that the authorities could intercept, no fellow terrorists who might be arrested and thereby enable the authorities to discover the plot, and so forth). But for women, who are programmed more than men to seek human connections, joining a terrorist group or cell would be the better route to take.

Paranoid Schizophrenia and Antisocial Personality Disorders Are Less Common in Women Than in Men

We saw in chapter 2 that one type of lone wolf is the idiosyncratic terrorist. These individuals, such as Theodore Kaczynski (the Unabomber) and Muharem Kurbegovic (the Alphabet Bomber), may have political or other agendas, but they also suffer from severe personality disorders that affect their behavior. In those two cases, each terrorist suffered from paranoid schizophrenia. The same was true for Jared Loughner, the young man who killed several people in a failed attempt to assassinate Arizona congresswoman Gabrielle Giffords. We find, therefore, among some lone wolves, severe personality and psychological problems.[49]

With men displaying "higher rates of disorders linked to violence, such as paranoid schizophrenia and antisocial personality disorders," than women, we have yet another reason for the scarcity of female lone wolves.[50] Paranoid schizophrenia is just one of several different types of schizophrenia, which is a mental illness in which a person loses touch with reality.[51] Furthermore, not only are men more likely than women to suffer from paranoid schizophrenia, but when they do, the symptoms tend to be more severe.[52] These symptoms include delusions; auditory hallucinations, such as hearing voices; anxiety; anger; emotional distance; and violence.[53]

The personality disorder most associated with violence, however, is antisocial personality disorder.[54] This disorder, which, as noted above, is found more in men than in women, "is a type of chronic illness in which a person's ways of thinking, perceiving situations and relating to others are abnormal—and destructive."[55] Among the symptoms are a disregard for right and wrong, persistent lying or deceit, using charm or wit to manipulate others, aggressive or violent behavior, and lack of remorse about harming others.[56] While there is no agreement among experts as to why men are more likely than women to have personality disorders that are linked to violence, some argue that the disorders are due to a combination of genetic and environmental factors.[57]

WOMEN ARE LESS LIKELY THAN MEN TO KILL A STRANGER

Another reason why women are virtually absent from the ranks of lone wolf terrorists is that they are less likely than men to kill a stranger when they engage in solo killings. The victims of female murders are usually people close to them, such as a child, parent, lover, or spouse.[58] One of the characteristics of lone wolf terrorism (as well as terrorism perpetrated by groups or cells) is that it usually involves attacks on victims the perpetrator does not know. Whether it be a car bombing, a hijacking, or a mass shooting, it is unlikely that a perpetrator has had prior contact with the victim(s). There are exceptions, of course, such as Maj. Nidal Malik Hasan's shooting of fellow soldiers and others at Fort Hood, Texas, but even in that case, it was a mass shooting, with Hasan firing indiscriminately into a processing center for soldiers at the base. John Gilbert Graham blew up a plane with his mother on board, but in that same attack, he killed scores of other people he did not know. To be a lone wolf terrorist, then, one has to be able to murder complete strangers and not have a group to fall back upon for emotional or moral support. Women seem to have a harder time than men in doing that.

WHEN WOMEN DO KILL BY THEMSELVES, IT IS MORE EMOTIONAL AND IMPULSIVE THAN PREMEDITATED

As compared to men, when women kill, it is more often based on emotion and impulse. As one expert writes, "The major portion of violent crimes committed by women are characterized by great impulsiveness. Most murders perpetrated by women have a strong emotional motive, are unpremeditated, and are carried out while the woman is in a depressed, desperate or anxious state of mind."[59] Another expert found "instrumentally motivated violence to be more characteristic of men's motivations, whereas women are more apt to use violence for expressive purposes or as a way of releasing accumulated tension."[60] While some lone wolves may also release pent-up emotions and tensions by committing a violent act, their terrorism is nevertheless always premeditated. The tendency for women to kill based more on emotion and impulse than on premeditation is yet another reason why we haven't seen many female lone wolves.

There may be additional explanations for why men seem to dominate the world of lone wolf terrorism. Men, for example, are more likely than women to be familiar and comfortable with using explosives, assault rifles, and other weapons that are favored by many lone wolves. Boys are more likely than girls to grow up in environments in which they are taught how to use various weapons for hunting and other purposes. Shooting guns and playing with other weapons is considered more of a masculine activity, and it is something that many girls would not be interested in. We therefore have a larger pool of potential male lone wolf terrorists. Furthermore, around the world, there are more men than women who have had training in the use of different types of weapons in militaries. Lone wolves such as Timothy McVeigh, Eric Rudolph, and Nidal Malik Hasan all served at some point in the US Army, with Hasan still in the military when he committed his mass shooting attack at Fort Hood.

Another reason for the relative absence of women as lone wolf terrorists is that committing a terrorist attack by oneself can sometimes fulfill a need for a sense of power, dominance, and control over others, traits more associated with men than with women. While lone wolves have many different motivations for their attacks, ranging from political and religious to criminal and idiosyncratic, there might still be at work on some psychological level, whether conscious or subconscious, the desire to strike a blow all by oneself against a larger and more formidable enemy. By perpetrating a terrorist attack that causes fear in a wide audience and elicits reactions from governments and societies, lone wolves can satisfy that need.

BREAKING DOWN THE BARRIERS TO WOMEN BECOMING LONE WOLVES

Although the factors contributing to the scarcity of female lone wolves are numerous and varied, there are indications that some of these may be changing. First, we have seen a plethora of conflicts erupt around the world during the first decade of the twenty-first century that will fuel the flames of anger, hatred, and retaliation among many individuals for years to come. Memories of what happened to relatives, friends, and others in the wars in Iraq, Afghanistan, and elsewhere will linger long after the conflicts end. A parable about two Druze in Lebanon best captures the endless nature of terrorism. One Druze is walking down the road with grenades, machine guns, and daggers weighing him down from head to foot. He passes by a fellow Druze, who inquires why his friend is carrying so many weapons. The first Druze replies that he is going to the Abdullah house to kill all the people there because they killed his ancestors one hundred years ago. The second Druze looks at his friend in amazement and exclaims, "One hundred years ago! What's the rush?"[61]

Time is indeed on the side of those who seek revenge, including women. The "black widows" of Chechnya and the female suicide bombers in Iraq demonstrated how women who have lost loved ones during a war can be recruited by militant groups to commit terrorist attacks. It will not be surprising to see more women from these and other war-torn countries turn to terrorism, even without the support and training of an extremist group. We have new generations of angry young men and women coming of age around the world, and they have been socialized by their experiences to accept violence and terrorism as the norm and to not be afraid to take action on their own.

Another factor that might bring more women into the ranks of lone wolves is the global economic crisis, which will take a long time to resolve. This has led to major disruptions in people's lives, as they lose their homes, jobs, savings, and more. A sense of hopelessness consumes their everyday existence. Some of these unfortunate people may therefore turn to violence, including individual terrorist attacks, to address their grievances. This could include lone wolf attacks by men or women on banks, financial institutions, government officials, and others.

The most important factor, however, that is likely to lead to a breakdown in women's reluctance to engage in lone wolf terrorist activities will be the continual growth and impact of the Internet. Two recent examples may be harbingers of what is in store as more women gain confidence and knowledge through the Internet to embark on terrorist missions.

THE ONLINE ODYSSEY OF JIHAD JANE

It all started in June 2008, when a diminutive, forty-five-year-old, blue-eyed, American blonde, Colleen LaRose, posted a comment on YouTube under the username "JihadJane," stating that she was "desperate to do something somehow to help" the suffering Muslim people.[62] LaRose, a convert to Islam, had a troubled past, which included two failed marriages, convictions for passing a bad check and driving under the influence, and an attempted suicide. She posted many more YouTube videos over time, most of them training videos or violent scenes she had taken from jihadi websites.[63] She had a MySpace webpage that contained photos of her wearing both a hijab, which is a headscarf worn by Muslim women, and a burqa, which covers the entire face and body.[64] LaRose also used the alias "Fatima LaRose" in her numerous Internet postings and communications. She communicated via e-mail with people in Europe and South Asia about mutual desires to become martyrs for the Islamic cause.

One e-mail message she received in December 2008 was from a man in a South Asian country who stated his desire to wage jihad and become a martyr. LaRose responded with an e-mail indicating that she, too, wanted to become a martyr. Then, in January 2009, LaRose received an e-mail from a woman in a western European country, stating that she "tried twice [to become a martyr] but i wasnt [*sic*] successful . . . [but] i will . . . try until Allah will m[a]ke it easy for me." LaRose responded with an e-mail that once again expressed her desire to become a martyr in the name of Allah.

The flurry of Internet activity continued in February 2009, when LaRose explained in an e-mail to the South Asian man why she could be valuable to the cause of Islamic extremism. She wrote that, because of her all-American physical appearance and US citizenship, she would be able to "blend in with many people," which "may be a way to achieve what is in my heart." LaRose was in communication with yet another man from a South Asian country in March. This man stated that he "can deal in bombs and explosives effecti[v]ely" and that LaRose "can get access to many places due to ur [*sic*] nationality." That man also asked LaRose to "marry me to get me inside europe [*sic*]." LaRose agreed to marry the man and wrote that she would obtain residency status in a European country. LaRose then contacted the Swedish Embassy in March via e-mail, requesting information on how to acquire permanent residency status in Sweden. Less than two weeks later, that same man sent LaRose an e-mail telling her to travel to Sweden to kill Lars Vilks, a Swedish illustrator who had angered Muslims throughout the world in 2007, when he drew a derogatory caricature of the Prophet Muhammad. LaRose enthusiastically agreed, e-mailing back that "i will make this my goal till I achieve it or die trying." The man then instructed LaRose to kill Vilks "in a way that the whole Kufar [non-believer] world get [*sic*] frightened."

Having made contact through the Internet with other like-minded potential terrorists, LaRose then posted an online solicitation for funds on July 1. Meanwhile, the FBI, which by now had become aware of her attempt to aid and join Islamic extremist movements worldwide, interviewed LaRose on July 17. She lied to the agents, telling them that she had never solicited funds for terrorism, had not made online postings to a terrorist website, and had not used the online username "JihadJane." Apparently not concerned or worried about the FBI interview, LaRose continued to try to recruit more people.

After being encouraged and emboldened through her Internet activity to wage jihad, LaRose took the next step and traveled to Europe on August 23. She had in her possession the stolen passport of her boyfriend, which she intended to give to a male member of her budding terrorist network. The purpose of her trip to Europe was to live and train with jihadists and to find and assassinate Vilks. She joined an online community while there that was hosted by Vilks. She also conducted online searches of Vilks and his location. On September 30, she sent an e-mail to the man she agreed to marry, stating that she considered it "an honour & great pleasure to die or kill for" him and pledging that "only death will stop me here that I am so close to the target!" However, she was arrested on October 16 after returning to the United States without completing her mission.

LaRose's arrest was not made public until March 2010, when

several people, including those with whom LaRose had communicated over the Internet regarding the plot to kill Vilks, were arrested
in Ireland. One of those detained was Jamie Paulin-Ramirez, another
American woman who had converted to Islam, whom LaRose had
recruited through e-mails for her planned terrorist activities. Paulin-
Ramirez returned voluntarily to the United States in April 2010 and
was arrested by federal agents in Philadelphia. She pled guilty in
March 2011 to conspiring to provide support to terrorists and faced
a fifteen-year prison sentence. She was scheduled to be sentenced in
November 2012. LaRose, meanwhile, pled guilty in February 2011
to four federal charges, including conspiracy to murder a foreign
target, conspiracy to support terrorists, and lying to the FBI. Her sentencing was scheduled for December 2012, where she faced the possibility of life in prison.[65]

We see in the case of Jihad Jane how a single individual, living
in a Philadelphia suburb, can, through the magic of the Internet,
build a terrorist network from scratch with online postings and communications. She demonstrated how an individual with no prior
contacts with extremists anywhere could announce her intention to
become a martyr for the Islamic militant cause and then just sit back
and see what unfolds. It would be hard to imagine LaRose being
able to reach around the globe for advice, support, funds, and comrades without the existence of e-mails, YouTube, MySpace, and other
Internet wonders.

The LaRose case, however, also illustrates a potential Achilles'
heel for lone wolves who act as recklessly on the Internet as LaRose
did. LaRose's flaunting of her desire to commit terrorist acts through
her numerous e-mails and her advocacy of Islamic extremism through
her many YouTube postings made her an easy target for identification by not only law enforcement agencies but also by others patrol-
ling the Internet to uncover extremist websites and those advocating
terrorist attacks. In fact, online monitoring groups such as My Pet
Jawa and YouTube Smackdown, whose volunteers pressure Internet
service providers to take down websites that are tied to extremist

groups or contain material in support of Islamic extremism, claim to have known about LaRose long before law enforcement discovered her activities and to have alerted the authorities about her growing militancy.[66] Therefore, one of the main advantages lone wolves have over organized terrorist groups and cells—namely, the ability to fly under the radar, since they usually work alone and do not leave a trail of communications that might be intercepted by authorities—can be compromised by those lone wolves who delve into the world of the Internet without taking precautions to cover their tracks.

BRITAIN'S FEMALE LONE WOLF: ROSHONARA CHOUDHRY

Whereas Colleen LaRose needed the emotional and logistical support of others to gain the confidence to plot a terrorist attack, all Roshonara Choudhry needed to gain the confidence to actually carry one out was a series of downloaded video sermons by the extremist cleric Anwar al-Awlaki. The American-born al-Awlaki, who was the spiritual leader of al Qaeda in the Arabian Peninsula, was killed in a US drone attack in Yemen in 2011. He could be considered the godfather of lone wolf terrorists, having influenced from afar a diverse array of extremists, including Maj. Nidal Malik Hasan. But it was his influence over Choudhry, a bright, young British woman whom he never met, e-mailed, or talked to, that demonstrates how rapidly one can be drawn into the web of terrorism via the Internet.

Choudhry was the eldest daughter of a poor family struggling to make ends meet. Her father was an unemployed Bangladeshi tailor. Her mother was born in Britain. Both her parents were living off benefits from the state and whatever income the children could raise through work. Choudhry was determined to make her life better than her parents', attending the prestigious King's College in London, where she studied English and communications and attained high grades. She also volunteered at an Islamic school. However, she inexplicably dropped out of college toward the end of her final year, despite the fact that she was expected to achieve a first-class degree, which is the highest level in the British university system.[67]

Unbeknownst to anybody, the model student began downloading the sermons of al-Awlaki in November 2009. She had given no prior indication of being sympathetic to those who espoused Islamic extremist views. But that is exactly what al-Awlaki did in his sermons. He preached "the need for violent action to combat the atrocities of the West against Muslims around the world, and urged followers to do what they could, when they could, no matter how small."[68] Choudhry downloaded and listened to more than one hundred sermons by al-Awlaki between November 2009 and May 2010. She would later tell police that she "became interested in Anwar al-Awlaki's lectures because he explains things really comprehensively and in an interesting way so I thought I could learn a lot from him and I was surprised at how little I knew about my religion so that motivated me to learn more."[69]

Choudhry's praise of al-Awlaki was similar to how Italian anarchists in the United States described the influence of another charismatic leader, Luigi Galleani, who, after coming to America in the early 1900s, became a lightning rod for the anarchist movement. His voluminous writings and spellbinding speeches quickly won him a loyal following. Those who heard him speak described him as a "forceful orator," "most effective debater," and the "soul of the movement." One anarchist recalled that "you hung on every word when he spoke," while another said that "he spoke directly to my heart." Other testimonials said that "he expressed what I wanted to say but couldn't because I didn't have the words" and that "you heard Galleani speak and you were ready to shoot the first policeman you saw."[70] The same could be said for al-Awlaki, who was able to do all of this over the Internet.

Choudhry didn't shoot a policeman. Instead, she targeted Stephen Timms, a member of parliament (MP) who supported the war in Iraq. She found a website that described his voting record and how he was among the most consistent supporters of the war. "That made me feel angry," Choudhry told police, "because the whole Iraq war is just based on lies and he just voted strongly for everything as though he had no mercy." She added, "I just felt like if he could treat the Iraqi people so mercilessly, then why should I show him any mercy?"[71]

Having decided to assassinate Timms, Choudhry purchased two knives and made an appointment to visit with him at one of his constituency meetings on May 14, 2010. Prior to the meeting, she paid off her student loan, relieving her parents of liability for the debt. After walking into Timms's office, she stated that she had to see the MP and not one of his assistants. Even though the security guard noticed that she seemed anxious, she was still allowed to wait for Timms. When Timms came out to greet her, he was surprised at what he saw. Choudhry, who was dressed in black and wearing traditional Muslim clothing, walked up to him as though wanting to shake his hand. He thought that was strange, since Muslim women dressed the way Choudhry was would not normally take the initiative to shake a man's hand. Choudhry then pulled a knife from her bag and stabbed him twice in the stomach. The security guard and one of Timms's assistants immediately restrained her until police arrived.[72]

Timms recovered from his wounds, and Choudhry was sentenced to life imprisonment with a minimum of fifteen years. Like most religious extremists, Choudhry showed no remorse and simply smiled when the sentence was announced. Timms expressed sympathy for the young woman, stating, "I think she wanted to be a teacher. Throwing all of that away because of what she saw on the web. I think that's tragic."[73] Choudhry thought it was noble: "I feel like I've ruined the rest of my life," she told police. "I feel like it's worth it because millions of Iraqis are suffering and I should do what I can to help them and not just be inactive and do nothing when they suffer."[74]

What baffled authorities was how Choudhry could fly so low under the radar. After her arrest, they searched her computers for contacts with Islamic extremists but found none. She had no connection to any Islamist group and had not attended any meetings.[75] She did not go to any mosque but instead prayed at home. One of the detectives questioning her could not believe she acted totally alone. "Forgive me," he said. "I just find it a little bit strange that you're doing all this on your own and not speaking to anyone else about [it]." Choudhry explained why she didn't talk to anybody about her militancy: "Because nobody would understand. And anyway, I didn't wanna tell anyone because I know that if anybody else knew, they'd get in trouble 'cos then they would be like implicated in whatever I do, so I kept it a secret."[76]

One can only imagine the discipline required for a young woman to keep to herself her journey from a diligent, top-of-her class student at a prestigious university to a fervent believer in jihad with the need to kill a politician based on his voting record in Parliament. Her suddenly dropping out of college, however, could have been a warning sign that something was amiss, similar to the practice of many suicide bombers who cut all ties with their families and friends weeks before they commit their attacks. But Choudhry's attack caught everyone by surprise. Not surprising, though, was the reaction of the British government, which called for websites hosting al Qaeda videos to be taken down. Security Minister Baroness Neville-Jones stated that the websites would be banned in Britain. "They incite cold-blooded murder," she said. "And as such are surely contrary to the public good."[77]

The Internet, however, is an irreversible fact of life in the twenty-first century, and for every militant site that is taken down, another one appears somewhere else in cyberspace, able to elude the authorities and appeal to impressionable and inquisitive people around the world. The void created by the killing of influential terrorists such as Anwar al-Awlaki and Osama bin Laden is quickly filled by others ready and willing to fan the flames of hatred and intolerance.

The Internet is also doing its part to convince some women that the risks of lone wolf terrorist activity are worth taking. In addition to offering valuable information on potential targets, weapons, tactics, and causes, it is also providing them with human interaction. Whether it is in the case of LaRose, who felt connected with others around the world through e-mails and other online activity, or in the case of Choudhry, who felt inspired by a voice and face that was always just one click away on her computer, nobody has to feel alone anymore when planning and implementing a lone wolf terrorist attack. The experiences of LaRose and Choudhry may just be the tip of the iceberg of more women joining the ranks of the lone wolves.

CHAPTER 5

LONE WOLF ASSASSINS

Long before the word *terrorism* was introduced to the world during the French Revolution,[1] another term associated with violence was already entrenched in the public's mind. The word *assassination* had its origins in a militant group, the Assassins, who were active in Persia and Syria between the eleventh and thirteenth centuries. Led initially by a charismatic figure, Hasan Sabbah, also known as the "Old Man of the Mountain," the group spread terror and fear throughout the region.

The Assassins came from the ranks of the Ismailis, a Shi'a Islamic sect, and were willing to die for their cause, which was to overthrow the Sunni establishment. They usually made no attempt to escape after thrusting daggers into their victims, who included princes, officers, and religious dignitaries.[2] The Assassins were fiercely loyal to their leader, who promised them entry into paradise if they obeyed his every command. As Bernard Lewis notes in his classic book *The Assassins: A Radical Sect in Islam*, the legend of the Assassins spread to Europe, where they caught the interest of poets, who became fascinated with the Assassins' devotion to their leader. "Just as the Assassins serve their master unfailingly, so I have served Love with unswerving loyalty," a Provençal troubadour told his lover. Another says: "You have me more fully in your power [than] the Old Man has his Assassins, who go to kill his mortal enemies."[3]

Assassination as a tactic of terrorists actually preceded the era of the Assassins. Jewish extremist groups—the Zealots and the Sicarii—used assassinations and other forms of violence as a means for provoking a revolutionary uprising against Roman rule in Palestine during the first century. That revolt failed, with more than nine hundred extremists taking their own lives rather than surrender to Roman forces, which were about to enter their fortress at Masada in the year 73 CE. Many other terrorist groups throughout history also employed assassination as a terrorist tactic, including Narodnaya Volya, which, as we saw earlier, waged an assassination campaign against the Russian government in the late-nineteenth century.

Assassinations can take many different forms. The Assassins and the Zealots stabbed their victims to death, while Narodnaya Volya used dynamite to kill its targets. Today's assassins can choose from a variety of weapons, ranging from assault rifles and sophisticated improvised explosive devices to secretive weapons such as poison-tipped umbrellas.[4] Yet, despite the widespread use of assassinations by groups, individuals, and states, it is not always accepted that this is indeed an act of terrorism. For example, one author writes: "The violence I discuss involves in most instances politically motivated activity by groups, not individuals. . . . [Terrorism is not] the isolated assassination of a government leader."[5]

However, the killing of a government leader, whether by a group, state, or individual, is never an "isolated" event, since it can have profound effects not just in the targeted country, but also around the world. "Among those who have fallen victim to the assassin's dagger, poison, bullet, or bomb are Roman tribunes, Arab caliphs, Ottoman sultans, European monarchs, US presidents, and scores of prime ministers and leading public figures," writes terrorism scholar R. Hrair Dekmejian. "All such assassinations, even those without a political motive, constitute acts of political violence because they have political consequences that alter the course of history. Although assassinations represent a micro-level technique of violence against state power, their impact often transcends the state to affect the international order."[6] Historian Franklin L. Ford further notes that assassinations have "demonstrated the capacity for affecting, often in the most dramatic fashion, situations which, in the absence of lethal violence, might conceivably have developed very differently."[7]

The idea of assassinations changing the course of history, or at least allowing us to speculate whether things would have indeed been different had a particular assassination not taken place, is a fascinating one. It is the reason why assassinations are a special form of terrorism. Whereas some terrorist incidents, such as the 9/11 attacks, can affect world events for many years afterward, most terrorist attacks have a short shelf life. A car bombing or hijacking, for example, can be quickly forgotten just months or even weeks after it occurs. Not so for most assassinations, which, even if they do not alter the future course of history, can still have a major impact on governments and societies. The fact that lone wolves are as capable as states and terrorist groups of perpetrating a major assassination is yet another reason why the individual terrorist demands our attention.

THE IMPACT OF LONE WOLF ASSASSINATIONS

What, then, have been some of the more notable lone wolf assassinations in history, and what have been the motivations and characteristics of these assassins? Before we can discuss this we have to first acknowledge the always interesting and controversial tendency for many people to see a "conspiracy" whenever a major event occurs in the world of terrorism. The Internet has given fuel to skeptics everywhere who can post their blogs and offer "credible" evidence that things did not really happen the way most people were led to believe they occurred. These blogs then get circulated around the world via the Internet, with countless others adding new "information" to the conspiracy. Among the far-flung conspiracy theories are those that claim it was elements within the US government—and not al Qaeda—that perpetrated the 9/11 attacks in order to build support for its own agenda, including a war on terrorism and the invasion of Afghanistan. Another revolves around the notion that it was a controlled demolition that brought down the Twin Towers and not structural failure due to the fire from the jet fuel of the hijacked planes that had crashed into the buildings.[8]

Assassinations, in particular, are favorite topics for conspiracy theorists. It is as though some people cannot accept the idea that a lone wolf, a virtual "nobody," can all by himself or herself kill a powerful leader. Surely, the thinking goes, it had to take elaborate planning, resources, strategy, and other coconspirators to successfully assassinate a president, king, or other ruler. Accepting the fact that a lone individual could kill a nation's leader also somehow psychologically makes that leader's death seem meaningless for many people. William Manchester, author of the bestselling book *The Death of a President*, put it best in a 1992 letter to the *New York Times* concerning the conspiracy theories regarding the assassination of President John F. Kennedy: "If you put the murdered President of the United States on one side of a scale and that wretched waif [Lee Harvey] Oswald on the other side," he wrote, "it doesn't balance. You want to add something weightier to Oswald. It would invest the President's death with some meaning, endowing him with martyrdom. He would have died for *something*. A conspiracy would, of course, do the job nicely."[9] Or as Jackie Kennedy said of her husband's death: "He didn't even have the satisfaction of being killed for civil rights . . . it had to be some silly little Communist."[10]

The lone wolf assassin has one major advantage over conspiratorial groups in committing an assassination—namely, the element of secrecy. The lone assassin "possesses his own secret which he will not consciously betray."[11] Groups or cells, on the other hand, have to worry about one of their members being arrested and revealing the plot before it can be carried out. "The critical facts are that very few lone assassins are apprehended before reaching the scene of the crime," writes terrorism expert David C. Rapoport, "while most conspiracies fail long before that point."[12] There have, of course, been many successful conspiratorial assassinations, including the murder of Archduke Franz Ferdinand, heir to the throne of Austria-Hungary, by a member of the Serbian nationalist movement "Union or Death" (also known as "The Black Hand" to its enemies) in Sarajevo in 1914, which was a major factor in the outbreak of World War I. But, as Ford points out, "conspiracy is certainly not the more common . . . [type of assassination] despite the eagerness of many observers to find elaborate collusion even in cases where little or no evidence for it exists."[13]

Planning and implementing an assassination is among the least complicated of all existing terrorist tactics. Whereas a kidnapping, hijacking, or other type of hostage situation requires the terrorists to plan for the aftermath of the attack (such as how long to hold the hostages, what demands to make, and so forth), an assassination is over once the bullet leaves the assassin's gun or the knife is thrust into the victim. Unless the assassination involves using an explosive device to kill the target, there is no need for an assassin to prepare the weapon, such as mixing the right ingredients to make a bomb or determining how to transport it to the target area. All of this makes the task much simpler for the lone wolf who wants to eliminate a head of state or some other high-profile individual. The challenge for the lone wolf assassin is to find the right opportunity to gain proximity to the unfortunate target and not have his or her weapon detected by whatever security personnel or devices may be in place.

Who, then, are these lone wolf assassins? A selective look at a few of the more notable ones in history reveals diversity in their backgrounds and motivations. What ties them together, though, is the ability to significantly impact events in a country, and sometimes in a region, by the single act of murder.

CHARLES GUITEAU AND THE ASSASSINATION OF PRESIDENT JAMES A. GARFIELD (1881)

In 1877, Leo Tolstoy penned one of the most famous opening lines in literature when he began his classic novel *Anna Karenina* by writing: "Happy families are all alike; every unhappy family is unhappy in its own way." Little did he know that, at that time, a product of a very unhappy family in America was well on a path to madness and murder that would transfix a nation and lead to the passage by Congress of one of the most important pieces of legislation in US history.

The usual explanation given in historical accounts for why Charles Guiteau assassinated President James A. Garfield on July 2, 1881, was that he was "a disappointed office-seeker."[14] The belief that denial of a request for a patronage job was a major factor in the assassination would play an important role in instituting civil-service reforms after Garfield's death. However, although Guiteau was obsessed with the idea that he should have been given a consular post in Paris for having supposedly once given a speech on behalf of Garfield when he was a presidential candidate, the real reason for the assassination was more complex. In Guiteau's twisted mind, he believed that something drastic had to be done to "remove" the president in order to save the nation from another civil war.[15]

Charles Guiteau was born in Freeport, Illinois, in 1841 to a mentally ill mother and an abusive father. His mother, who barely ventured outside the house, died when he was just seven years old. Her death was attributed to "brain fever," but she was probably insane. "I always felt I never had a mother," Guiteau would later say. His father, who one physician also believed was insane, would beat Charles in a vain effort to cure the youngster's speech impediment. The only positive force in his life was his older sister, Frances, who helped raise him and provided him with both moral and financial support throughout his life. However, she, too, would eventually be committed to an insane asylum. Many of Guiteau's other relatives were also mentally ill, including at least two uncles, one aunt, and two cousins.[16]

The young man was finally able to escape his dysfunctional family when he left home to attend college. But after just a couple semesters at the University of Michigan, he quit and went to live at the utopian Oneida Community in upstate New York, which was a religious commune that also practiced free love. It wasn't long before Charles managed to alienate many people at the commune with his belief that only he was divinely ordained to lead the community and that one day he would become president of the United States and, after that, ruler of the world.[17]

Guiteau left Oneida in 1865 for New York City, where he pursued a variety of failed endeavors, including trying to establish a daily religious newspaper. He also tried to extort money from the Oneida Community by threatening to make public some of the commune's sexual practices and alleged financial improprieties, but that also failed.[18] For the next fifteen years, Guiteau roamed aimlessly between New York and Chicago, winding up with dead-end jobs, including work as a debt collector. That job didn't work out, as he pocketed for himself all the debts he collected. He next somehow managed to pass the Illinois bar and become a lawyer without ever attending law school, although the bar exam consisted of just three or four questions. Not surprisingly, he was a terrible lawyer. In one case, his client was a petty larcener, and Guiteau made an hour-long speech to the jury, screaming and rambling incoherently and shaking his fists at the startled jurors. The latter rendered a guilty verdict without ever leaving the jury box. Guiteau also tried his hand at evangelism, but that also ended without success. He eventually got married, but his wife soon divorced him after he emotionally and physically abused her.[19]

By 1880, Guiteau had become immersed in politics, and he followed that year's presidential campaign closely. It was a tumultuous time for party politics in America, with the Republican Party split at its national convention in Chicago in June between two warring factions. On one side were "the Stalwarts," known for being unapologetic advocates of the spoils system, where elected officials would use patronage to distribute jobs to their friends and supporters, regardless of their qualifications for the particular job. On the other side were the reformers, known as "the Half-Breeds." The Stalwarts's candidate was former president Ulysses S. Grant, who would be serving a third term if elected, while the Half-Breeds had two contenders, John Sherman (brother of General William Sherman) and Senator James G. Blaine of Maine. When none of the leading candidates could win a majority of votes at the convention, the delegates turned to a dark-horse compromise candidate on the thirty-sixth ballot, James A. Garfield, who had been a general during the Civil War and was now a senator from Ohio.[20]

The nomination of Garfield caught everyone by surprise, including Guiteau, who had expected Grant to be the nominee. Guiteau was an admirer of Grant and the Stalwart faction, believing that the spoils system was the best way for him to attain a high-level government job. He had prepared a speech titled "Grant against Hancock" (the latter being the expected nominee of the Democratic Party), but once Garfield got the nomination, he simply changed the title to "Garfield against Hancock" and left virtually everything else the same.[21] It was this speech that Guiteau would later claim helped win Garfield the presidency. And Guiteau believed that he should be rewarded by the new administration. The speech, which may have once been delivered to a small audience in Troy, New York, asserted that if the Democrats won the presidency, it would lead to a resumption of the Civil War because the Democrats had only sectional, rather than national, loyalties.[22] "I think I have a right to claim your help on the strength of this speech," Guiteau wrote in a personal note to Blaine, the newly appointed secretary of state, shortly after the March 1881 inauguration of Garfield. "It was sent to our leading editors and orators in August. It was the first shot in the rebel war claim idea, and it was their idea that elected Garfield. . . . I will talk with you about this as soon as I can get a chance."[23]

Guiteau was relentless in hounding Blaine and Garfield about being politically rewarded. These were the days when citizens had easy access to elected officials, and Guiteau took full advantage of it. He would walk the corridors of the State Department and White House, seeking to talk with Blaine and Garfield whenever he spotted them, or he would have personal notes delivered to them. His continual requests for a high-level appointment to Paris finally angered Blaine, who in May 1881 shouted at him: "Never speak to me again on the Paris consulship as long as you live!"[24]

Around this time, two major figures in the Stalwart faction,

Senators Roscoe Conkling and Thomas Platt, both resigned from the Senate to protest President Garfield's refusal to follow their recommendations for patronage appointments. This was the inspiration Guiteau needed to finalize his plans to assassinate Garfield. He could now consider himself part of the Stalwarts, a comrade-in-arms, and no longer feel alone in his frustrations with the new administration. "Now, for the first time in his oddly chaotic life," political scientist James Clarke writes, "Guiteau found himself sharing his outsider status with men he admired: Conkling and Platt and the other Stalwarts. And it was in this realization—not the denial of the various appointments he had sought—that his assassination scheme germinated."[25] Guiteau believed that the "removal" of the president would unite the two factions of the Republican Party and save the government from "going into the hands of the ex-rebels and their northern allies," causing another civil war. In Guiteau's mind, it would be patriotism, not personal revenge, which would lead him to kill the president.[26]

He also found inspiration in a message he claimed came from God one night in May, telling him that "if the President was out of the way every thing would go better."[27] By June, Guiteau was well on his way to carrying out the assassination. He had purchased a .44-caliber, ivory-handled revolver for $10. He could have bought a wooden-handled model for $9, but he believed the more expensive one would look better in a museum or library, where he was sure it would be put on display after he killed Garfield. Guiteau had one small problem though. He was afraid of firearms and didn't know how to shoot a gun. So he went to the bank of a canal and practiced shooting at a small tree growing in the water. He also paid a visit to the jail he expected to be taken to after the assassination. He wanted to make sure it was both comfortable and secure. He was afraid that there might be lynch mobs after him, but he believed that would not last long, since the American people would ultimately understand why he killed the president and would eventually hail him as a hero.[28]

Guiteau also prepared several letters and notes that he knew would be read by the public after the assassination. In one letter, which he titled "Address to the American People," he wrote: "I had no ill-will to the President. This is not murder. It is a political necessity."[29] In another letter, he wrote: "The President's removal is an act of God. I am clear in my purpose to remove the President. Two objects will be accomplished: It will unite the Republican party and save the Republic, and it will create a great demand for my book, 'The Truth.' This book was written to save souls and not for money, and the Lord wants to save souls by circulating the book."[30]

Meanwhile, the thirty-nine-year-old Guiteau stalked the president, this time not seeking a job, but instead looking for the best opportunity to kill him. On one occasion, he attended Garfield's church with the loaded revolver in his pocket, but he decided against killing the president that day. On another occasion, after learning of the president's travel schedule from newspaper stories, Guiteau went to the Baltimore and Potomac Railroad Station in Washington, DC, with the intention of shooting Garfield. He changed his mind, however, when he saw that Garfield was accompanied by his wife. "My heart would not allow me to remove him in the presence of Mrs. Garfield," he would later testify at his trial. "She was a sick lady, and the shock might have killed her. That was my reason for not doing it. I only had authority to remove the President."[31] That "authority," which Guiteau would continually describe in his trial and in the letters he wrote preceding the assassination, came from God.

On yet another occasion, the evening of July 1, he sat on a park bench across from the White House and followed Garfield on foot as the president walked a few blocks to the home of Secretary of State Blaine. Again, Guiteau had his revolver with him but did not use it. He then followed both Blaine and Garfield as they walked together back to the White House, but, again, Guiteau chose not to kill either man that night. Guiteau was enraged at seeing Blaine, who had told him to never speak to him again, walking with Garfield. He believed that Garfield had "sold himself body and soul to Blaine." Guiteau promised himself that he would not hesitate at the next opportunity to assassinate the president.[32]

That would come the next morning, when he fired two shots at Garfield as the president was walking through the waiting room of the Baltimore and Potomac Railroad Station. Garfield was traveling from Washington to New Jersey, where he would pick up his wife, who was recovering from an illness at their summer home by the ocean, and then they planned to travel to Williams College in Massachusetts for Garfield's twenty-fifth class reunion. Guiteau had read about the president's travel plans and made sure that he would be in the waiting room when Garfield walked through, accompanied once again by Blaine. The first shot sliced through the president's right arm, while the second bullet went into his back. As Garfield crumpled to the floor, Guiteau attempted to escape, but he was promptly captured by a police officer and others who had witnessed the shooting. An angry crowd quickly formed after the shots rang out. As cries of "Lynch him!" echoed through the station, the police officer ushered Guiteau outside and transported him to police headquarters and then to jail. There had also been a mob gathering outside the station wanting to lynch the assassin.[33]

The president, meanwhile, was attended to by a growing stream of doctors who were called to the station. Garfield was later transported back to the White House at his own request, where it was not believed he would survive the night. However, when he made it through the first forty-eight hours, doctors became more optimistic, with one stating that the president would make a full recovery. That buoyed everyone's hopes, but his condition then worsened. It would still take two and a half months before he would die. His last days were spent at his seaside cottage in New Jersey, where he passed away on September 19. The cause of death was a rupturing of an aneurysm in the splenic artery.[34]

The president's slow death was one of the most agonizing periods in American history. People across the country woke up each morning wanting to know what the latest prognosis was for the president. What became apparent after his death was that the treatment he received was abhorrent. Garfield "had miraculously survived the initial trauma of the bullet wound, [but] was so riddled with infection that he was literally rotting to death."[35] The infection was caused mainly by his doctors' refusal to use sterilized procedures in treating Garfield. The practice of antiseptic surgery was still controversial in the United States (but not in Europe) at the time. Garfield's doctors repeatedly probed his wound with unsterilized hands and instruments in an attempt to locate the bullet. "Far from preventing or even delaying the president's death," wrote one historian, "his doctors very likely caused it."[36]

It wasn't long after Garfield died that his assassin was put on trial. Guiteau's lawyer, who was his brother-in-law, argued that his client was insane and should be found not guilty. The potential for Guiteau to "get away with murder," however, worried many Americans who wanted him hanged.[37] The prosecutor, retired judge John K. Porter, put it best in his closing argument when he laid the groundwork for why the jury should convict Guiteau even if they thought he was insane:

> If men like the prisoner were irresponsible [due to insanity], who would be safe? What household would be secure? What church would protect its worshipers, even with the aid of the law? . . . If it were true that . . . [all] insane [men] . . . are licensed to murder you and yours, they are equally licensed to forge your name, to enter your house by midnight burglary, to stab your wife as she sleeps by your side, to force your strong box and seize your wells, to ravish your daughters. This is the nature of the license, for which the counsel for the prisoner contends.[38]

Porter didn't have to fret about the jury's decision. Although the trial lasted more than two months, the jury found Guiteau guilty after just one hour of deliberation. Throughout the trial, Guiteau claimed that God instructed him to assassinate Garfield and that the murder was not related to his not receiving a political appointment. "I have told you a hundred times," a frustrated Guiteau told Porter in response to yet another question about his motivations, "that my getting or not getting the Paris Consulship had nothing to do with my removing the President."[39] In his disturbed mind, Guiteau believed that he would be preventing another civil war by killing Garfield. "I do not pretend that the war was immediate," he testified, "but I do say emphatically that the bitterness in the Republican Party was deepening hour by hour, and that by two or three years at least the Nation would have been in a flame of war."[40] He also told the court, "I am not a disappointed office-seeker."[41]

Guiteau was hanged on June 30, 1882. The lone wolf assassin would have been shocked, and maybe even amused, to learn that his moment of violence actually helped lead to one of the most significant government reform acts in American history. The perception that Guiteau was just "a disappointed office-seeker" led to the end of the "spoils system," whereby the majority of jobs in government went to the political friends and supporters of the president. Congress passed, and President Chester A. Arthur signed, the Pendleton Act in 1883, which provided that federal government jobs be awarded on the basis of merit and that government employees be selected through competitive exams. The law also protected government workers from being fired or demoted for political reasons. Other aspects of this revolutionary law made it illegal for supervisors and others to require employees to give political service or contributions. Finally, the US Civil Service Commission was established to enforce this act. The new law "transformed the nature of public service." When it went into effect, only 10 percent of the federal government's 132,000 employees were covered, while today, more than 90 percent of the approximately 2.7 million federal workers are covered.[42]

Unfortunately, another legacy of the Garfield assassination was ignored. The easy access any potential killer had to a president of the United States did not change with the killing of Garfield. Even though Americans had lost President Abraham Lincoln to an assassination less than twenty years earlier, the Garfield assassination did not result in an outcry that the president must now be protected. The American public "did not believe . . . that Garfield had been assassinated because he had walked into the train station, just as he had traveled everywhere since the day of his election, wholly unprotected."[43] The idea of placing Secret Service agents or other guards around presidents permanently and thereby distancing presidents from the public "seemed too imperial, too un-American."[44] It would take yet another assassination barely two decades later to change that perception.

LEON CZOLGOSZ AND THE ASSASSINATION OF PRESIDENT WILLIAM McKINLEY (1901)

At the dawn of the twentieth century, the United States was in the midst of building a powerful empire overseas while dealing with continuing labor strife at home. The United States had acquired the Philippines, Guam, and Puerto Rico, and had become the protectorate of Cuba, following a three-month war with Spain in 1898, and it had also sent troops to China in 1900 to put down the Boxer Rebellion.[45] But the foreign policy of the United States was not the major concern for a young man who was the son of working-class immigrants from Prussia. Leon Czolgosz was concerned most with what was happening inside America, and he didn't like it.

Czolgosz was born in Michigan in 1873 and spent most of his young life working in factories and mills. It was a time of escalating conflicts between labor and management in the United States, including the 1886 Haymarket Square bombing in Chicago that killed eleven people, with seven policemen among the casualties. Several anarchists were arrested, tried, and convicted. Four anarchists were hanged, and one committed suicide in his cell, even though there was no evidence linking any of them to the bombing. This angered many in the labor movement, including those who were just working in the factories, such as the teenaged Czolgosz.[46] He became further radicalized as time went on and additional violent incidents occurred between labor and industry. Losing his job at a steel mill due to a strike and being blacklisted afterward left an indelible mark on the young Czolgosz. He saw former coworkers in the same situation forced to leave town in the hopes of finding work, while those who stayed would hang around street corners hoping to hear about potential jobs. His brother would recall that it made Czolgosz "quiet and not so happy" and that he began to question his prospects for a good life.[47] He ultimately came to believe "that the oppressive American corporate structure could only be changed through revolution."[48]

Czolgosz was drawn to the writings and speeches of the anarchists and ultimately considered himself to be one of them. Anarchists called for the rejection of authority and the elimination of existing political, economic, and religious institutions. While some anarchists practiced the "propaganda by deed" credo, most anarchists in the United States were opposed to bombings, assassinations, and other violent acts. They believed that violence would only turn the public against their movement and that it would also be at odds with the utopian ideals of anarchism.[49] Czolgosz, however, came to believe that violence was justified. He attended a speech by the famed anarchist Emma Goldman in Cleveland in May 1901. Although Goldman told the crowd that anarchists were opposed to violence to achieve their ends, she understood why some anarchists rejected that approach. She said that some people were so consumed with passion that they could not sit back and do nothing as they watch injustices being committed. The speech "overwhelmed Czolgosz" and gave him the "inspiration" he needed to become one of those who would not sit idly by. "He hadn't worked [it] out exactly, and probably only vaguely understood what it meant," writes author Scott Miller, "but Czolgosz seemed from this night on to have resolved to pursue the life of a radical social revolutionary."[50]

The anarchists, however, wanted no part of Czolgosz. He was viewed suspiciously by those he met, with some believing he was a government infiltrator. He asked too many questions, wanted to be introduced to other anarchists around the country, and was advocating violence that not all the anarchists prescribed to. The editor of a major anarchist newspaper, *Free Society*, felt compelled to warn others about Czolgosz on September 1, 1901. After giving a physical description of Czolgosz and claiming he was a government spy, the editor wrote, "His demeanor is of the usual sort, pretending to be greatly interested in the cause, asking for names or soliciting aid for acts of contemplated violence. If this same individual makes his appearance elsewhere, the comrades are warned in advance and can act accordingly."[51]

Having been rebuffed by those he admired and wanted to join, Czolgosz took matters into his own hands. There was speculation that the assassination of President McKinley may have been motivated, in part, by the *Free Society* warning about Czolgosz, who likely read it and then wanted to prove himself to be a loyal anarchist. He stated after his arrest that "something I read in *Free Society* suggested the idea." However, he never indicated that it was the warning about him that made him take action against the president. As political scientist Clarke notes: "The overall pattern of his behavior suggests that he had the assassination in mind long before the notice [about him] appeared."[52]

On September 6, 1901, Czolgosz was among the first standing in a reception line that was being allowed to greet McKinley at the Pan-American Exposition in Buffalo, New York. He had intended to kill McKinley the day before when the president gave a speech at the exposition, but he was too far back in the crowd to attempt a shot. He even followed McKinley when the president and his party took a short sightseeing trip to Niagara Falls on the day of the assassination, but again, Czolgosz couldn't get near the president to carry out his nefarious plot.[53] When McKinley returned to the exposition to shake peoples' hands, however, Czolgosz was ready. He hid his .32-caliber pistol in his right hand, which was wrapped in a handkerchief. He approached McKinley as if to shake his hand but instead shot the president twice, in the chest and abdomen. Czolgosz was wrestled to the ground as an angry crowd shouted its desire to lynch him.[54] The nation was spared the ordeal of seeing another president suffer a slow and agonizing death, as was the case with President Garfield. Nevertheless, it still took eight days for McKinley to die.

There would not be a lengthy trial, as there had been in the case of Charles Guiteau, the assassin of Garfield. Czolgosz was tried and convicted in a two-day trial that began on September 23, 1901. He was sentenced to death and executed by electric chair just a month later. The assassin hardly spoke during his short trial. He frustrated his lawyers, two former New York State Supreme Court judges who didn't really want the case but were nevertheless appointed by the trial judge. Addressing the jury, one of the lawyers, Loran Lewis, lamented, "Now, gentlemen, we have not been able to present any evidence upon our part. The defendant has even refused on almost every occasion to even talk with his counsel [and] he has not aided us."[55] Lewis also wanted everyone to know how much he despised being Czolgosz's lawyer. "I wish to say that I am accepting this assignment against my will," he said earlier at Czolgosz's arraignment, "and while it is more repugnant to me than my poor words can tell, I promise to present whatever defense the accused may have."[56]

That defense would be insanity. Lewis tried in vain to convince the jury that his client should be acquitted because he was not sane:

> All that I can say, to aid you, is that every human being . . . has a strong desire to live. Death is a spectre that we all dislike to meet, and here this defendant, without having any animosity against our President, without any motive, so far as we can see, personal motive, we find him going into this building, in the presence of these hundreds of people, and committing an act which, if he was sane, must cause his death. How, could a man, with some mind, perform such an act? Of course, the rabble in the street would say, "No matter whether he is insane or sane, he deserves to be killed at once," but the law says, no; the law says, consider all the circumstances and see whether the man was in his right mind or not.[57]

Lewis's precedent for making his argument was the M'Naghten Rule, which the courts generally followed as the test of criminal insanity. It basically stated that a defendant is insane if, at the time of the incident, he did not know what he was doing and did not know that it was wrong.[58] Czolgosz, though, gave every indication in statements he made to police and doctors before the trial that he knew the difference between right and wrong, and contrary to his lawyer's claim that he did not have any animosity toward McKinley, it was clear that he harbored deep resentment against the president.[59] He had informed the police that he believed it was his "duty" to shoot McKinley. He was upset with what he described as the president's indifference and hostility toward the working people of this country. "I didn't believe," he said, "[that] one man should have so much and another should have none."[60] Czolgosz told doctors who examined him that "McKinley was going around the country shouting prosperity when there was no prosperity for the poor man. I am not afraid to die. We all have to die sometime."[61] He also told the doctors that "I don't believe in the Republican form of government and I don't believe we should have any rulers. It is right to kill them."[62] Finally, he gave the prosecution all that it needed for a conviction when he said before the trial began: "I fully understood what I was doing when I shot the President. I realized I was sacrificing my life. I am willing to take the consequences."[63]

The consequences of his act of violence were enormous for many parties. For Czolgosz, of course, it meant death. For the anarchists, it led to a government crackdown on the movement that could best be described as the equivalent of contemporary society's "war on terrorism." This time, though, it was a war on anarchism, with the new president, Theodore Roosevelt, denouncing anarchism in his first State of the Union Address in December 1901 as "a crime against the whole human race." He added that "all mankind should band against the anarchist." Roosevelt said that an anarchist

is not the victim of social or political injustice. There are no wrongs to remedy in his case. The cause of his criminality is to be found in his own evil passions and in the evil conduct of those who urge him on, not in any failure by others or by the state to do justice to him or his. He is a malefactor and nothing else. He is in no sense, in no shape or way, a product of social conditions. . . . Anarchist speeches, writings, and meetings are essentially seditious and treasonable.[64]

Congress responded to Roosevelt's address by passing an immigration law in March 1903 that excluded from American shores "anarchists, or persons who believe in or advocate the overthrow by force or violence of the Government of the United States, or of all government, or of all forms of law, or the assassination of public officials."[65]

The assassination of McKinley also led to a new era of social reform in America. "If any assassination can be said to have changed history," writes historian Lindsey Porter, "McKinley's at least brought to public attention the social conditions of America's immigrant poor and paved the way for the policies of his successor, Theodore Roosevelt, and the Progressive Era."[66] Those policies included increased government regulation of business, such as the breaking up of monopolies and the protection of workers and consumers, and conservation polices, such as the establishment of several national forests and national parks. In foreign affairs, Roosevelt was more aggressive than McKinley, who was reluctant to go to war with Spain in 1898. Roosevelt's "walk softly and carry a big stick" policy sought to expand American power throughout the world, and he took every occasion possible to demonstrate to other nations the growing influence of the United States. For example, he once sent several warships to Morocco to demand the release of what was thought to be an American hostage, but it turned out to be an individual who had actually given up his US citizenship years before. Meanwhile, one of the crowning achievements of the Roosevelt presidency was the building of the Panama Canal.

One can only speculate on how much America was changed by the single terrorist act of a lone wolf assassin. It appears, though, that McKinley would most likely not have initiated the domestic reforms and tougher stance against big business that Roosevelt did and would not have been as assertive overseas as the new president. It also seems reasonable to argue that any hopes the anarchist movement had for increasing its ranks and getting its message across to the American people were dashed with the assassination and the wave of antianarchist sentiment that swept across the nation afterward.

LEE HARVEY OSWALD AND THE ASSASSINATION OF PRESIDENT JOHN F. KENNEDY (1963)

No assassination in American history has spurred more interest and more conspiracy theories than the killing of President John F. Kennedy in Dallas, Texas, on November 22, 1963. Gerald Posner, author of the bestselling book *Case Closed*, observed in 1993 that more than two thousand books had been written about that tragic day in Dallas, with most of them attacking the government-appointed Warren Commission's finding that Lee Harvey Oswald was the lone assassin.[67] There have probably been hundreds more written in the ensuing decades. And in today's computer age, conspiracy theorists can find outlets for their views on the assassination by posting blogs, articles, and other material on the Internet.

The fascination with the Kennedy assassination can be attributed to its special place in American history. Despite the fact that there had been an assassination attempt on President Harry S. Truman in 1950 by Puerto Rican separatists, most Americans by the early 1960s were not thinking about their leaders being the target of assassinations or other acts of political violence. In one respect, the public's mind-set was similar to that of the American people in the early 1990s, when it was thought that the US homeland was insulated from the terrorism that was rampant around the world. It took the truck bombing at the World Trade Center in 1993 to shatter that illusion, just as the JFK assassination shattered the illusion that the United States would not experience the political assassinations and other acts of terrorism that were common in other countries.

The Kennedy assassination, however, can probably be even better described as that era's 9/11. Although there weren't hijacked planes crashing into buildings, killing thousands of people and launching a global "war on terrorism," there was an equivalent sense of loss and despair throughout the country as well as a feeling that things were never going to be quite the same again. How all this came about can be seen in the troubled life of a lone assassin and a controversial investigation into the killing of a president.

Illustration of Charles Guiteau shooting President James A. Garfield at the Baltimore and Potomac Railroad Station in Washington, DC, on July 2, 1881. Garfield survived for more than two and a half months before succumbing to his wound. Guiteau, who was mentally ill, was found guilty and hanged on June 30, 1882. (Library of Congress)

Illustration of the assassination of President William McKinley on September 6, 1901. Leon Czolgosz, an anarchist, shot the president at the Pan-American Exposition in Buffalo, New York, with a concealed revolver in his right hand, which was wrapped in a handkerchief. McKinley died eight days later. (Library of Congress)

LEON CZOLGOSZ, WHO SHOT PRESIDENT McKINLEY.

The above pictures are snap-shots of the assassin taken just after his arrest.

LEON F. CZOLGOSZ, THE ASSASSIN.

Photographs of Czolgosz taken shortly after his arrest. He told police he thought it was his "duty" to shoot McKinley due to what he believed was the president's indifference and hostility toward the working people of the United States. (Library of Congress)

Czolgosz was tried and convicted in a two-day trial in September 1901 and executed one month later. The assassination of McKinley led the new president, Theodore Roosevelt, to declare the equivalent of a "war" on anarchism. (Library of Congress)

The Wall Street bombing on September 16, 1920, represented the first vehicle bombing in the United States. A horse-drawn wagon exploded in front of the J.P. Morgan and Company bank headquarters, killing thirty-eight people and injuring more than two hundred others. The bombing is believed to have been the work of a lone wolf terrorist, Mario Buda, who fled the country shortly after the attack. (Library of Congress)

A United Airlines executive points to the spot on the reconstructed plane where an explosion took place shortly after takeoff from Denver on November 1, 1955, killing all forty-four people onboard. The incident represented the first major midair plane bombing in US history. (AP Photo/Edward O. Eisenhand)

John Gilbert Graham sits with his wife, Gloria, outside a district courtroom in Denver. Graham had placed several sticks of dynamite in his mother's luggage on the United Airlines plane in order to collect a $37,500 insurance policy he had taken on her life. The bombing made the public and the government aware for the first time of the need for airline security measures. Graham was executed in 1957. (AP Photo)

Muharem Kurbegovic held Los Angeles in fear during the summer of 1974 with a bombing at Los Angeles International Airport and a series of subsequent terrorist threats. He became known as the "Alphabet Bomber" because his attacks were supposed to spell out the name of his fictitious group, "Aliens of America." The first attack at the airport represented the letter "A." (AP Photo/Wally Fong)

Yigal Amir, the assassin of Israeli prime minister Yitzhak Rabin, in a Tel Aviv court. Amir killed Rabin on November 4, 1995, because he felt Rabin was betraying Israel in peace negotiations with the Palestinians. (AP Photo/Motti Kimchi)

The Unabomber's mansion in Montana. Theodore Kaczynski lived in this shack, where he constructed package bombs that he either sent to his victims or left at the scene of the attack. Over the course of seventeen years, beginning in 1978, he was responsible for a total of sixteen bombings throughout the United States that killed three people and injured twenty-three others. (AP Photo/Elaine Thompson)

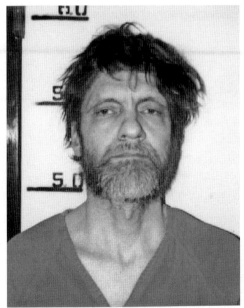

Kaczynski was arrested in April 1996 after his brother, David, informed the FBI that writings he discovered by Kaczynski resembled the Unabomber manifesto that had been published in the *Washington Post*. Kaczynski pled guilty and received a sentence of life in prison without the possibility of parole. (Federal Bureau of Investigation Photo)

Search and rescue crews attend a memorial service in front of the Alfred P. Murrah Federal Building in Oklahoma City. Until the September 11, 2001, hijacking-suicide attacks in the United States, this bombing by Timothy McVeigh on April 19, 1995, which killed 168 people, represented the worst act of terrorism on American soil. (AP Photo/Bill Waugh)

McVeigh being escorted by law-enforcement officials from the Noble County Courthouse in Perry, Oklahoma. The fact that the perpetrator of the Oklahoma City bombing was a homegrown terrorist surprised and shocked many Americans. McVeigh, who was a right-wing, antigovernment extremist, would later say: "The truth is, I blew up the Murrah Building. And isn't it kind of scary that one man could reap this kind of hell?" (AP Photo/David Longstreath)

Eric Rudolph was responsible for a bombing at the 1996 Summer Olympic Games in Atlanta as well as a series of bombings in subsequent years at abortion clinics and a gay nightclub. He was finally apprehended in May 2003. (*Huntsville Times,* Dave Dieter)

FBI agents wearing biohazard suits pour a liquid into a drum outside the American Media Inc. building in Boca Raton, Florida. Envelopes filled with anthrax spores were sent to several targets in September and October 2001, including media and congressional facilities. Five people died and seventeen others were infected due to the attacks. (AP Photo/Steve Mitchell)

REWARD
UP TO $2,500,000

For information leading to the arrest and conviction of the individual(s) responsible for the mailing of letters containing anthrax to the New York Post, Tom Brokaw at NBC, Senator Tom Daschle and Senator Patrick Leahy:

AS A RESULT OF EXPOSURE TO ANTHRAX, FIVE (5) PEOPLE HAVE DIED.

The person responsible for these deaths...

- Likely has a scientific background/work history which may include a specific familiarity with anthrax

- Has a level of comfort in and around the Trenton, NJ area due to present or prior association

Anyone having information, contact **America's Most Wanted** at
1-800-CRIME TV or the FBI via e-mail at amerithrax@fbi.gov

All information will be held in strict confidence. Reward payment will be made in accordance with the conditions of Postal Service Reward Notice 296, dated February 2000. Source of reward funds: US Postal Service and FBI $2,000,000; ADVO, Inc. $500,000.

The FBI and the US Postal Service released a reward poster offering up to $2.5 million for information leading to the arrest and conviction of the person responsible for the anthrax letter attacks. The poster included copies of the envelopes with handwritten addresses used in some of the attacks. (AP Photo/Brian Branch-Price)

Bruce Ivins was a microbiologist at the US Army Medical Research Institute of Infectious Diseases, located at Fort Detrick in Frederick, Maryland. He was working on an anthrax vaccine at the time of the letter attacks. The US Justice Department concluded that he sent the letters, in part, to increase interest and funding for his vaccine. Ivins committed suicide in July 2008. (AP Photo/*Frederick News Post*, Sam Yu)

One of the oldest terrorists in history was James von Brunn. A longtime neo-Nazi and white supremacist, he opened fire inside the US Holocaust Memorial Museum in Washington, DC, on June 10, 2009, killing a guard. Brunn was eighty-eight at the time of the shooting. (Talbot County Sheriff Office)

Major Nidal Malik Hasan was responsible for the worst terrorist attack ever to take place at a US domestic military installation. He shot and killed thirteen people and injured thirty-two others at Fort Hood, Texas, on November 5, 2009. Hasan was partly influenced via the Internet by Anwar al-Awlaki, an Islamic extremist cleric living in Yemen at the time. (Bell County Sheriff's Department)

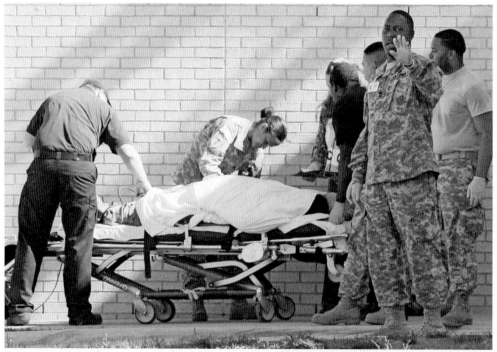

Emergency personnel transport one of the soldiers from the Soldier Readiness Processing Center at Fort Hood, where the mass shooting took place. Hasan, who was wounded by return fire, did not expect to survive the attack. (AP Photo/*Killeen Daily Herald*, David Morris)

A memorial service was held at Fort Hood on November 10, 2009, for the victims of the shooting. Here, chaplain of III Corps, Col. Michael Lembke, addresses the audience. (Department of Defense Photo/Cherie Cullen)

The US military collected biometrics from civilians, detainees, and others throughout Iraq and Afghanistan during the wars in those two countries. The information was used, in part, to identify known or potential terrorists. Here, an Afghan woman is having her iris scanned in September 2010, prior to being seen at a hospital in the Parwa province of Afghanistan. (Department of Defense Photo/Spc. Kristina L. Gupton, US Army)

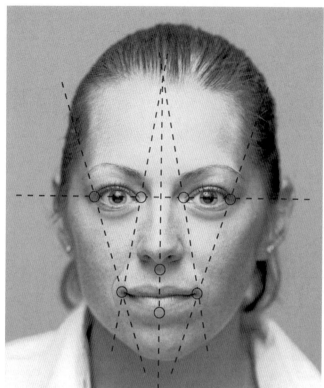

Face recognition is one of the biometrics being used by governments, militaries, and businesses for the identification of a person or for verification. Identification concerns determining who a person is, while verification concerns determining whether a person is actually who he says he is. (Federal Bureau of Investigation Photo/Criminal Justice Information Services Division)

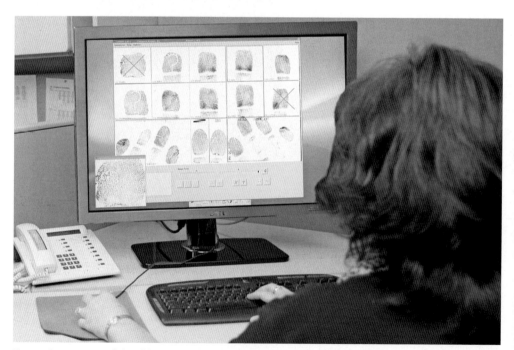

Fingerprints are one of the oldest and still most widely used biometrics. In 2011, the first phase of the FBI's Next Generation Identification (NGI) system was introduced, which improved the accuracy of fingerprint searches and added enhanced processing speed, automation, and searching capabilities. (Federal Bureau of Investigation Photo/Criminal Justice Information Services Division)

The FBI's Criminal Justice Information Services (CJIS) Division in Clarksburg, West Virginia. The new Biometrics Technology Center is scheduled for completion in 2014. (Federal Bureau of Investigation Photo/Criminal Justice Information Services Division)

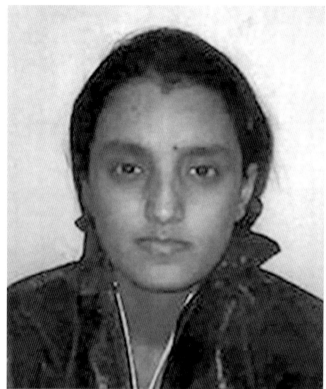

Roshonara Choudhry attempted to assassinate Stephen Timms, a British member of Parliament who supported the war in Iraq, on May 14, 2010. Choudhry acted after she had downloaded and listened to more than one hundred sermons over the Internet by the Islamic extremist cleric Anwar al-Awlaki. (Metropolitan Police)

Colleen LaRose, an American who called herself "Jihad Jane," used the Internet to appeal for help in becoming a martyr for the Islamic cause. She traveled to Europe during the summer of 2009 with the intent to kill Lars Vilks, a Swedish illustrator who had angered Muslims throughout the world by drawing a derogatory caricature of the Prophet Muhammad. She was arrested in October 2009 after returning to the United States without completing her mission. (Tom Green County Jail)

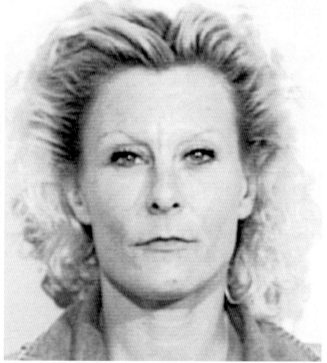

The world was shocked on July 28, 2011, when an anti-Islamic, right-wing lone wolf terrorist, Anders Breivik, massacred sixty-nine people, mostly youths, at a summer camp on Utoya Island in Norway. The camp was attended by the youth wing of the ruling Labor Party. Breivik had just hours earlier set off a car bomb that killed eight people in Oslo near government offices, including the prime minister's. Here, Norwegian flags and flowers are displayed near the island, which is in the background. (AP Photo/Lefteris Pitarakis)

A defiant Breivik upon arriving at his trial in Oslo. He had posted a fifteen-hundred-page manifesto online shortly before his attacks, in which he called for an end to "the Islamic colonisation and Islamisation of Western Europe" and the "rise of cultural Marxism/ multiculturalism," blaming Norwegian politicians for allowing that to happen. (AP Photo/Lise Aserud/Scanpix Norway/POOL)

Anwar al-Awlaki could be considered the godfather of lone wolf terrorists, having influenced many of them either over the Internet or in person. The American-born al-Awlaki, who was the spiritual leader of al Qaeda in the Arabian Peninsula, was killed in a US drone attack in Yemen in 2011. (Wikipedia Creative Commons/ Muhammad ud-Deen)

Lee Harvey Oswald had a lot of things going against him from the moment he was born in New Orleans in October 1939. For starters, his father had died two months earlier, forcing his mother, Marguerite, to make difficult choices regarding Lee and his brother and half brother. Not able to care for them on her own after having to get a job, she put the two older children in an orphanage and would have done the same with Lee except that the orphanage wouldn't take him because he was too young. Marguerite, who was described by Lee's brothers as quarrelsome, domineering, and "not easy to get along with when she didn't get her own way," had her sister, housekeepers, and babysitters care for Lee, moving to different places five times before finally putting three-year-old Lee in the same orphanage where she'd left his brothers. He was there for a little over a year before Marguerite decided to move to Dallas and took him and her two other sons with her. She then remarried and placed the two older children in a military boarding school. She traveled with Lee and her new husband extensively, since he was required to do so for his job with a utility company.[68]

Marguerite and her husband, whom Lee had grown close to, fought a lot and eventually got divorced. By the time Oswald was thirteen years old, both brothers had joined the military. Marguerite then moved with Lee to New York, where one of her sons was stationed in the coast guard. It was a difficult time for Oswald, who was teased by other students for his southern accent and shabby clothes. He failed most of his classes in junior high school, which wasn't surprising, since he usually didn't even bother to attend the school. He grew increasingly angry and difficult to control. On one occasion, he pulled a knife on his brother's wife and then punched his mother in the face when she told him to put the knife away.[69] On another, he was sent for psychiatric observation, where the examination report stated that he was "an emotionally, quite disturbed youngster who suffers under the impact of really existing emotional isolation and deprivation, lack of affection, absence of family life and rejection by a self-involved and conflicted mother."[70]

It was around this time that the seeds were sown for the assassination of President Kennedy many years later. When he was only fourteen years old, Oswald was given a Marxist pamphlet protesting the trial and impending execution of Julius and Ethel Rosenberg, who were eventually executed in 1953 for passing secret information about the atomic bomb to the Soviet Union. Oswald, at that young age, "began to see himself as a victim of capitalist oppression," which he blamed for all his problems.[71] He would continue to harbor those sentiments even when, a few years later, he enlisted in the marines. He learned to speak Russian while in the service and was not afraid to express his Communist sympathies.[72] It was remarkable that no action was taken against him in the military for his pro-Russian sentiments. It was his behavior, however, that got him in trouble, including his resentment at being told what to do as a marine. He was court-martialed and put in the brig for one month due to disputes he had with his superiors. He eventually obtained an early discharge from the marines, claiming he had to care for his allegedly disabled mother.[73]

Oswald had no intention of going back to his mother. Instead, he planned to defect to the Soviet Union, believing he would be welcomed there with open arms. He traveled to Moscow, where he tried to convince skeptical Soviet authorities that he had valuable military intelligence to give to them based on his marine experience. He denounced the United States and waited for the Russians to give him a good job and hopefully Soviet citizenship. However, when the Russians told him that he could not stay in their country, he attempted to kill himself by slashing his wrists. He was eventually allowed to stay for a couple years, but he was unhappy with life in the Soviet Union. He returned to America in June 1962 with his Russian wife, Marina, and their infant daughter.[74]

From that point until the November 1963 assassination, Oswald's life was a dizzying array of anti–US government activity, including walking the streets of New Orleans, where he lived for a while, to hand out pro-Cuba leaflets with the hope of eventually moving to that Communist country. His life also consisted of continual fighting with his wife, losing a job as a result of what he believed to be FBI harassment, and a failed attempt to assassinate right-wing, former major general Edwin Walker in Dallas in April 1963.[75] By November, Oswald was working in the Texas School Book Depository in downtown Dallas, a seven-story warehouse with a clear view of the route President Kennedy's motorcade was to take during his visit to Dallas. It was the moment Oswald had been waiting for his whole life, an opportunity to strike a major blow against the hated US government by assassinating its president and, at the same time, become known around the world.[76]

Perched by a window on the sixth floor of the warehouse, Oswald fired three shots from a mail-ordered rifle at the motorcade on November 22, fatally wounding Kennedy and also injuring Texas governor John Connally, who was riding in the same open-top limousine as the president. The Warren Commission, which investigated the assassination, concluded that one of the bullets exited Kennedy and struck Connally (the so-called single bullet theory, a finding that critics of the investigation have challenged). Oswald, meanwhile, was captured about an hour after the shooting, hiding in a movie theater after having also killed a policeman who stopped him in the street. Two days later, Oswald was himself shot and killed by a nightclub owner, Jack Ruby, as Oswald was being transferred from the Dallas city jail to the county jail. The killing of Oswald was seen live on television by millions of people.

The role of television during the Kennedy assassination was a watershed for the still-infant industry. For four long days, from the assassination on a Friday to the funeral and burial of the president on a Monday, the nation was transfixed by television coverage of the tragedy. But unlike some terrorist incidents that would unfold on television in later decades and cause great anxiety and fear among the public, the television coverage of the Kennedy assassination actually had a calming effect on the nation. People watching the events unfold on television were able to feel like they were part of the process. Many were comforted knowing that there were others sharing the same emotions as them. Nobody had to feel alone and isolated.[77] As Marshall McLuhan, the famous communications theorist, wrote: "The Kennedy assassination gave people an immediate sense of the television power to create depth involvement on the one hand, and a numbing effect as deep as grief, itself, on the other hand. Most people were amazed at the depth of meaning which the event communicated to them."[78]

Most people also refused to acknowledge that a lone wolf assassin was responsible for the shooting. In the immediate aftermath of the assassination, only 29 percent of the American people believed that Oswald had acted alone. There was no dearth of possible suspects as far as the public was concerned, with people claiming the assassination was planned by the Mafia, Fidel Castro, the Soviet Union, the far right in the United States, or others.[79] Adding to the confusion were conflicting reports on how many shots were actually fired. Some argued that one shot came from the front of the motorcade and not from the back, where Oswald did his shooting, meaning that there was a second gunman on a grassy knoll near where the motorcade passed. There were also disputes over the interpretation of a live film of the assassination and criticism of the Warren Commission. When the Commission, chaired by Supreme Court chief justice Earl Warren, reached its conclusion in 1964 (in an 888-page report with twenty-six accompanying volumes) that Oswald acted alone, many pundits criticized the findings. The title of one book summed up best the frustration of the skeptics: *Rush to Judgment.*[80] Its author, a former New York State legislator, Mark Lane, claimed that the conspiracy to kill Kennedy involved people, whom he did not name, at the highest levels of government.[81]

Other factors that contributed to conspiracy theories regarding the assassination included the Watergate scandal in the early 1970s, which led to a general distrust of government throughout the country, a reopening of the assassination investigation by Congress in the mid-1970s, and a controversial film by Oliver Stone in 1991, *JFK*, which mixed fact with fiction and portrayed the assassination as a conspiracy.[82]

The conspiratorial theories will undoubtedly continue, particularly as new interest arises coinciding with the fiftieth anniversary of the Kennedy assassination in November 2013. Computer reconstruction of the assassination has, however, supported the Warren Commission's finding that a single bullet struck both Kennedy and Connally from behind.[83] There has also been no convincing evidence yet presented to refute the view that Oswald alone killed the president. For a new edition of his book, which had argued that Oswald acted alone, Gerald Posner wrote in 2003 that "there has simply been no information or developments during the past decade that have changed the conclusions reached in *Case Closed*. Rather, the release of millions of pages of assassination related documents have bolstered the history originally set forth in the book. My only change for [the title of the new edition of the book] . . . might be to call it *Case Still Closed*."[84]

The impact that a lone wolf assassin can have on a government and a society can clearly be seen in the Kennedy assassination. One brief moment of violence led to the loss of innocence for the American people regarding political violence in the homeland. While there had already been violence associated with those who were opposed to the civil-rights movement of this period, the loss of the young president to an assassin's bullet had a special meaning for many Americans. The image of Camelot that had been built up while Kennedy was in office came crashing down with his death. The assassinations of Martin Luther King Jr. and Robert Kennedy a few years later would drive home the point that the United States was just as vulnerable as any other country in the world to having its leaders and other prominent individuals become the victims of assassins.

But it is in the realm of the Vietnam War that the impact of Kennedy's assassination has been one of the most hotly debated issues among scholars and other observers. The key question is whether the change in leadership from Kennedy to Lyndon Johnson had any significant effect on US involvement in Vietnam, a war that cost more than fifty-eight thousand American and over two million Vietnamese lives and divided American society throughout the 1960s until the war ended in 1975.[85] Princeton historian Sean Wilentz believes it did, arguing that "Kennedy probably would not have Americanized the war in Vietnam, as Robert McNamara and McGeorge Bundy on reflection have conceded. After the [Cuban] missile crisis, he was embarked on a course to wind down the cold war and stop nuclear testing and proliferation."[86]

There does appear to be enough evidence that points to Kennedy having the intention of ending US involvement in Vietnam had he been reelected in 1964. He had approved a plan to withdraw one thousand of the sixteen thousand American advisors by the end of 1963 and most of the rest by the end of 1965—there were no combat troops in Vietnam during the Kennedy years, while there would be five hundred thousand during the Johnson administration.[87] This, of course, does not mean he might not have reversed his decision as the situation in South Vietnam deteriorated and the Communist insurgents made significant gains in the country. But the groundwork had at least been laid for a de-escalation of US involvement in South Vietnam before Kennedy was assassinated. Some observers have even argued that no matter what the situation was in Vietnam after 1963, Kennedy, had he still been president, would not have changed his mind on the eventual withdrawal of all American advisors from that country.[88]

Meanwhile, the man responsible for this nation's grief and all the speculation on what might have been was buried in Fort Worth, Texas, on the same day that President Kennedy was buried. Whereas dignitaries from around the world attended the president's funeral in Washington, DC, and millions of people watched the proceedings on television, Lee Harvey Oswald had only his immediate family (his wife, Marina, their two children, his brother Robert, and his mother Marguerite) and a few other people at his burial. Oswald, who was such a troubled individual in life, would not even have the satisfaction of being able to rest in peace. Marina had his body exhumed in 1981, convinced by conspiracy theorists that it was not her husband in the coffin but rather a KGB agent. When it was determined that it was indeed Oswald, he was put in a new coffin, due to the deterioration of the original one, and reburied. The funeral home kept the original coffin and sold it at auction in 2010 for more than $87,000. Robert Oswald, who had tried to block the auction, then sued the funeral home, providing yet one more example of the never-ending saga of the Kennedy assassination.

YIGAL AMIR AND THE ASSASSINATION OF PRIME MINISTER YITZHAK RABIN (1995)

It is not surprising to hear about terrorist attacks related to the Israeli-Palestinian conflict. The modern era of international terrorism is usually traced back to 1968, when Palestinian extremists began hijacking and blowing up planes, among other incidents, while the Israelis struck back in retaliatory and sometimes preemptive attacks. Assassinations committed by both sides were a common feature of this ongoing battle. Yet it was a single assassination in the mid-1990s by an Israeli citizen against his nation's leader that had major repercussions that are still being felt today.

On November 4, 1995, Yigal Amir, a twenty-five-year-old religious Jewish extremist, fired three shots at Israeli prime minister Yitzhak Rabin at a peace rally in Tel Aviv, fatally wounding him and also injuring a security guard. Although the assassination shocked the country, it was not surprising. Rabin, along with foreign minister Shimon Perez, had long been the target of a vitriolic campaign by segments of the Israeli population. There were also some in the orthodox Jewish communities both in Israel and the United States who did not shy away from calling for his death. The reason for the hatred was Rabin's support of the 1993 Oslo Accords that, among other things, called for Israel to give up land in exchange for peace with the Palestinians. If ever there was an assassination that was just waiting to happen, the killing of Rabin would fit that bill. Despite all the rhetoric against Rabin, nobody took action except for Amir. How he came to be the one to carry out the assassination reveals some of the dynamics of the making of a lone wolf assassin.

Amir was born in the Israeli city of Herzilya in 1970 to a lower-middle-class family of Yemenites. His mother, Geula, the dominant figure in the family of eight children, was known for her extremist views. She even once made a pilgrimage to the grave of Baruch Goldstein, the Jewish extremist who killed twenty-nine Palestinians in February 1994 when he opened fire at worshippers at a mosque in the West Bank city of Hebron. Amir's father, who was an Orthodox Jew working as a calligrapher transcribing Jewish holy books, did not make much money, and it was left to Geula to become the family's breadwinner. She ran a private nursery in the family's backyard. Yigal, meanwhile, was sent to ultra-Orthodox schools. He also served in the army in the occupied territories during the first intifada (Palestinian uprising) that began in late 1987.[89]

It was when he enrolled at Tel Aviv's Bar-Ilan University to study law and computer science after leaving the army in September 1993 that Amir became radicalized. This was the same time as the signing of the Oslo Accords, which infuriated Amir and other Israelis. The accords called for Israel to recognize the Palestinian Authority as the governing body of the Palestinian people and grant the Palestinians self-government in parts of the West Bank and Gaza Strip. The Palestine Liberation Organization in turn recognized Israel's right to exist and renounced its intent to attack and destroy Israel.[90] The Amir family, like most Israelis, was divided over the Oslo Accords. Amir argued with his father, Shlomo, who supported the peace process. When Shlomo would say at the dinner table that Rabin should be given a chance, Yigal would angrily reply that Rabin was giving away the sacred land of Israel. When the discussion would come to an end, his mother, Geula, would sum it up and declare, "Yigal is right."[91]

Amir became involved in right-wing political activity while at Bar-Ilan University. He was the driving force behind student protests and led discussion groups on the future of Israel. He also organized solidarity weekends in Hebron to show support for the Jewish settlements there. Despite his activities, Amir "was a loner who felt uncomfortable as a registered member of any ideological movement or cell." Nevertheless, he would tell people that he felt an obligation to kill both Rabin and Perez. Nobody took him seriously.[92]

However, the notion of the right to kill Rabin, who as prime minister was the person most responsible for implementing the Oslo Accords, was a salient one in ultra-Orthodox communities both in Israel and in the United States. It was based on an obsolete Halakhic [Jewish law and tradition] precept of *din rodef,* which stated that it is the duty of Jews to kill a Jew who imperils the life or property of another Jew. Through a broad interpretation of *din rodef,* a number of Orthodox rabbis "reached the conclusion that relinquishing territory in the West Bank and Gaza Strip to non-Jewish rule endangered Jewish lives, making *din rodef* applicable to anyone who did so."[93] It was the Jewish equivalent of a *fatwa,* an Islamic religious ruling on any matter, only in this case it dealt with the justification for the death of a leader. Yigal Amir believed that he had received one, as can be seen in his explanation to investigators for why he assassinated Rabin:

> Without believing in God—a belief in the afterlife—I would never have had the strength to do it. In the last three years I came to realize that Rabin is not the leader who can lead the people. . . . He didn't care about Jews, he lied, he had a lust for power. He brainwashed the people and the media. He came up with ideas like a Palestinian state. Together with [Palestine Liberation Organization chairman] Yasser Arafat, the murderer, he was awarded the Nobel Peace Prize, but he failed to address his people's problems. He divided the people. He marginalized the settlers and didn't care about them. I had to save the people because they failed to understand the true situation, and that is why I acted. . . . If not for a Halakhic ruling of *din rodef* made against Rabin by a few rabbis I knew about, it would have been very difficult for me to murder.[94]

Amir stalked Rabin on several occasions before the assassination. He attended a ceremony in Jerusalem for victims of the Holocaust in January 1995, expecting Rabin to be there, but the prime minister canceled his visit. Then, he went in April to a folk festival that Rabin was to attend, also in Jerusalem, but Amir got nervous and left the site with his loaded gun. In September, he went to another ceremony near the city of Herzliya that Rabin was scheduled to attend, but Amir again lost his nerve and left before Rabin arrived.[95] He finally carried through with his plan when he shot Rabin in the back as the prime minister was walking to his car after a peace rally in Tel Aviv.

Amir was convicted and sentenced to life in prison for assassinating Rabin. He was also convicted, along with his brother Hagai and a friend, Dror Adani, on separate charges of conspiring to kill Rabin and to attack Palestinian Arabs. Amir, his brother, and their friend had often talked about killing Rabin, with only Yigal being totally serious about the assassination.[96] Hagai, who was an amateur gun enthusiast, had amassed a vast arsenal of guns and explosives in the Amir home in Tel Aviv. He also prepared the hollow-point bullets that Yigal used to kill Rabin. However, it was not determined whether Hagai had given Yigal these bullets with knowledge that his brother was actually going to follow through with the assassination. Investigators concluded that Yigal acted alone in killing Rabin on the night of November 4.[97] From all his statements and actions prior to the assassination, Yigal did not seem like the type of person who needed the help of others in killing Rabin. He was determined to do so no matter what, and it was just a matter of time before he found the best opportunity. His family, however, believed that it was a breakup with a girlfriend in January 1995 and her subsequent marrying of one of Amir's friends that set him on the path of throwing his own life away by assassinating Rabin. He became depressed after the breakup and, according to his brother, began talking about sacrificing himself.[98]

The assassination naturally shocked and saddened the country. One left-wing member of the Knesset described the assassination as "the most shocking political disaster in Israeli history."[99] Despite the anti-Rabin rhetoric that had been heard from those opposed to the Oslo Accords, "the vast majority of organizations and individuals who spoke the language of delegitimation and engaged in character assassination had not really wished to see Rabin dead."[100]

The assassination did, however, achieve one of the goals of the anti-Rabin sector; it slowed down the peace process.[101] Shimon Perez, who became the new prime minister upon Rabin's death, was only able to stay in office for a few months. He was defeated by Benjamin Netanyahu, leader of the conservative, right-wing Likud Party, in the May 1996 elections. Netanyahu would himself only stay in power for a few years, losing to Labor's Ehud Barak in the 1999 elections. (Netanyahu returned to office as prime minister after winning the elections in 2009.) The topsy-turvy of Israeli politics, therefore, continued as usual despite the assassination of Rabin. However, one can speculate as to whether Rabin would have been able to defeat Netanyahu in the 1996 elections and eventually successfully implement the Oslo Accords. Former US president Bill Clinton believes so, writing on the fifteenth anniversary of the assassination, in 2010, that had Rabin lived, "within three years we would have had a comprehensive agreement between the Israelis and Palestinians."[102]

Regardless of how things might have turned out, Yigal Amir nevertheless demonstrated the impact of a lone wolf assassin. His act of violence, at the very least, created uncertainty at the time in Israel and beyond about the Mideast peace process and caused concern in Israel about the ramifications of one Jew killing another. Some even worried that the assassination might eventually be seen as "the first shot in the Israeli civil war."[103]

A court-ordered psychiatric evaluation of Amir found him to be neither mentally ill nor emotionally disturbed. He did, however, have "narcissistic and schizoid tendencies and sees the world in terms of black and white."[104] He was also found to have the complex personality of a highly intelligent individual "who sought love and admiration at any price. He had a desire to prove to himself, his mother, his friends, and others that he could go further than anybody else."[105] He was afraid that somebody else might kill Rabin before he did and thereby stand in the way of his chance for fame. Perhaps most indicative of his self-aggrandizement was the following statement Amir made as he reflected upon the assassination: "My deed will be understood in the future. I saved the people of Israel from destruction."[106]

OBSERVATIONS FROM THE CASES EXAMINED

This brief look at four different cases of lone wolf assassins is certainly not enough to generalize about the characteristics and impact of all lone wolf assassins. It does, however, provide us with some interesting observations that may also apply to other lone wolf assassins.

First, in terms of their psychological makeup, only one of the assassins, Charles Guiteau, would qualify as being mentally ill. Guiteau was so delusional that he believed he deserved the top US envoy position to France, even though he had no government or diplomatic experience. A speech he had once made on behalf of President Garfield when the latter was a candidate was enough, in Guiteau's mind, to earn him the prestigious post. He was also convinced that God told him to kill Garfield in order to save the country from another civil war, a thought not based on reality. He believed that a grateful nation would eventually see the justification for the assassination and set him free. Yigal Amir also believed that God approved of his actions ("I have no regrets," he told the court. "Everything I did was for the sake of God."[107]) and that his country, too, would ultimately understand and honor him. He was not mentally ill. His belief—that if Yitzhak Rabin was removed from power, then the Oslo Accords might not be implemented—was not an irrational thought and was shared by many others. Leon Czolgosz and Lee Harvey Oswald were also not mentally ill, but both were similar to Guiteau and, to some extent Amir, in that they, too, were basically unhappy, depressed individuals with few friends.

Other studies of lone wolf assassins have found differences in the psychological makeup of the assassins. For example, terrorism scholar R. Hrair Dekmejian divided lone wolf assassins into two basic categories—pathological and political. Pathological assassins "target leaders or other symbols of authority as an expression of their individual pathologies such as paranoia, identity crisis, cognitive disorders, and feelings of inferiority, helplessness, rejection, or marginality." Dekmejian placed Guiteau (along with Arthur Bremer, who shot Governor George Wallace, and John Hinckley Jr., who shot President Ronald Reagan) into this category. Political assassins, on the other hand, who may have psychological problems, are nevertheless motivated primarily by political causes "based on ideology, ethnicity, or religion." Czolgosz, Oswald, and Amir are placed into this category by Dekmejian.[108]

In another study, political scientist James Clarke divided sixteen American assassins and would-be assassins (including both lone wolves and those who worked with coconspirators) into four basic categories that he simply named Type I, II, III and IV. The Type I assassins "view their acts as a probable sacrifice of self for a political ideal. . . . Their extremism is rational, selfless, principled, and without perversity." Czolgosz (along with John Wilkes Booth, among others) was put into that category. Type II assassins, on the other hand, are "persons with overwhelming and aggressive egocentric needs for acceptance, recognition, and status." Clarke put Oswald (along with female would-be assassins Lynette Fromme and Sara Jane Moore, both of whom attempted to assassinate President Gerald Ford) into this category. Type III assassins are "psychopaths (or sociopaths) who believe that the condition of their lives is so intolerably meaningless and without purpose that destruction of society and themselves is desirable for its own sake." Clarke placed Giuseppe Zangara (who attempted to assassinate President Franklin Roosevelt) and Arthur Bremer (who attempted to assassinate Governor George Wallace) into this category. Finally, Type IV assassins "are characterized by severe emotional and cognitive distortion that is expressed in hallucinations and delusions of persecution and/or grandeur." Clarke placed Guiteau, among others, into this category.[109]

While there were differences in the psychological makeup of the four lone wolf assassins we looked at, they were similar in one respect.

They all had a major impact upon government and society with their violence and, in some cases, may have altered the course of history. The assassinations of Garfield, McKinley, Kennedy, and Rabin each shocked their respective publics and, of course, led to new leadership. While the Garfield assassination resulted in the passing of a sweeping civil-service reform act a couple years later, beyond that, it did not appear to greatly alter the course of US domestic or foreign policy. The same could not be said for the assassinations of McKinley and Kennedy. The rise to power of Theodore Roosevelt was accompanied by major domestic reforms, including government regulation of business and the protection of workers, an assertive foreign policy, and a "war on anarchism" that might not have occurred if McKinley was still in power. In the case of Kennedy, many observers believe that, had he lived, the United States would not have escalated its involvement in the Vietnam War. And the speculation as to whether the Oslo Accords would have been implemented had Rabin lived continues today, as the goal of Mideast peace remains elusive.

The four lone assassins were also similar in that none of them "came out of nowhere," as is often said about lone wolf terrorists in general. All four lone assassins had exhibited erratic and other similar types of behavior that in some cases the authorities were aware of and, in other cases, other people knew about. Guiteau, for example, was known to President Garfield and his advisors, including Secretary of State Blaine, who became so exacerbated with the strange man wanting the appointment to Paris that he screamed at him one day to leave him alone. Czolgosz had alienated other anarchists with his odd behavior and his call for violent action. In the case of Oswald, the FBI was well aware of him, based on his defecting to the Soviet Union and his anti-US activity, including protests in favor of Communist Cuba when he returned to the United States. Amir, meanwhile, was known to Israeli authorities through his organizing of protests on behalf of the settlements in the occupied territories. None of this by itself would be a predictor that an individual would assassinate a head of state, but it at least indicates that these individuals did not become radicalized overnight and then decide to kill their leader.

The question of how to identify the early warning signs of lone wolf terrorism, whether in the form of assassinations or other types of terrorist activity, is one of the most difficult challenges facing law enforcement, intelligence agencies, and others whose job it is to combat terrorism. There is no group or cell to infiltrate, no members to arrest and interrogate for information, and no communications to intercept when it comes to lone wolves. By working alone, lone wolves hold a major advantage over the government and society they intend to attack. What, then, can be done to prevent and respond to this growing form of terrorism? We now turn to that important challenge.

CHAPTER 6

STRATEGIES FOR DEALING WITH LONE WOLF TERRORISM

Combating terrorism is one of the oldest professions in the world. Beginning with the Zealots and the Sicarii of the first century, who walked up to their targets with short swords hidden in their long coats, and continuing today with extremists utilizing a wide variety of tactics and weapons, governments have waged an endless struggle to prevent, deter, and respond to terrorism.

It has been a mixed record. For every plot uncovered or bomb discovered, there have been a far greater number of terrorists who have succeeded in carrying out their attacks. The task for those dedicated to fighting terrorism is quite daunting. Terrorists can strike anywhere, anytime, while it is impossible to protect every target, everywhere. That is why there can never realistically be an end to terrorism. There will always be vulnerable targets somewhere for a group, cell, or individual with varying motivations to exploit in a terrorist operation.

Depending on the type of terrorist involved, there are different actions that can be taken to deal with the threat. For example, when a terrorist group has the sponsorship of a government, or a government is using its own agents in terrorist attacks, the counterterrorist options are virtually unlimited. The targeted country can use all the tools at its disposal to attempt to end the state sponsor's activities. During the 1980s and 1990s, for example, the United States utilized diplomatic, economic, and financial sanctions against Libya for its role in sponsoring anti-US terrorist attacks. The United States also launched a retaliatory military raid against Moammar Gadhafi's regime in 1986, in response to the bombing by the Palestinian terrorist group, Abu Nidal, of a nightclub in West Berlin that was frequented by American troops. That incident illustrated the value of good intelligence in combating terrorism. US intelligence had intercepted conversations between Libyan diplomats in East Berlin and Gadhafi's headquarters in Tripoli that indicated Libya was behind the bombing that killed two US soldiers and one Turkish woman, and injured hundreds of others, including scores of American servicemen.

When dealing with a terrorist group that is independent of a state sponsor, as is the case for most terrorist groups around the world today, the options become more limited. Diplomatic and economic sanctions (i.e., trade embargoes and so forth) do not obviously apply for such groups. However, there are still many counterterrorist policies available, including cutting off terrorists' financing, as President George W. Bush did in the aftermath of the 9/11 attacks. Executive Order 13224 froze the US-based assets of those individuals and organizations that were known to be involved with terrorism, including those who had provided support or who were associated with terrorists and terrorist groups.

Military measures can also be used against terrorist organizations. This includes the targeted killing or capture of high-value terrorists overseas, such as group or cell leaders and bomb makers. Good intelligence and law-enforcement activities are also valuable assets that are used against terrorist groups, including the interception of their communications, using informants to learn about plots, and so forth. Cooperation among different nations' intelligence and law-enforcement agencies is an important part of this strategy. And, of course, good physical security measures, such as metal detectors, x-ray machines, and full-body scanners at airports, embassies, and other buildings and facilities that terrorists might strike, as well as closed-circuit television surveillance monitors and other devices, are all critical in helping to reduce the risk of terrorist attacks.

It is when the terrorist threat involves lone wolves and cells not affiliated with a central terrorist organization that problems arise in trying to design effective strategies. With regard to the unaffiliated cells, a lot of attention has been given in recent years to the threat posed by decentralized Islamic cells throughout the world. As noted in chapter 1, Marc Sageman has described these cells as "leaderless jihad." They act independent of "al Qaeda Central" (i.e., the core leadership), with no directions or communications coming from al Qaeda leaders in Pakistan or from al Qaeda–affiliated groups in Europe, Africa, Asia, and elsewhere. Oftentimes, the leaderless jihad cells are comprised of just a few individuals who decide to conspire together to promote jihad; they are basically "'homegrown' wannabes [who] form a scattered global network."[1]

Leaderless cells, however, can inflict as many casualties and cause as much destruction as the larger, more organized terrorist groups. Authorities often do not know who these individuals are or where their cells are located, in addition to various other factors that inhibit taking effective action against them. The threat, as Sageman points out, "has evolved from infiltration by outside trained terrorists against whom international liaison cooperation and border protection are effective to inside homegrown, self-financed, self-trained terrorists against whom the most effective countermeasures would be to stop the process of radicalization before it reaches its violent end."[2] The way to do this, Sageman proposes, is to take the glory and thrill out of being a terrorist, diminish the sense of moral outrage over US policies and actions, counter the enemy's appeal, end discrimination against Muslims, and eliminate terrorist networks.[3]

How, though, do we deal with lone wolf terrorists? Not all are attracted to notions of jihad or Islamic extremism. Among the lone wolves I have discussed in this book are politically motivated, non-religious extremists; white supremacists; single-issue militants; lone assassins; idiosyncratic individuals; and others. An end to Islamic extremism would not affect their activities. And there can always be new causes and issues that will arise and attract new types of lone wolves. It is, therefore, necessary to design a creative mix of policies and actions to deal with the unpredictable nature of lone wolf terrorism. This involves identifying both the preventive and responsive measures that hold the most promise.

PREVENTIVE MEASURES

"You don't prevent bank robberies," said James Thompson, former governor of Illinois. "You solve bank robberies after they happen. . . . The notion of trying to prevent attacks by radicalized Americans, or people in this country lawfully, is almost impossible."[4] The National Security Preparedness Group also expressed frustration regarding the prevention of lone wolf terrorism. In a report reviewing US counterterrorism efforts on the tenth anniversary of the 9/11 attacks, the group wrote that "it is simply impossible to know the inner thinking of every at-risk person. Thus, self-radicalization poses a serious emerging threat in the U.S."[5] And reporter and television commentator Geraldo Rivera, also writing on the tenth anniversary of the suicide attacks, noted that, while the United States was in a better position to prevent another 9/11-type attack from occurring, the lone wolf threat was a different story. "The one thing we can't prevent is not these vast [terrorist] plots but it's the lone wolf who gets it in his head to get a gun and shoot people. That's the danger going forward."[6]

The thinking that lone wolf terrorism cannot be prevented is understandable. Whereas governments, militaries, and law-enforcement agencies can devise comprehensive strategies to go after state sponsors of terrorism or terrorist groups themselves, the individual terrorist poses special problems due to his or her ability to "fly under the radar." It is ironic that we spend so much money and resources on the group terrorist threat—more than one trillion dollars was spent on homeland security in the United States in the decade following the 9/11 attacks[7]—with the goal of "defeating" terrorism, yet when it comes to the lone wolf terrorist, the tendency is to throw up our hands and say that there is very little we can do about it.

Why, though, should we concede the battle to the lone wolf when we spend so much time and resources on the other aspects of terrorism? While we can't expect to prevent every act of lone wolf terrorism, we can, however, take some preventive measures to help reduce the risk of lone wolves succeeding in their nefarious plans.

Improved Detection Devices

When one thinks about the millions of people who pass through airport security systems each day and the millions of pieces of mail that are sent daily around the world, it is amazing that we do not experience more terrorism than we have already. Finding every potential knife, gun, explosive, or other weapon that is either hidden in luggage or on a person who is traveling, as well as screening for every type of explosive that may be in an envelope or package that goes through postal offices, is an incredibly difficult task.

Protecting against terrorism has been a never-ending technological race against terrorists. As soon as new devices are designed and installed at airports, post offices, and other places to detect weapons, terrorists change their tactics to defeat them. It is a battle of wits, and the terrorists hold the ultimate advantage. No matter how many times security measures are effective in preventing terrorist attacks, the terrorists need to penetrate the system only once to demonstrate its weakness. Security personnel are then blamed for allowing the incident to occur. For example, Pan American World Airways was found guilty by a federal jury in 1992 of "willful negligence" for failing to prevent the 1988 bombing of Pan Am 103 over Lockerbie, Scotland, in which 270 people were killed, including all 259 on board and 11 others on the ground.[8]

Lone wolves have proven particularly adept at exploiting the postal service to send bombs or hazardous material. One of the most famous cases is that of Theodore Kaczynski, the Unabomber, whom I discussed in chapter 2. Kaczynski successfully sent bombs to targets throughout the United States for more than seventeen years. As noted in chapter 2, his campaign of violence led the United States Postal Service (USPS) and the FBI to warn the public about not opening letters or packages that had oily stains on the wrapping, since that could indicate leakage from batteries and/or other devices that were parts of a bomb. The public and postal employees were also warned about wires protruding from packages or letters, oddly-shaped packages (or ones of unusual weight given their size), excessive postage, hand-addressed letters or packages (perhaps with misspellings and no return address), or those with a return address that did not match the postmark. A law was also enacted requiring any letter or package weighing over thirteen ounces to be presented in person at a post office. That took some of the anonymity away from a potential lone wolf package bomber.

The sending of letter and package bombs was nothing new. As noted earlier in this book, an anarchist group, the Galleanists, sent thirty package bombs to various targets in April 1919, while Muharem Kurbegovic, the Alphabet Bomber, claimed to have sent nerve gas through the mail to the US Supreme Court justices in 1974, which turned out to be a hoax. Palestinians and Israelis traded letter bombs throughout the 1970s. And in October 2010, the Yemen-based al Qaeda in the Arabian Peninsula (AQAP) sent two cargo packages containing bombs hidden in the ink cartridges of printers to a Jewish synagogue and a Jewish community center in Chicago. The packages were intercepted by security personnel in Britain and Dubai after a tip from Saudi intelligence.

The experience of the British police with the AQAP package bombs is indicative of the tough job police, security, and intelligence personnel have with respect to discovering bombs in packages. London's Metropolitan Police Department Bomb Squad was called to the East Midlands Airport in central England in the early-morning hours of October 29, 2010, to inspect a United Parcel Service package from Yemen that Saudi intelligence believed contained a bomb. Bomb squads get calls all the time about suspicious packages that turn out to be harmless, but the Saudi tip made this one seem not likely to be a hoax. The police inspected a printer from the package, including lifting out its ink cartridge, but found no explosives. They also used specially trained bomb-sniffing dogs and put the printer through an x-ray scanner. When no explosives were detected, the bomb squad thought their day was over. But Saudi intelligence asked them to look again, because they were convinced that there was a bomb hidden in the printer. Sure enough, the second examination of the printer revealed four hundred grams of high-explosive pentaerythritol tetranitrate (PETN) hidden inside the ink cartridge. PETN was also found inside the ink cartridge of the package at the Dubai airport.[9]

AQAP taunted the West after the bomb attempt with the following statement: "[Our goal was to] force upon the West two choices: You either spend billions of dollars to inspect each and every package in the world or you do nothing and we keep trying again."[10] Since screening for cargo is not as extensive as the screening of passengers and their luggage and other possessions, AQAP had found a vulnerability and exploited it. And even when the British authorities were looking for the bomb, they still could not initially find it, since it is difficult to distinguish the plastic explosive PETN from similar nonlethal powdered substances.

Fixing this loophole in the airport security system is critical, since the AQAP package bombs had been placed on passenger jets as cargo during the first legs of their journeys.[11] A lone wolf could just as easily have constructed a PETN bomb and succeeded where AQAP failed. The AQAP bomb was discovered only because Saudi intelligence had information that the terrorist group was planning such an attack. Such intelligence is unlikely to be available to uncover a lone wolf plot, making the screening of cargo that much more significant. The single-view x-ray machines, which is the technology used at a large number of cargo warehouses around the world, lacks the resolution necessary to thoroughly inspect the contents of packages. New-generation multiview x-ray machines and explosive-trace-detection devices, which the British did not have at the time they inspected the package bomb, have a better chance of finding explosives such as PETN, but they are not used for all cargo flights.[12] Even if a lone wolf brings down a cargo flight rather than a passenger flight, there will still be casualties and worldwide reaction. Continuing to improve airline security measures for cargo is therefore an important preventive measure for potential lone wolf terrorist attacks.

Meanwhile, following the Unabomber attacks, the USPS made detecting letter and package bombs a top priority. However, due to the volume of mail sent daily, it was not feasible to screen all letters and packages for explosives. Since letter and package bombs are intended to kill or injure the recipient, it is the latter who has to play one of the key roles in preventing these attacks from being successful. This includes following the precautions noted above (being on the alert for letters or packages that have excessive postage, are hand-addressed with possible misspellings, contain oily stains, and so on). Letter and package bombs can also be intercepted by the alert mail carrier or other postal employees. For example, in June 2007, a mail carrier in Missouri found a suspicious package in a collection box addressed to the West Plains, Missouri, police. The Missouri State Highway Patrol's bomb squad x-rayed the package and discovered a pipe bomb inside. After rendering it safe, they sent the components to the US Postal Inspection Service's forensic laboratory in Dulles, Virginia, where it was traced to purchases made at a retail store. Copies of a surveillance photo and a reward poster were distributed to the media, and the suspect, Donald Wayne Schamber, was arrested shortly afterward. Schamber, who pled guilty and was sentenced in May 2008 to ten years in prison, told postal inspectors that he was trying to frame his ex-wife's husband as the mailer of the pipe bomb.[13]

Corporations and other large businesses that may be targets of lone wolves can also take preventive measures by utilizing various mail-screening technologies that are available. These range from low-cost desktop electronic devices that can automatically detect improvised explosive devices in letters and packages to more complex, conveyorized x-ray screening systems that are used in the aviation industry.[14]

While preventive measures can work with respect to letter and package bombs, it is more difficult when it comes to detecting biological agents. Bruce Ivins opened the eyes of the security world with his successful anthrax letter attacks in 2001. Now, in addition to worrying about package bombs, postal services, government agencies, and the public everywhere had to be concerned that lone wolves and others would be sending deadly biological agents through the mail. Most, if not all, deadly biological agents, however, cannot be detected until *after* they have been released into the environment. That is why there has been a major effort in the United States and elsewhere to improve the response time to a potential bioterrorist attack. Devices that can measure if anthrax, ricin, or any other biological agent has been released are important for providing early warning that an attack is underway. Accurate diagnosis and speedy treatment of victims can save many lives.

Among the devices utilized by the USPS following the anthrax letter attacks is the Biological Detection System, which is set up to screen the air above mail processing machines as an early warning sign that a biological agent has been released.[15] The US government has also deployed air monitors in thirty major cities, covering approximately 80 percent of the US population, to test for the presence of biological warfare agents.[16] However, until the day comes when detection devices are developed (if possible) that can accurately detect biological agents before they are released into the environment, terrorists, including lone wolves, will still have a major advantage over security systems everywhere.[17]

Expansion of Closed-Circuit Television (CCTV) in Public Settings

Nobody likes being watched. Yet the price for security against terrorism requires a little watching. How much, though, is always open to debate. Since the 9/11 attacks, the number of closed-circuit television (CCTV) cameras that monitor your every move in public settings has skyrocketed around the world. Britain, the United States,

China, and India are just a few of the countries that are utilizing CCTV to prevent crime, terrorism, and other illegal activities. In Britain alone, which is considered the CCTV capital of the world due to the prevalence of these cameras, it is estimated that there are nearly two million CCTV cameras, with the average Londoner being caught on camera approximately three hundred times each day.[18] Yet, in the case of Britain at least, CCTV has not been proven to have reduced crime or been responsible for catching a single terrorist before she or he went into action. Because of this, many observers have questioned its value. "CCTV leads to massive expense and minimum effectiveness," said David Davis, a British member of Parliament. "It creates a huge intrusion on privacy, yet provides little or no improvement in security."[19]

The CCTV cameras have, however, been effective in tracking down lone wolves and other terrorists after an incident and therefore preventing these individuals from striking again. One of the earliest examples occurred in April 1999, when David Copeland (mentioned in chapter 1), a British neo-Nazi who became known as the "London Nailbomber," embarked upon a thirteen-day bombing campaign that killed three people and injured 139 others. His target was the black, Asian, and gay communities of London. Copeland planted home-made nail bombs in public locations over three successive weekends. The first bomb exploded outside a supermarket in Brixton, South London, a district with a large black and minority ethnic popula-tion. The second bomb detonated in Brick Lane, East London, an area with a large South Asian community. The third bomb went off in a pub in Soho, Central London, which was frequented by the gay community.[20]

After the first bombing, the authorities viewed more than one thousand CCTV videotapes of the area, which contained approxi-mately twenty-six thousand hours of footage. Since the police had been able to recover a black sports bag that had contained the bomb, they looked on the videotapes for people carrying similar bags. They eventually saw images of a man carrying such a bag, and he became their prime suspect. After releasing the CCTV images to the media, the police received hundreds of calls and other information from the public. Their best lead came from one of Copeland's coworkers (an engineer who had worked with him on the London Underground), who recognized him from the released CCTV images.[21] But before the police could go to his home to arrest him, Copeland struck again with the Soho bombing. "I was devastated because we'd released the images . . . and we were actively following lots of information that had come through," said Detective Chief Inspector Maureen Boyle. "We'd not succeeded in arresting . . . him before he committed his next offence."[22] The arrest, however, did help prevent additional attacks, since Copeland confessed that he had three more multicultural areas in London on his list of future targets.[23]

CCTV cameras were also used in the aftermath of the July 2005 London bombings to identify the four suicide terrorists responsible for the attacks in the subway that killed fifty-two people and injured seven hundred others. Another example of effective CCTV use occurred during the November 2008 terrorist attacks in Mumbai, India, that killed more than 160 people. CCTV cameras were able to record the terrorists' movements during the shooting spree, which aided in the investigation of the incident. During riots in London and other cities in August 2011, British authorities posted CCTV images of looters and others, leading to information from the public that allowed them to make several arrests. And it wasn't just facial images that the British authorities used in their investigations. Since many of the rioters were aware that there were cameras watching, they hid their faces with scarves, bandannas, and hooded sweatshirts. But the CCTV cameras weren't fooled. "We can identify people on how they walk, their height, their clothes, shoes—all manner of things," noted Martin Lazell, chairman of the Public CCTV Managers Association, a body that represents council-run CCTV networks throughout Britain. "People recognized people by what they wear and often, despite having full wardrobes, we tend to wear the same clothes most of the time. These people won't be going home and burning their jeans, trainers, jackets, or coats so they can be identified and placed in an area."[24] The CCTV system also allows for tracing the earlier movements of suspects, by following them back in time to a period when their face was not hidden or where they might have gotten off a train, bus, or car, thereby yielding more clues as to where they live and other vital information.

CCTV systems, however, have to be more than just an investigative tool if they are to be of value for identifying lone wolves or any type of terrorist *before* such an individual acts. One factor that plays into the hands of police, intelligence agencies, and others whose job it is to protect against terrorism is the need for some lone wolves, just like other terrorists, to conduct onsite surveillance of potential targets. The use of the Internet for virtual surveillance has somewhat reduced the need for the physical inspection of targets. Still, terrorists usually do not just go off on a mission without some previous scouting of whom or what they are going to attack. This makes lone wolves vulnerable to detection by CCTV before they strike. And since they do not have others to assist them in the surveillance, lone wolves can become even more susceptible to discovery than "professional" terrorists. As one security expert noted: "A person unskilled in the art of surveillance, especially one who is mentally disturbed, will frequently commit many errors of demeanor. Thus, their odd behavior and crude surveillance technique—they frequently stalk and lurk—make them easy to pick out."[25] For example, Yigal Amir lurked in a parking lot prior to assassinating Israeli prime minister Yitzhak Rabin. Volkert van der Graaf hid for two hours in the bushes outside a building before killing Dutch politician Pim Fortuyn. And Abdulhakim Mujahid Muhammad (who changed his name from Carlos Bledsoe) had cased a Little Rock, Arkansas, military recruiting center before opening fire on two soldiers standing in front of the building, killing one and injuring the other in June 2009.[26]

As CCTV technology advances, there will be an even greater potential for these systems to prevent some lone wolf attacks. Imagine cameras that can "think" for themselves and automatically notify authorities that something "suspicious" is occurring at some point in a city, airport, train station, or other location? That is exactly what the next generation of CCTV technology is aiming for. It is known as "smart CCTV," or "video content analysis." The idea behind this is to solve the problem of there being too much video captured by CCTV for one person or even a group of people to view and interpret in a timely manner. Computer technology is therefore being developed that can recognize "suspicious" behavior in public places and then instantly send the information to a control room, where the CCTV controllers can decide what to do, such as notify nearby police about the situation.[27]

The problem, naturally, is how to define "suspicious" behavior. (We will see in the next section how advances in biometrics are attempting to solve that problem). Somebody who is just nervous, but not a threat, may still be spotted by the CCTV. The key is to teach the CCTV system what to look for. The system can learn what is and what is not normal behavior by analyzing and modeling behavior patterns. For example, a system might be able to locate people who are stopping in unusual places, wandering around a specific area, or leaving a bag behind.[28] One system that is being developed is based on a "surveillance profile" that is built into the CCTV cameras. It measures "various physical parameters such as size, shape, speed, time, movement, density, and location of a particular scene and [compares] these to a preselectable surveillance profile. If any parameters are exceeded, the cameras then spring into action and follow closely such unusual occurrences."[29]

Some camera systems are being developed in the hopes that they will be able to identify an individual who may be hiding a bomb under his or her clothes. The camera software would detect the bomb by assessing the way the individual walks or by focusing on tiny sensors that may be able to detect chemicals that were used to make the improvised explosive devices.[30] The US military used videostream sources to identify possible terrorists during the wars in Iraq and Afghanistan. "We [would] look at those videos," said a retired

Department of Defense intelligence analyst who did not want to be identified. "[One of the factors would be] the way they're dressed. They may be wearing a big outfit, and if we find that it looks too suspicious, we analyze the data a little bit further. The first thing we do is the facial recognition to see if that particular individual is in any of our databases so we can identify who that individual is. If he is not in our database, we may search someplace else to try to come up with a match." If the individual turns out to be somebody new who is not in any database, then that person will be given an identification code. "If we see them again in another video stream, then at least we'll be able to track it," said the former intelligence analyst.[31]

The widespread use of CCTV and other video sources can also serve as a deterrent to the lone wolf who is planning an attack. The more he or she knows that there are cameras watching, the less likely it may be that he or she will strike in that area. That does not mean, of course, that lone wolves and other terrorists will not adapt and strike at other targets or try evasive measures to avoid the cameras, but CCTV is still at least one more measure that can be taken to try to reduce the probability of a successful lone wolf terrorist attack.

The Lure of Biometrics

As promising as CCTV is for preventing lone wolf terrorism, biometrics may hold even greater hope for stripping away the anonymity of the lone wolf. Biometrics are the measurable physiological and behavioral characteristics that can be used to identify people. It is based on the principle that certain characteristics of the human body and certain behavioral patterns are unique to an individual. The history of biometrics can be traced back to fourteenth-century China, where merchants used fingerprints as a form of signature to settle business transactions and parents may have used both fingerprints and footprints as a way to differentiate children from one another.[32] In the late-nineteenth century, an anthropologist, Alphonse Bertillon, who was working as a record clerk in a Paris police station, developed a method for identifying criminals by taking precise measurements of their faces and bodies. This included, among other measurements, the length of the head, middle finger, and left foot. He also took frontal and profile photographs of suspects (i.e., the "mug shot").[33] The Bertillon System, as it became known, was based on the science of anthropometrics and was soon used throughout the world. However, it was eventually replaced by fingerprinting, which proved to be a more accurate measure of identification.[34] In 1924, a young J. Edgar Hoover, who had recently been named the director of the Bureau of Investigation, the forerunner of the FBI, created an identification division and introduced one of the first systematic uses of fingerprints to track down and identify criminals throughout the United States.[35] For most of the remainder of the century, fingerprints continued to be the main biometrics used by the FBI and other law-enforcement and government agencies around the world.

But a revolution in biometrics was in the making by the dawn of the twenty-first century. Advances in computer technology had allowed for the testing of various biometrics during the latter part of the twentieth century, but it was a combination of domestic and international events affecting the United States that propelled biometrics into the forefront of the public's consciousness. The first event was the 9/11 attacks on the homeland, which made security against terrorism a top priority for the nation. The US Visitor and Immigrant Status Indicator Technology (US-VISIT) program was initiated in 2004, using face recognition to screen photos of visa applicants in order to identify individuals who were previously denied, had their visas revoked, or were seeking multiple visas under different names.[36] US-VISIT, which is part of the Department of Homeland Security, operates the Automated Biometric Identification System, known by the acronym IDENT. This system maintains fingerprints, photographs, and biographic information on more than 126 million people and conducts approximately 250,000 biometric transactions each day, averaging ten seconds or less for each transaction.[37]

The wars in Afghanistan and Iraq also made biometrics a top

priority for the US government, which led the Department of Defense to deploy its own biometric system in 2004, also known as the Automated Biometric Identification System (ABIS). This system utilized palmprint, face, and iris matching to support US military operations overseas, with data taken from enemy combatants, captured insurgents, and other individuals.[38]

The FBI, meanwhile, had established the Integrated Automated Fingerprint Identification System (IAFIS) in 1999, facilitating the exchange of information regarding fingerprints of criminals, suspected terrorists, and others.[39] By 2011, the first phase of the FBI's Next Generation Identification (NGI) system was being introduced, which improved the accuracy of fingerprint searches and added enhanced processing speed, automation, and searching capabilities.[40] "We're finally in a position where we get reliable information, biometrically based fingerprints in a timely fashion that's accessible to the guys that need it," said William M. Casey, the program manager for the FBI's Biometric Center of Excellence, Criminal Justice Information Services (CJIS) Division, which is located in Clarksburg, West Virginia. "Getting the right information to the right people in a timely fashion is, I think, the whole thing about how information can be useful."[41] An ongoing goal of the US government is to attain interoperability among all the major biometric systems.

The advances that have been taking place in biometrics are truly breathtaking. Fingerprinting, which was the standard-bearer of biometrics for so long, has already been joined, as noted above, by several other physiological biometrics. These include, among others, face recognition, which measures and analyzes the overall structure, shape, and proportions of the face; iris recognition, which scans different points of the iris (the colored elastic and connective tissue that surrounds the pupil); retina scanning, which focuses on the blood vessels at the back of the eye; palmprint matching, which, like fingerprinting, analyzes friction ridge impressions; hand and finger geometry, which measures and analyzes the overall structure, shape, and proportions of the hand; and DNA analysis, which involves taking and examining samples of DNA from an individual's blood, saliva, hair, and so on. Ear and tattoo recognition are additional physiological biometrics that are emerging.

In addition to physiological biometrics, there are several behavioral biometrics that governments, militaries, law-enforcement agencies, and businesses are using. These include the following: voice recognition, signature recognition (which measures and analyzes the physical activity of signing, such as the stroke order, the pressure applied, and the speed), keystroke analysis (which measures the rhythm, time, and way an individual types on a keyboard), and gait analysis (which examines the way an individual walks).[42] The FBI's NGI system, in addition to dealing with fingerprints, is also examining these new biometrics. "NGI is looking out ten years as to what other modality biometrics are out there," said Stephen G. Fischer Jr., the unit chief for the FBI's CJIS Division's Multimedia Productions Group. "We're kind of still in the beginning stages of that."[43]

There are two basic ways that biometrics are currently used. One is for identification of an individual, while the other is for verification. Identification concerns determining who a person is. This involves finding a match for an individual's biometric data in a database containing records of people and their characteristics. For example, there could be a match of fingerprints or of a face, iris, or retina. This is also known as "one-to-many" matching, since one person is being matched against an entire database. (Additionally, there could be searches for multiple characteristics, which are known as "multimodal" biometrics and can improve the accuracy of the match.) Verification concerns determining if a person is actually who he says he is. This involves comparing an individual's biometric data to the previously recorded data for that person to ensure that it is the same person. Verification is mainly used for access control to buildings, computer systems, and other entities or systems that require verifying a particular individual. Verification is also referred to as "one-to-one" matching, since the person is being matched to only one other person in the database.[44]

The obvious drawback to using biometrics to prevent lone wolf terrorism, or any type of terrorism for that matter, is that a person has to be "enrolled" in a biometric system for it to be effective. In other words, there has to be a database that contains that individual's physiological or behavioral biometric characteristics. Otherwise, an individual who plans to travel to the United States to commit a terrorist attack will not raise a red flag when his or her biometric data is taken at some point before entry into the United States. As noted above, the long wars in Iraq and Afghanistan have yielded biometric data on many of these individuals, providing a safeguard against their trying to enter the United States under false identities.

An example of how biometrics could be used to prevent a lone wolf from emigrating to the United States to carry out an attack can be seen in the case of Mohammed Merah, a Frenchman of Algerian descent, who, in March 2012, launched three separate terrorist attacks in just over a week in France, killing four men and three children before he himself was killed in a shootout with French police. Merah claimed to be a member of al Qaeda, but no evidence supported that claim. (While he may have had some ties to al Qaeda and been under the influence of his brother, who was a radical Islamist, he basically acted alone in the attacks). He had traveled to Afghanistan and Pakistan and, at one point, was arrested by the Afghan police, who turned him over to the US military, which most likely took his fingerprints, iris scan, and facial image before transferring him to the French authorities. Merah was also put on the FBI's "no-fly" list, which contains the names of individuals who are not allowed to fly into, around, or out of the United States because they are deemed to pose a terrorist risk.[45] Even if Merah wanted to travel to America under a different name with a false passport, his biometric data would have alerted US authorities to his true identity.

In another case, an individual who had overstayed his visa in the United States attempted to gain employment at a nuclear power plant using a false document under a false identity to prove his legal status to reside and work in this country. The US-VISIT program, however, was able to use biometrics to determine his true identity, and the man was subsequently arrested.[46] While not a terrorist, the case nevertheless illustrates how the true identity of those who seek to work in critical infrastructure areas such as nuclear power plants can be determined through biometrics.

The homegrown lone wolf, however, poses many more problems regarding discovery than the foreign-based terrorist. If the home-grown terrorist has not done anything to put himself or herself on anybody's radar or into any biometric database, then it will be dif-ficult to identify that person as a potential terrorist, criminal, or someone using a false identity. And even if a person is in a biometric database and is found to have lied about his or her identity or is dis-covered to have been linked to a previous crime, it does not mean that the individual was planning a terrorist attack.

That is why the real promise of biometrics as a tool for pre-venting lone wolf terrorism lies in the second-generation biometrics that are currently being researched and tested. These biometrics go beyond the first-generation biometrics, such as fingerprints, iris scanning, facial images, and so forth, which are used to identify or verify who a person is. The second-generation biometrics are instead now aimed at predicting *what* a person is likely to do, similar to the goal of the "smart CCTV" cameras. The new biometrics basically try to detect suspicious behavior and gauge an individual's motivation and intent.[47]

There are several programs underway to develop and test sensors that can predict future human actions. One of the biggest is the Future Attribute Screening Technology (FAST) project being devel-oped by the US Department of Homeland Security (DHS). The project is based on the "theory of malintent." Malintent is the intent to cause harm. The idea is that someone with malintent "may act strangely, show mannerisms out of the norm, or experience extreme physiological reactions based on the extent, time, and consequences of the event."[48] Although the project is mainly focused on improving airport security, it may be applied to other venues as well, such as at border crossings or at large public gatherings, including sporting events and conventions.[49]

Among the types of sensors that are being developed to detect malintent are the following: a remote cardiovascular and respiratory sensor to measure heart rate and respiration; a remote eye tracker that uses a camera and processing software to track the position and gaze of the eyes and measure pupil diameter; thermal cameras that provide detailed information about changes in thermal properties of facial skin and help assess electrodermal activity and measure respiration and eye movements; a high-resolution video camera that, aside from generating highly detailed images of the face and body for image analysis to determine facial features and expressions and body movements, also has an audio system for analyzing human voice for pitch change; and other sensors for pheromones detection.[50]

The FAST system, and similar ones such as the European Union–funded Automatic Detection of Abnormal Behavior and Threats in Crowded Spaces (ADABTS), has been compared to the movie *Minority Report*, where Tom Cruise enlists the help of "precog mutants" to see into the future to determine who is going to commit a crime. The authorities then make a "pre-crime" arrest. But instead of using "precogs," FAST, ADABTS, and other systems are automated.[51]

If all this sounds futuristic, it is. The FAST program is still in the early stages of development, and the DHS has stated that they have no plans yet to deploy the technology publicly.[52] That has not stopped its many critics from voicing their opposition to the idea that one can predict hostile behavior by using remote sensors. "I believe that the premise of this approach—that there is an identifiable physiological signature uniquely associated with malicious intent—is mistaken," said Steven Aftergood, a senior research analyst with the Federation of American Scientists. "To my knowledge, it has not been demonstrated. Without it, the whole thing seems like a charade."[53] Another critic, Stephen Fienberg, a professor of statistics and social science at Carnegie Mellon University, notes that "it's mainly baloney. What evidence do we have coming out of physiology, psychology, or brain imaging that we can do any of this? Almost all of what I've seen and heard is hype."[54]

Time will tell if the critics are correct. FAST and other systems still have a long way to go before being fully tested and deployed in various places throughout the United States and possibly in other countries as well. Privacy issues will have to be addressed, including the willingness of the public to have their facial expressions, eye movements, heart rates, breathing patterns, and other characteristics captured by sophisticated sensors wherever they go in order for a decision to be made by others concerning what they *might* be intending to do. The potential for a high rate of "false positives" (i.e., people identified as "malintents" who are not intending to do anything criminal or terrorism-related) also has to be addressed. Defenders of the system, however, claim that it can work and that it has the ability to "tell whether a racing heart and sweaty skin are those of a nervous terrorist or merely a person who had to run to catch a plane."[55] If they're right, then a major breakthrough in preventing some terrorist attacks, including those of lone wolves, might be on the horizon.

Monitoring Lone Wolf Use of the Internet

Lone wolves like to talk a lot. This is one of the surprising findings from my study of lone wolf terrorists throughout history. Even loners have a basic human need for contact with others. It was harder in the days before the Internet, since they could not just sit at home and send e-mails around the world, post YouTube videos, create Facebook pages, or engage in other online activity to satisfy their need to express their views on various issues. But they still found ways to communicate their messages or sentiments to whoever would listen. Muharem Kurbegovic, the Alphabet Bomber, who terrorized Los Angeles during the summer of 1974, taunted the Los Angeles Police Department with audiotapes that eventually led to his identification and arrest. Theodore Kaczynski, the Unabomber, demanded that a manifesto he wrote be published in a newspaper, which it was, and which eventually led to his arrest after his brother recognized the writing style and notified the authorities.

The Internet, however, has made it easier and faster for lone wolves to communicate whatever messages and statements they want. Some recent examples of lone wolves who used the Internet to reach out to others, and, in doing so, may have tipped their hand as to their violent plans, include the following:

> *Colleen LaRose* (also known as Jihad Jane)—She used MySpace, YouTube, and e-mails to express her desire to become a martyr for the Islamic cause. She was in contact with other extremists online and traveled to Europe in August 2009 to be involved in an assassination plot.
>
> *Nidal Malik Hasan*—He communicated through e-mails with Anwar al-Awlaki, an American-born radical Islamic cleric who was living in Yemen, before he opened fire on fellow soldiers at Fort Hood, Texas, in November 2009, killing thirteen people and wounding thirty-two others.
>
> *Anders Breivik*—He posted an anti-Islamic manifesto on the Internet before he embarked on a terrorist mission that involved setting off a bomb in Oslo and massacring scores of youths on a Norwegian island in July 2011.
>
> *Joseph Stack*—He posted an anti–US government manifesto on the Internet before flying a plane into a building in Austin, Texas, in February 2010. The building contained offices of the Internal Revenue Service. One person was killed, in addition to Stack himself.
>
> *Richard Poplawski*—He frequented a neo-Nazi chat room on the Internet and was responsible for killing three police officers in Pittsburgh, Pennsylvania, in April 2009.
>
> *James von Brunn*—He posted anti-Semitic and racist writings on the Internet for years before killing a secu-

rity guard at the Holocaust Memorial Museum in Washington, DC, in June 2009. He also sent several e-mails with violent content to a friend in the weeks before the attack.

Bruce Ivins—He sent several alarming e-mails to a former colleague in the year before he launched the 2001 anthrax letter attacks that killed five people. In the e-mails, he described how he was experiencing "incredible paranoid, delusional thoughts at times."

Nicky Reilly—He was in contact over the Internet with extremists in Pakistan who encouraged him to commit a suicide terrorist attack in Britain, which he attempted to do in May 2008. The attempt failed when one of three nail bombs he was preparing in a restroom of a restaurant exploded in his hands.

Even Roshonara Choudhry, the "purest" of lone wolves, in that nobody knew anything about her radicalization and intentions to commit a violent act, still inadvertently revealed herself by downloading more than one hundred sermons by Anwar al-Awlaki, who influenced many lone wolf terrorists from his base in Yemen until he was killed in 2011. While the downloading of the al-Awlaki material by itself might not have been enough to alert the authorities to her desire to commit a terrorist attack (had they been monitoring everyone who was downloading his inflammatory sermons), when that information is combined with her suddenly dropping out of college near the end of her final year, even though she was expected to graduate with honors, it very well could have been a warning sign that she might be planning a terrorist mission.

The radicalization of individuals via the Internet, however, is not always the result of their just reading extremist groups' websites or downloading documents. Sageman argues that terrorist websites only reinforce what these individuals already believe in.[56] He notes that it is the online forums commonly known as "chat rooms" that are among the most influential aspects of the Internet for inspiring terrorist attacks by those who might otherwise never consider going to such extremes. Sageman writes:

> The interactivity is what is important. . . . Since physical militant sites, like radical mosques, are closely monitored by law enforcement authorities, militants have moved online. The new forums have the same influences that these radical mosques played in the previous generation of terrorists. It is the forums, not the images of the passive websites, which are crucial in the process of radicalization. . . . It is the . . . interactive exchanges in the chat rooms that inspire and radicalize.[57]

Regarding Islamic lone wolves, Sageman notes: "These loners appear as 'lone wolves' only offline. Most are part of a forum, where they share their plans and are encouraged by chat room participants to carry them out."[58] The same could be said for any lone wolf who has interactions with other extremists, or "wanna-be extremists," over the Internet. They are "lone wolves," but their desire for communication and human interaction via the Internet can give them away to the authorities. The monitoring of extremist chat rooms, which law-enforcement agencies in many countries already do, together with the identification of who the anonymous "chatters" are, is one way to get a head start on identifying potential lone wolves, whether they are Islamists, antiabortion militants, environmental extremists, right-wing militants, or others.

More problematic, of course, is how to discover the lone wolves who do not frequent any extremist chat rooms yet are still using the Internet to advance their plans. How to uncover that activity without violating law-abiding individuals' civil liberties is one of the more difficult tasks concerning Internet monitoring. However, real-time monitoring of the Internet for the posting of inflammatory manifestos, and the ability to react quickly, might have given some warning, albeit just a few hours, of Breivik's carnage in Norway and Stack's suicide plane mission in the United States. Both men posted their manifestos online the day of their attacks. It is not known if the authorities in either country knew about the postings before the attacks took place.

Governments around the world have been increasing their efforts to monitor Internet activity, although not always just for signs of potential terrorist threats. The US Department of Homeland Security, at its National Operations Center, monitors social media networks such as Twitter and Facebook. It has the authority "to provide situational awareness" for government officials "in the event of a natural disaster, act of terrorism or other man-made disaster" and to "ensure that critical terrorism and disaster-related information reaches government decision makers."[59] It was discovered, though, that a 2011 DHS manual called on analysts to identify and write reports about discussions on social media networks concerning "policy directives, debates and implementations related to DHS."[60] It was not determined whether DHS analysts actually produced such reports, but it is those kinds of revelations that alarm many people regarding government monitoring of the Internet.

Let us suppose, though, that the day will come when people believe that compromising some civil liberties and privacy rights in the name of being protected against terrorism is worth the trade-off, even to the extent of having their Internet activity monitored. After all, we have already made several trade-offs in the name of preventing terrorism, ranging from agreeing to pass through metal detectors and submit to full-body scans at airports (although the full-body scans have raised the ire of some people) to being watched by CCTV cameras when we enter buildings, attend events, or even just walk around a city. And our Internet activity is already being monitored by Google and other companies for advertising and marketing purposes. In 2011, for example, Google generated an estimated $36.5 billion in advertising revenue "by analyzing what people sent over Gmail and what they searched on the Web, and then using that data to sell ads."[61] However, even if everybody's Internet activity were monitored in order to identify the lone wolves or other types of terrorists among us, it would still probably not be effective. It would be very difficult, if not impossible, to distinguish a terrorist from a student, researcher, Internet surfer, and the like. For example, had such a monitoring system been in place as I wrote this book, then I would probably be at the top of the list of potential lone wolf terrorists. During the time that I conducted research, I visited numerous extremist web pages and postings; conducted Google searches for "bomb," "anthrax," "mass casualties," and other related words and phrases; and downloaded various documents about terrorism that would likely have raised a red flag.

There is little doubt, however, that the Internet is an indispensable tool in combating lone wolf terrorism. In some cases, Internet activity by lone wolves may be the only intelligence that the authorities have prior to an attack. Intercepting the e-mails of lone wolves who are in communication with radical extremists abroad, monitoring militant chat rooms and blogs, and uncovering online postings of the final manifestos by lone wolves, in which they basically announce their plans, are just some of the Internet preventive measures that can be taken.

In addition, the online purchase of large amounts of precursor chemicals that can be used for making improvised explosive devices or even chemical warfare agents is another possible indicator of lone wolf activity. For example, Anders Breivik, the Norwegian lone wolf, was put on a watch list, as noted in chapter 2, after purchasing large quantities of ammonium nitrate fertilizer from an online store in Poland. He was taken off the list after he explained to the authorities that the fertilizer was for use on a farm he had rented. However, he used it instead to produce the car bomb that he set off in Oslo as part of his dual terrorist attacks. Another suspicious online purchase would be for large amounts of seeds from the castor bean plant by an individual without any legitimate reason for doing so. The seeds can be used to produce the deadly toxin ricin. Although Breivik was not planning an attack with a weapon of mass destruction, the next lone wolf might be, and he or she could use the Internet to purchase the necessary ingredients for the weapon.

Before the advent of the Internet it was often said that there was a symbiotic relationship between terrorists and the media. Each needed and used the other for mutual benefit. The terrorists needed the media to publicize their cause(s), generate fear in the targeted country's population, and win new recruits around the world. The media, meanwhile, needed terrorist crises and other terrorist-related events to generate ratings for television and increased circulation for newspapers and magazines. While this is still the case regarding "traditional" media, the Internet has changed the dynamics of this relationship. Terrorists now have another option besides traditional media for getting their messages across, and they have certainly taken advantage of that with their websites, YouTube videos, Facebook pages, and other material they generate on the Internet. But this is a one-sided relationship; terrorists need the Internet more than the Internet needs them. And that fact may prove helpful to law-enforcement and intelligence agencies aiming to prevent lone wolf attacks.

Early Warning Signs

In addition to tipping their hands through their Interact activity, there are several other early warning signs that an individual may be on the road to becoming a lone wolf terrorist. One would be individuals who have broken away, been expelled, or been rejected by extremist or other fringe-type groups. These types of individuals can be dangerous, since they are sometimes viewed as too unstable or too extreme for membership in a terrorist or other type of militant group. Without the group decision-making apparatus to control their activities, these individuals may decide to launch their own terrorist attacks. I noted in chapter 2 that Timothy McVeigh began plotting the bombing of the federal building in Oklahoma City after a Michigan militia group distanced itself from him because its members found his views to be too radical. "Many lone wolves approached extremist groups but were rejected for being too extreme and unstable," observed Mark F. Giuliano, assistant director of the FBI's Counterterrorism Division. "The groups do not want to attract the attention of the FBI so they don't want these people as members."[62] Identifying who these individuals are may help prevent some lone wolf attacks.

Another characteristic often exhibited as an early warning sign of lone wolf terrorism is individuals who have had a troubled past, have displayed abnormal behavior, or have various personality issues. For example, the *New York Times* quoted an FBI bulletin that described people with difficult work and personal relationships and who have stood out to others due their erratic behavior as potential lone wolves. "Often there are early warning signs concerning these individuals that could be useful to law enforcement," the bulletin stated. "Many lone extremists, for example, have a history of functioning poorly within traditional communities, such as educational institutions, churches, and places of employment."[63] However, how to distinguish these types of individuals from those with similar behavioral patterns who, instead of becoming lone wolves, actually become very successful in life is difficult to determine.

Yet many lone wolves have exhibited psychological and personality disorders that, given their jobs and access to weapons and targets, should have been an early warning sign of trouble. Bruce Ivins, the perpetrator of the anthrax letter attacks, had a history of mental problems that, as a panel of behavioral scientists concluded, should have prevented him from attaining a security clearance and from being allowed to work with biological warfare agents. Maj. Nidal Malik Hasan, the Fort Hood shooter, also displayed abnormal behavior for a person employed by the US Army. As noted in chapter 2, an instructor and a colleague each described him as a "ticking time bomb," and he once told his supervisor that, as an infidel, she would be "ripped to shreds" and "burn in hell."

Sudden changes in behavior could be another indication that an individual is considering an act of violence. Several suicide terrorists in the Middle East and elsewhere withdrew from their family and friends once they decided, or were persuaded, to embark upon a suicide attack. Others, who may have had personal problems, suddenly appeared calm and relaxed to their friends after they decided they would launch an attack that would result in their death. The flip side of this are those individuals who are normally calm and friendly but who suddenly become extremely agitated and angry. This was true of Joseph Stack, who, as mentioned earlier, flew a plane into a building containing IRS offices in Austin, Texas. Stack, who was described by most people who knew him as easygoing, became increasingly angry in the weeks before his suicide mission, leading his wife to leave their house with their daughter the night before the attack.[64]

Another early warning sign of potential lone wolf terrorism is the suspicious purchase of various materials that can be used in constructing bombs or other weapons. In addition to monitoring the online purchases of such material, it is also important that law-enforcement agencies be able to know who has made such purchases in person at various stores throughout the country. The FBI, therefore, has a program in place known as Operation Tripwire, which enlists the aid of businesses in identifying such individuals. FBI agents meet with owners and employees of gun stores, chemical companies, beauty supply stores, and other industries to explain what types of suspicious activities to look out for. This includes, among other things, large purchases of precursors for making explosives (beauty shops, for example, sell hydrogen peroxide for coloring hair and acetone for removing nail polish, two ingredients that can also be used to make peroxide-based explosives, also known as "liquid bombs"), purchases of short lengths of pipe for constructing pipe bombs, and using cash for large transactions. The FBI urges these businesses to engage their suspicious customers in conversation, asking them questions and observing their responses, to gauge whether something doesn't sound quite right. If an interaction or transaction seems unusual, the business owners and workers are advised to contact the FBI's Joint Terrorism Task Force, which has offices throughout the United States.[65]

Lone wolves may also give themselves away by their recent travels.

Visits to countries or regions known for their presence of militants, terrorists, and the like should obviously raise red flags for any nation's security personnel. While such travel is not necessarily an indicator of being part of a terrorist plot or having ties to a militant organization, individuals who have recently traveled to these areas might nevertheless return home more radicalized and more susceptible to the influences of extremist groups and other militants than they were before they left their home country.

Countering the Message of Terrorists

Part of the battle against terrorism is a propaganda war. Al Qaeda has been among the best at the game of exploiting the Internet and traditional media for maximum benefit. Its media arm, al Sahab, has produced numerous videos and other online content over the years. Related groups, such as AQAP, have also played the propaganda game very well, particularly al-Awlaki, who, until he was killed in 2011, was the most influential media personality in terms of reaching potential lone wolves around the world. It remains to be seen if anybody else will be able to replace him as the Internet star that he became, but just like a corporation that has a high-profile vacancy at the top, there are likely to be several militants eager to advance their careers by taking his place.

How to counter the message of not just al Qaeda and related groups but also other extremist movements has been a major challenge for governments around the world. With respect to Islamic extremism, working with Muslim moderates to convey the message that the terrorism preached by al Qaeda and other militant groups goes against the teachings of the Koran has been one approach tried. The message that bin Laden and others "hijacked Islam" has been heard many times. However, as Sageman points out, there are limits to the effectiveness of counter-ideology as a strategy against terrorism. "I am not sure," Sageman writes, "that this strong emphasis on ideology, religion, and fighting 'extremist Islam' is fruitful. . . . I have come to the conclusion that the terrorists in Western Europe and North America were not intellectuals or ideologues, much less religious scholars. It is not about how they think, but how they feel. Let us not make the mistake of over-intellectualizing this fight. It is indeed a contest for the hearts and minds of potential terrorists, not an intellectual debate about the legitimacy of an extreme interpretation of a religious message."[66]

One of the recommendations that Sageman and others make, as noted earlier in this chapter, is to "take the glory out of terrorism."[67] Many impressionable youths around the world view terrorists as their heroes and only see the thrill and glory in engaging in terrorist attacks, not the suffering it causes to innocent victims and their families. The more these other types of images can be conveyed, as well as portrayals of terrorists as criminals and not glorified combatants or fighters, the better the prospects for countering the appeal of some terrorist movements. To that extent, as Sageman notes, high-profile press conferences announcing the arrest or capture of a terrorist can be counterproductive and only serve to elevate that terrorist to a higher status and generate more publicity. Indeed, one of the lessons about terrorism that has been ignored throughout history is that overreaction by governments, media, and the public to various incidents and attacks allows terrorist groups, cells, and lone wolves to achieve a status they would not ordinarily attain due to their size, power, and influence.

Another strategy that can be used to reduce the ranks of those who become attracted to terrorism via the Internet is to demonstrate the reality of a terrorist lifestyle. As one terrorism scholar notes, "Radical clerics and ideologues often glamorize and aggrandize the life of activists and martyrs and ignore the real-world lack of romance associated with this role. . . . [A] special emphasis must be placed on highlighting [online] the inglorious nature of a terrorist's life and daily separation from family and undisputedly denouncing the concept of martyrdom and use of violence for political ends."[68]

An innovative approach to countering the message of extremists is the community outreach program that President Barack Obama unveiled in August 2011. The idea behind it is to have the federal government "support and help empower American communities and their local partners in their grassroots efforts to prevent violent extremism." The strategy is aimed at "improving support to communities, including sharing more information about the threat of radicalization; strengthening cooperation with local law enforcement, who work with these communities every day; and helping communities to better understand and protect themselves against violent extremist propaganda, especially online."[69] The program, however, has been criticized for allegedly collecting intelligence on individuals in some cases, primarily in Muslim American communities, under the guise of working as a community partnership.

Increased Public Awareness

The idea that an alert and aware public can be an important element in preventing not just lone wolf terrorism but any type of terrorism is commonly accepted in many countries. Israel, for example, has experienced its share of terrorism over the years, and Israelis are therefore always on the lookout for unattended packages, suspicious individuals, and other things that may portend a terrorist attack. In other countries, such as the United States, however, the lack of sustained terrorist incidents has led to a sense of complacency among the public concerning the terrorist threat. Government officials have contributed to this perspective with the numerous terrorism warning alerts of previous years, including the ill-fated color-coded alert system that needlessly worried people about impending attacks that never materialized. The heightened public awareness regarding terrorism that occurred following 9/11 and the anthrax letter attacks eventually dissipated as the years went by without another major incident.

Nevertheless, the value of an alert public in preventing terrorism has been demonstrated in several cases, including, as noted in chapter 1, the case of passengers and crew onboard a Northwest Airlines flight who overpowered Umar Farouk Abdulmutallab, a Nigerian man who was connected with al-Awlaki's AQAP, when he attempted to detonate a bomb as the plane flew over Detroit on Christmas Day in 2009. Passengers and crew also subdued Richard Reid, a British citizen linked to al Qaeda, as he was trying to ignite explosives hidden in his shoes onboard an American Airlines flight in December 2001. Meanwhile, in Britain, a worker in a market in Brixton spotted one of the bombs left by David Copeland, the notorious nail bomber who set off three bombs in London neighborhoods in 1999, and alerted police. Although the bomb still went off, injuring scores of people, many more would have been hurt had an evacuation of the market not already been underway.

RESPONSIVE MEASURES

When a lone wolf succeeds in an attack, a combination of strategies can then be employed in response. Some of these overlap with the preventive measures just discussed, such as using CCTV cameras to identify and track the movements of the lone wolf both before and after the incident and using biometrics to identify the perpetrator. Other preventive measures, including the monitoring of Internet activity, can also be used to determine who may have been responsible for the incident. Diplomatic, economic, financial, and military countermeasures will not be effective, as noted earlier, in responding to lone wolf terrorism. (Though, in one case, the killing of al-Awlaki by a drone attack did eliminate an inspirational and influential figure for many lone wolves around the world.) Law-enforcement crackdowns on suspected terrorist groups will also not be likely to yield any information on a terrorist who works alone. However, there are still a number of response measures that may prove valuable for dealing with the lone wolf terrorist.

Use of Forensic Sciences

Forensic sciences, often referred to simply as forensics, is the application of scientific knowledge to legal issues. This is commonly known as the "crime scene investigation" of evidence. Television shows such as *CSI*, among others, have made many people familiar with the use of forensics by law-enforcement agencies for solving all types of crimes, including terrorist attacks. Investigators wearing special protective gloves sift through every piece of evidence at a crime scene, meticulously gathering physical biometrics such as latent fingerprints and DNA from blood, hair, fibers, and other material. For terrorism investigations, in addition to the above, forensics can also include, among other things, collecting explosives residue to help uncover the type of bomb used and where the bomb-making material may have been purchased, which, in turn, can lead to the identification of the terrorist or terrorists involved. Forensics for car or truck-bombing incidents also includes recovering the vehicle identification number (VIN) for the vehicle used in the explosion, which then leads investigators to who may have purchased or rented the vehicle.

The case of Faisal Shahzad, the Times Square bomber, illustrates how forensics, along with other investigative tools, can help catch a terrorist. Although Shahzad was not a lone wolf, since he had received some training in Pakistan on how to build a bomb prior to his attack and had received some funding from extremists in that country, the way he was identified and captured would have been similar had he worked entirely alone without anybody's knowledge. On the night of May 1, 2010, Shahzad drove an SUV containing a fertilizer-based bomb hidden in the trunk into Times Square in New York City. He set the bomb to explode in approximately five minutes' time and then walked away to a safe distance. He waited to hear the explosion, but instead the bomb malfunctioned, leaving a trail of smoke that attracted the attention of an alert street vendor who notified the police. Shahzad went home, thinking he would be more successful the next time.[70]

However, the police were able to trace the sales history of the SUV using its VIN. There were no fingerprints or DNA recovered, but the VIN led them to the previous owner, who then was able to provide more information that led to Shahzad's identity. Surveillance cameras in a Bridgeport, Connecticut, shopping center—Shahzad bought the car through an Internet ad from a woman who did not know what it was going to be used for—recorded him taking the SUV for a test drive before purchasing it. Other information, including an e-mail and a cell-phone call Shahzad had made to the woman regarding the purchase, led to him being arrested on a plane that was taxied on the runway at Kennedy Airport in New York, ready to take off on a flight to Dubai. The entire investigation leading to his arrest took just two days from the time of the incident.[71]

The lightning speed with which Shahzad was tracked down was unusual for most terrorist investigations. The search for Theodore Kaczynski, the Unabomber, took more than seventeen years, while the search for Eric Rudolph, who set off bombs at the 1996 Summer Olympics in Atlanta and bombed abortion clinics, took nearly seven years. Those investigations, however, were in those ancient days of the latter part of the twentieth century, before state-of-the-art automated systems greatly facilitated the analysis of evidence discovered at the scene of an incident. Technology, particularly advances in biometrics, will likely improve the results of many investigations of lone wolf terrorist attacks.

As noted in the previous section, biometrics can be used for both preventive and responsive measures to terrorism. For forensic investigations, fingerprints are the most widely used biometric, since there is a large database available to match against those fingerprints discovered at the scene of a crime or terrorist incident. As of 2011, the FBI's Integrated Automated Fingerprint Identification System had more than 70 million criminal fingerprints, 31 million civil fingerprints, and 486,000 unidentified latent fingerprints (i.e., those left behind at a crime or terrorist scene) from which to look for a match.[72] If a CCTV camera or other video device is able to capture the facial image of a lone wolf at the scene of an attack, then that image can be compared to a database containing facial images of individuals to determine the identity of the lone wolf, provided that the lone wolf's photo is already in the database.

One of the more interesting applications of biometrics in forensic investigations involves enhancing artist sketches of suspects so that these can be used in facial recognition software. When there is no facial image of a suspect captured on a CCTV camera but there are witnesses, a police artist will sketch an image of the suspect based on the eyewitness accounts. Using super-resolution (hallucination) techniques, that image can then be made into a high-resolution, picture-like image to be used for facial-recognition analysis.[73]

Another creative application of biometrics for forensics is the use of tattoos. As more people ink their bodies, law enforcement agencies are finding novel ways to use such artwork in their investigations. "You wouldn't think of tattoos as a biometric," said the FBI's Stephen Fischer Jr., "but we're starting to work on a tattoo database. Scars, marks, and tattoos we call it. Is it positive identification? No. But it's a good investigative lead."[74] The FBI's Biometric Center of Excellence recently launched the TattooID pilot program, which allows users to initiate a search utilizing a test image to find similar images. Users can also enter keywords or characters related to a tattoo to see if there are matching images. The idea behind the program is that individuals can be matched by the design and location of their tattoo(s).[75]

As the database of tattoos increases, it could become a valuable asset not only for identifying people who are using a false identity, but also for helping to locate and arrest an individual who has committed a crime or terrorist attack. For example, if a lone wolf placed a bomb in a shopping area, and his face was hidden from CCTV cameras, there still could be images captured of other parts of his body where there is a tattoo. If the lone wolf had a previous criminal record and was in the tattoo database, then the tattoo image captured by the video can be compared to tattoos in the database to reveal the identity of the perpetrator. "All these kids who put the tattoos on their necks and stuff like that," said the FBI's William Casey, "[don't realize that] if they rob a bank, the camera usually gets those types of [images]."[76] For all the parents who are not thrilled with the idea of their children getting tattoos, they may have now finally found a way to persuade them not to get one.

Psychological Profiles and Psychological Warfare

When lone wolves are not killed or captured shortly after their attacks, psychological profilers usually emerge to offer their expertise on who the lone wolves might be and what may have made them do what they did. It is a controversial endeavor, however, since psychological analysis is offered by professionals who have never met with the person they are profiling and do not know anything firsthand about the individual's personality or mind-set. Everything is based on assessing the type of attack, weapon used, target, victims, and so forth, to derive a psychological profile. If the lone wolf decides to communicate after the attacks, then his or her written messages, handwriting, or Internet-posted material become part of the profile.

While a psychological profile by itself cannot result in the specific identification of the lone wolf, it can still narrow the gap in knowledge about the type of person who committed the attack. It can also be used to design a "psychological warfare" program aimed at increasing the stress level of the lone wolf in the hope that he or she will make a mistake that will result in an arrest.

Austrian police used this strategy against Franz Fuchs, a right-wing extremist who launched a bombing campaign in Austria and Germany in the 1990s. Fuchs's targets were immigrants and organizations and individuals he believed were friendly to foreigners. Between 1993 and 1996, he sent twenty-five mail bombs and planted three pipe bombs that killed four people and injured fifteen others. Most of the bombings occurred in Austria, where the authorities turned to criminal psychologists for help in their search for the individual known as "Austria's Unabomber."[77]

Thomas Mueller, who was one of the psychologists consulted, developed a five-phase program aimed at capturing Fuchs. He referred to it as a "psychological duel," a way to break the anonymity of the bomber and force him to make a mistake. Mueller had a lot to work with, since Fuchs had sent several letters to the authorities during his bombing campaign. The first phase was to publicly acknowledge the skills of the bomber, emphasizing his detailed knowledge of electronics, physics, and chemistry. The second phase was to make Fuchs feel guilty for his crimes, an attempt to instill a "bad conscious" in him. Since they knew of his militant, right-wing sentiments based on his letters and the victims he chose to attack— and that he also liked small children—Mueller released a recording to the media of an interview he conducted with a neo-Nazi who was initially suspected of the bombings but was put in prison for other

offenses. In the interview, the neo-Nazi lamented that he had not yet been permitted to see his newborn daughter. Mueller hoped that would make Fuchs feel responsible for the situation.[78]

The third phase of the psychological duel involved giving inside information to two journalists who then wrote a book about the bombing campaign, which included Mueller's profile of the bomber. The profile described the bomber as an Austrian male in his fifties who probably completed secondary education, lived in a family house, and possessed specialized tools along with a hobby workplace. He was described as a Catholic who had knowledge of hierarchies and religious titles and liked order and tidiness. He was also portrayed as somebody who had knowledge of chemistry and an interest in history. The police hoped the bomber would read the book and realize that they knew a lot about him. It was thought that adding pressure might increase the bomber's level of anxiety, which might in turn lead him to make a crucial error. (The book, however, was not found among Fuchs's possessions after he was arrested.) The fourth phase of the plan involved a government announcement that the police were now being given more powers to collect intelligence on the bombing campaign, and the final phase included a government statement that ten Austrians were prime suspects in the bombings and that they were under close and continuous observation.[79]

The strategy, particularly the government announcement that suspects were being watched, appeared to work, as Fuchs grew more apprehensive about being caught. He became suspicious of two women who drove by his house twice one night in October 1997, shortly after the government's announcement. Thinking that they were undercover policewomen, he followed them, which of course doesn't seem like a good strategy if you believe the authorities are watching you. One of the women thought Fuchs was a stalker and called police. When police stopped Fuchs, he thought they were about to arrest him for the bombings. He tried to commit suicide by setting off an improvised explosive device. He survived the blast but lost both hands and injured a nearby policeman. Fuchs, who was convicted of the bombing campaign and sentenced to life in prison in March 1999, eventually succeeded in committing suicide the next year.[80]

Another example of police using psychological profiling and psychological warfare to arrest an anonymous lone wolf terrorist was the case of George Metesky. Known as the "Mad Bomber," Metesky terrorized New York City between 1940 and 1957 by planting thirty-three improvised explosive devices, of which twenty-two exploded, in public settings including movie theaters, libraries, train stations, and other locations. There were no fatalities, but fifteen people were injured by the bombings. The bombs became more powerful as the years went by. Just like the Unabomber case years later, the bombing campaign frustrated and embarrassed the police, who seemed helpless to deal with the violence.[81]

The first bomb, which did not explode, was left at the utility company Consolidated Edison (also known as Con Ed), in November 1940, with a note calling the company "crooks." Metesky had worked there and was denied disability benefits, despite being injured on the job. A second, similarly constructed pipe bomb without a note was discovered nearly a year later, lying on the street a few blocks from the Con Ed offices. Then there was a hiatus for many years. Metesky wrote letters stating that he was halting his bombing campaign out of patriotism for US involvement in World War II. Years later, in March 1950, a third unexploded bomb was found in Grand Central Station. Police were beginning to think that the lone wolf terrorist never intended to have his bombs explode. That belief was proven wrong when additional bombs that Metesky had placed in Grand Central Station and the New York Public Library exploded in 1951. Over the next several years, many more bombs would explode in public places.[82]

Frustrated with their inability to catch the Mad Bomber, police turned to a psychiatrist, Dr. James Brussel, in 1956, to produce one of the first-ever psychological profiles of a terrorist. Brussel surmised, based on the many letters that Metesky had sent to newspapers, police, and Con Ed over the years, as well as the phallic construction of the bombs and other facts of the case, that the bomber was a single man between forty and fifty years old, disinterested in women, an introvert, unsocial but not antisocial, egotistical, moral, honest, and religious. He was portrayed as a skilled mechanic, an immigrant or first-generation American who was neat with tools, and a present or former employee of Con Ed, with a possible motive for the bombings being that he was discharged or reprimanded. Brussel also concluded that the bomber's resentment kept growing and that it was probably a case of progressive paranoia. Some of the other characteristics in Brussel's profile of Metesky included that he was meticulous and feminine, possibly homosexual, and most likely living with his parents or sisters. Brussel also predicted that when the police finally caught up with the Mad Bomber, he would be wearing a buttoned, double-breasted suit. (Metesky was arrested at home in his pajamas but changed into a buttoned, double-breasted suit for the ride to the police precinct!)[83]

Brussel urged the police to publicize the profile as a way of goading

Metesky to communicate with the authorities. Part of the profile was published in the *New York Times* and other New York newspapers on Christmas Day in 1956. Brussel soon received a call from Metesky in which he said, "This is F.P. speaking. Keep out of this or you'll be sorry." (F.P., it would later be learned, stood for "Fair Play," the name Metesky was using in all his communications.) Although the call was too brief to be traced, Brussel felt that it would only be a matter of time before Metesky's arrogance would cause him to make a mistake.[84]

Metesky's mistake occurred when the *Journal-American* news-paper, in conjunction with the police, published an open letter to the bomber the day after the profile had been published, urging Metesky to give himself up in return for guarantees of a fair trial and an opportunity to publish his grievances in the newspaper. Metesky, arrogant and overconfident, just as Brussel had predicted, declined the offer in his response, writing, "Where were you people when I was asking for help? Placing myself into custody would be stupid—do not insult my intelligence—bring the Con Edison to justice." The *Journal-American* published his letter and requested more informa-tion from Metesky about his grievances. Metesky complied with a second letter that included the fact that he had pursued a workman's compensation claim against Con Ed. After publishing that response, the newspaper asked him for more details and dates about the com-pensation case so that a new and fair hearing could be held. Metesky fell into the trap and wrote back that he was injured on September 5, 1931. (In his original letters to Con Ed, Metesky claimed he was knocked down by a backdraft of hot gasses from a boiler, which later caused him to develop tuberculosis.) The authorities now had an exact date to check against Con Ed's records. They had already been given Metesky's file by an alert employee at Con Ed, who, after going through old records, noticed similarities in the wording of his original letters requesting compensation and his recent letters in the news-paper. Among the phrases that caught her attention was the threat to "take justice in my own hands." Police had no trouble locating him, since he was still living with his sisters at the same Waterbury,

Connecticut, address that was listed in his work file. The fifty-three-year-old Metesky was arrested in January 1957. He was found by psychiatrists to be "an incurable paranoid schizophrenic with a strong impulse to martyrdom" and was committed to an asylum for the criminally insane. Upon his release in December 1973 he returned to his home in Waterbury, where he died in 1994.[85]

As with the Fuchs case, it cannot be said that the profiling alone caught Metesky. The "Mad Bomber" was discovered by falling into the psychological trap that was placed for him with the invitation to write about his motivations to the newspapers. Fuchs was caught because he felt the mounting pressure of the government's public announcements that they were closing in on the anonymous mail bomber. But in both cases, the profiles gave the authorities a better idea of who they were dealing with and contributed to the psychological campaigns that were aimed at getting the lone wolves to make a mistake.

One of the more famous cases in which psychological profiling and psychological warfare had little effect was that of the Unabomber. Despite a seventeen-year search for Theodore Kaczynski, with numerous assessments provided by psychiatrists, psychologists, and others, the only reason he was caught was due to his jealousy over the attention that Timothy McVeigh, the Oklahoma City bomber, was receiving, which motivated him to threaten more bombings unless his manifesto was published in the newspapers. It was that publication, and his brother turning him in after recognizing the writing style and phrases as those of Kaczynski, that led to his capture.

Entice the Lone Wolf to Communicate

Perhaps the most important aspect of any psychological campaign against lone wolves is encouraging them to communicate in any way possible. The more information a lone wolf provides, the more likely it becomes that he or she will be identified. It worked with Metesky, who unwittingly revealed enough about himself in his communications to lead to his arrest. Sometimes no encouragement is needed, as in the case of Muharem Kurbegovic, the Alphabet Bomber, who sent in several audio tapes to the media during his terror campaign in 1974. It was those tapes that led to his identification and arrest. The same was true for Kaczynski, who desperately sought an outlet for the dissemination of his antitechnology, anti-industrial-society views. The irony is that had the Internet been accessible during his reign of terror, he probably would have used it to post his manifesto online early in his terrorist career (despite his distaste for technology). The same scenario that played out years later, when his brother turned him in after reading the manifesto in a newspaper, would have likely occurred once his brother read it online. Subsequent attacks may have therefore been prevented.

The desire to talk, which, as noted earlier, is a universal human need and can be used to identify lone wolves before they launch their first attack, can also be used after an attack to track them down. Lone wolves are dying to let somebody, anybody, know what they have done. After succeeding with an attack, there is no fun in just retreating back into their isolated world and keeping totally quiet about what has transpired. We are living in an age in which the ability to communicate and get one's message out to the world is easier than in any other time in history. Lone wolves who want to complain about perceived injustices that were done to them or to others, brag about their recent terrorist attack, or taunt the authorities do not have to bother with sending in secret notes in block letters that are cut and pasted from newspapers, magazines, or books, as kidnappers used to do in the old days when they wanted to let their victims' families know that they had their loved ones in captivity. All they have to do now is go to their computer, or use one from a library, Internet café, or some other venue, to send out a message.

If lone wolves are not communicating on their own after an attack and need encouragement to do so, then law-enforcement agencies need to devise plans to bring them out into the open. In the Metesky case, police worked with the *Journal-American* to entice him to reveal more information about himself through open letters published in the newspaper. It turned out, though, that Metesky, who had already been writing letters for years to Con Ed, politicians, and others about his grievances, had always wanted to communicate but had never received a response, which reinforced his anger and resentment. In one of his published letters to the *Journal-American*, he promised to suspend his bombings for a while due to the newspaper's efforts on his behalf. "In about 3 weeks," he wrote, "the N.Y. Journal American accomplished what the authorities could not do in 16 years. You stopped the bombings."[86]

The Metesky case illustrates that the process of drawing out a lone wolf has to be gradual. With each letter from Metesky, the newspaper deftly asked for a little more information under the guise of helping him with his compensation claims. This avoided his becoming suspicious and abruptly ending the communications. In today's Internet world, the chances are that a lone wolf would probably choose an online outlet over a newspaper to conduct any communications. The challenge for law enforcement, therefore, is how to get a lone wolf to choose the authorities' online presence over the multitude of others that comprise the virtual world of the Internet. In a way, their dilemma is the flipside of the one faced by terrorists, who want to gain the attention of the world when they commit an attack. The terrorists need to do something different or more spectacular than has been done previously in order to ensure that their activity, and therefore their message and cause, will not get lost or forgotten among the daily terrorist events occurring around the world. The authorities need to do the same, either through public announcements or some other activity, to ensure that they have the attention of the lone wolf and that he or she will begin a dialogue with them. The advice of psychologists, psychiatrists, criminologists, sociologists, and others might be helpful in determining what actions or statements would have the best chance of motivating a particular type of lone wolf to begin communicating with the authorities.

COUNTER ANY "HERO STATUS" A LONE WOLF MAY BE GENERATING

There is always the risk that a lone wolf may gain a cult following after an attack. People can live vicariously through the exploits of an individual who takes on larger, more formidable foes. The Internet has only made this easier, as people can post on Facebook pages or send out tweets on Twitter in support of a lone wolf. It happened in the Eric Rudolph and Joseph Stack cases. Rudolph, the antiabortion militant who, in addition to bombing abortion clinics, set off an improvised explosive device at the 1996 Summer Olympics in Atlanta, was able to elude the FBI for many years. As noted in chapter 2, there were T-shirts made supporting his activities (showcasing phrases such as "Run, Rudolph, Run" and "Eric Rudolph—Hide and Seek Champion of the World") as well as messages posted on the Internet labeling him a hero after his arrest. "What some hatemongers and extremists are saying is, this person is a hero whose crusade against abortion and the government is noble and praiseworthy," Abraham Foxman, the national director of the Anti-Defamation League, said after Rudolph's arrest in 2003. "What is even more troubling is that some of the chatter [on the Internet] is calling for violence or lone-wolf acts to be carried out in Rudolph's name."[87] Internet support for Stack also appeared shortly after he crashed his plane into IRS offices in Dallas. Several pro-Stack Facebook groups emerged on the Internet just hours after the attack. There were many postings describing Stack as a hero and patriot on both mainstream and extremist websites.[88] His daughter initially described him as a hero but later retracted that statement.[89]

Countering the hero status of lone wolves is difficult, particularly in the Internet age, where positive descriptions of a terrorist can come from many different people and then get disseminated through Twitter, Facebook, and other outlets. And this support is not always based on somebody necessarily agreeing with the issue or grievance that the lone wolf is purportedly basing the attack on. Sometimes, it could just be an expression of David-and-Goliath syndrome, in which anything a lone wolf does against the big, bad government or business is viewed in a positive vein by many people. One possible way to counter this would be to emphasize the innocent victims who may have died or been injured in the lone wolf attack. Media interviews with victims and their families may lead some people to rethink their admiration for a lone wolf terrorist. Another strategy would be to avoid antagonizing those who are agreeing with the issues that the lone wolf claimed motivated the attack. Acknowledging that there are legitimate grievances that should be addressed but that there were nonviolent alternatives available to express those sentiments will not convince everybody, but it could still help defuse some of the support a lone wolf may be generating among the public.

The above are just some of the response strategies available for dealing with lone wolf terrorism. Others include preparing for the aftermath of a lone wolf bioterrorist incident. Lone wolves such as Bruce Ivins have already proven that a single individual can launch a bioterrorist attack that causes widespread fear throughout the nation. The irony of bioterrorism, however, is that, while it has the potential to cause many more casualties than "traditional" terrorist incidents, more lives can nevertheless be saved in its aftermath than in a conventional explosion. Whereas most of the fatalities in a conventional terrorist bombing occur immediately or shortly after the incident, in a bioterrorist attack the incubation period for the virus, bacterium, or toxin could be several days. As noted earlier in this chapter, accurate diagnosis and speedy treatment will be needed to save lives. The medical and health communities will therefore be playing the most significant role in responding to a potential lone wolf bioterrorist attack. There is thus a need for hospitals to have adequate supplies (or ways to quickly obtain these supplies) of antibiotics and antitoxins that can be used to treat those exposed to biological agents. Medical and emergency-services personnel also need to be trained to recognize the different symptoms of various biological agents so that those exposed can be treated quickly.[90]

We have seen how preventing and responding to lone wolf terrorism is a complex task requiring a mix of strategies and actions. Terrorists, whether they are lone wolves or part of a larger group or cell, will always have the advantage of reversing all perceptions of progress in the battle against terrorism with just one major successful attack. Even though it is an endless struggle, efforts must continue to improve our readiness to deal with all forms of terrorism, including those initiated by just one individual.

UNCOVERING THE LESSONS LEARNED

One of the most memorable quotes concerning the need to learn lessons from past experiences comes from the American philosopher George Santayana, who, in 1905, wrote: "Those who cannot remember the past are condemned to repeat it."[1] In those brief words, he captured the essence of why it is crucial for governments, societies, and individuals to understand past mistakes so as not to repeat them in the future. Without usually acknowledging Santayana, virtually every hearing held and report issued after a major terrorist attack follows his advice. "Lessons learned" is a crucial part of any investigation into a terrorist incident. These "lessons" can include practically any issue, ranging from intelligence failures and lapses in physical security to understanding how various policies and actions by a government or military may have led to the terrorist attack.

When it comes to lone wolf terrorism, however, uncovering lessons learned becomes a little more difficult. This is due to the fact that we're dealing with an individual terrorist and not a group or state sponsor. Intelligence failures, for example, are usually not cited, since it is hard to blame an intelligence or law-enforcement agency for not knowing about a plot when the terrorist was not part of any conspiracy and had minimal or no communications with others prior to the attack. The same is true for pointing to various foreign or military policies as the cause of a terrorist incident, since some lone wolves can be oblivious to what is happening in the world yet still launch a devastating attack. There have been, nevertheless, a sufficient number of lone wolf attacks over the years from which we can derive lessons that can guide us in better understanding this growing phenomenon.

ISLAMIC MILITANTS DO NOT HAVE A MONOPOLY ON THE LONE WOLF TERRORIST THREAT

Despite all the attention that has been given to Islamic extremism since the 9/11 attacks, we have seen in this book that lone wolf terrorism is indeed a diverse threat. While there have been lone wolves ascribing to Islamic militancy, there have also been many secular, single-issue, criminal, and idiosyncratic lone wolves. In fact, the two worst lone wolf terrorist attacks in history were perpetrated by non-Islamic terrorists. Timothy McVeigh, a right-wing, antigovernment extremist, blew up the federal building in Oklahoma City, killing 168 people. Anders Breivik, a right-wing, anti-Islamic extremist opposed to multiculturalism in Europe, was responsible for the massacre of sixty-nine people, mostly teenagers, at a Norwegian youth camp, in addition to killing eight other people in a bombing earlier that same day in Oslo.

These two incidents demonstrate how misperceptions about terrorism can dominate the public agenda. While al Qaeda and other Islamic terrorist groups and cells have been the most active extremists around the world in recent years, lone wolves have come from all parts of the political, religious, and cultural spectrum. For every Nidal Malik Hassan (who went on a shooting rampage at Fort Hood, Texas, as a protest against the wars in Iraq and Afghanistan), there is a Bruce Ivins, who sent out anthrax-laden letters, in part, as a means for gaining more funding for his anthrax vaccine. For every Colleen LaRose (also known as "Jihad Jane," who traveled to Europe to kill in the name of jihad), there is a James von Brunn, who attacked the Holocaust Memorial Museum in Washington, DC, due to his hatred of Jews and other minorities.

That is why any effort to understand the radicalization process as a means for preventing, or at least greatly reducing, the incidence of lone wolf terrorism is doomed to fail if it only focuses on Islamic radicalization. The process by which individuals become right-wing, antigovernment militants, white supremacists, antiabortion and environmental extremists, and so forth has to also be included in any research project or community outreach program. Otherwise, no matter how much success may be achieved regarding reducing lone wolf Islamic terrorism, we will still be left with the likes of Timothy McVeigh, Anders Breivik, and Bruce Ivins.

Related to this is the fallacy of believing that changes in US foreign and military policies will significantly affect the threat of lone wolf terrorism. While several lone wolves may find inspiration for their violence in protesting specific US foreign policies, there are still plenty of others who are motivated to act for different reasons, including the environment, abortion, white supremacy, and other factors. And even if the United States were to retreat from all its commitments overseas and follow an isolationist policy, there would still be individuals who would commit terrorist attacks due to their irreversible perception of what American society represents, such as capitalism, consumerism, and materialism.

It is also important that we do not fall into the trap of believing that the main source of lone wolf terrorism today is emanating from the call by al Qaeda and other Islamic terrorist organizations for lone wolves to attack the West. Following the death of Osama bin Laden and the increased difficulty of initiating large-scale, complex operations like those of 9/11 (due to the loss of their central training grounds in Afghanistan, improved security in many countries, and a series of setbacks over the years), al Qaeda is now emphasizing "individual jihad" in its calls for attacks against the West. In June 2011, just one month after bin Laden's death, an American-born al Qaeda spokesman, Adam Gadahn, released a video message titled "Do Not Rely on Others, Take the Task upon Yourself" on the Internet, in which he urged Muslims living in the United States to carry out individual terrorist operations. "What are you waiting for?" he asked in the video. He pointed out that it would be easy for anybody to go to a gun show and leave with an automatic assault rifle. He urged his followers to target major institutions and influential public figures.[2] The role of al Qaeda in influencing lone wolves clearly has intelligence officials around the world worried. "I must say that my colleagues in Britain, in Australia and the United States think the same thing—we are already seeing an increase in the number of people who are acting as individuals and that really makes our lives complicated," said Richard Fadden, the head of the Canadian Security Intelligence Service, in April 2012. He predicted that the number of al Qaeda–inspired lone wolf attacks would increase.[3]

However, it would be a mistake to focus exclusively on al Qaeda as the cause of the growing lone wolf threat. There is always a tendency when faced with a complex problem to think of it in black-and-white terms. That allows one to think there is a solution that can be achieved. This happened in the 1970s and 1980s, when some terrorism experts, such as Claire Sterling, in her influential book *The Terror Network*,[4] argued that the Soviet Union was the main source of international terrorism and that if the United States and its allies could counter Soviet influence, then a big part of the terrorist problem would be solved. That proved to be wrong, as terrorism during that era had many origins, as is true today. We have to be careful that we don't perpetuate the legacy of al Qaeda based on what it accomplished with the 9/11 attacks and subsequent incidents. They are certainly part of the lone wolf problem, but they are not the major source. The fact that there is no central source for lone wolf terrorism is one of the key lessons to be learned about this form of terrorism.

The diversity in lone wolf terrorism also means that, just like terrorism overall, it can never truly be "defeated." As long as there are individuals and groups who believe that terrorism is justified in the name of some cause, we will always have terrorism. Furthermore, as noted earlier, one does not even have to have a "cause" as we usually think of one in order to qualify as a lone wolf terrorist. If an individual is only motivated by money, greed, personal revenge, or some other purpose, his or her violent actions can still be considered terrorism if the effect on government and society is the same (i.e., heightened security, fear) as if the act had been committed by a terrorist with a political or religious agenda.

LONE WOLVES ARE NOT AS CRAZY AS MANY PEOPLE ASSUME

Whenever there is a terrorist attack, one doesn't have to wait too long for some observers to describe the terrorists as "madmen" or irrational human beings. Typical of this view is the description given by one psychologist, who wrote that most terrorists are "battered children forced into madness."[5] The thinking is that who but mentally ill people would kill innocent victims in the mistaken belief that they were furthering a cause. This, of course, ignores the harsh reality that, in many cases, terrorism pays off. It is a way for small groups and individuals to obtain results otherwise unobtainable, such as winning concessions from a targeted government during a hijacking or other type of hostage incident, creating a crisis atmosphere in the targeted country, gaining worldwide publicity, sabotaging peace efforts, and so forth.[6] The limited number of psychological studies of members of terrorist groups has confirmed that most terrorists are indeed quite "normal."[7]

When it comes to the lone wolf, however, the consensus among scholars and others is that the individual terrorist is somewhat different in terms of psychology and personality from those who join terrorist organizations. For example, one scholar argues that "although most terrorists are normal, the rate of psychological disturbance is certainly higher among the loners."[8] However, that conclusion was based on limited data; only twenty-seven American lone wolves were studied, with just six of them showing signs of mental illness.[9] In another study of lone wolves in a few different countries, the author concluded that "lone wolf terrorists are relatively likely to suffer from some form of psychological disturbance," even though only five lone wolves were examined, with three of them diagnosed with personality disorders and one with obsessive-compulsive disorder.[10]

What I suspect is occurring with the psychological explanations for lone wolf terrorists is that we tend to know more about them after an incident than we do about members of a terrorist group. After all, there are fewer lone wolves than there are terrorist group members, and while some terrorist group members (such as the perpetrators of the 9/11 attacks) are analyzed and their background characteristics become well known, the majority of terrorists simply fade into oblivion after their attacks. There are just too many of them for researchers to conduct detailed psychological histories. It may very well be that if it were possible to get psychological data on every terrorist in the world, a few would undoubtedly have personality disorders and perhaps even mental illness.

Some of the lone wolves I discussed in this book clearly were mentally ill, such as Theodore Kaczynski (the Unabomber), Muharem Kurbegovic (the Alphabet Bomber), Bruce Ivins (the sender of the anthrax letters), and Charles Guiteau (the assassin of President James Garfield). Others had psychological problems, such as Nidal Malik Hasan (the Fort Hood shooter) and Anders Breivik (the perpetrator of the Norway massacre). But many other lone wolves were not "abnormal" in the psychological sense, such as Timothy McVeigh, Eric Rudolph, Roshonara Choudhry, and others. While some of them may have had views that were too extreme for membership in a group, or the groups may have viewed them as too unstable, they were still not "crazy," which is the label often used by those who throw up their hands and claim that there is nothing we can do about the lone wolf terrorist. And while it may be true that some lone wolves combine personal grievances and problems with a political, religious, or single-issue cause in order to justify their violence, they are no less dedicated to the issues for which they are fighting for than the "regular" terrorists. As terrorism expert John Horgan wrote about terrorists in general: "Many attempts exist to denigrate terrorists and their cause by purposefully regarding them as psychopathic."[11] The same could be said about the misguided labels many people apply to the lone wolf.

THE INTERNET IS A DOUBLE-EDGED SWORD FOR LONE WOLVES

The march of technology has been good for all terrorists, including lone wolves. It has given them targets with large numbers of people to attack, such as airplanes that can now carry over eight hundred passengers; more powerful and sophisticated weapons; advanced communication and navigational devices, including GPS units; and, of course, the most important gift of all—the Internet. If the Internet did not exist, terrorists would probably have had to invent it. Just as it's hard to imagine any of us conducting our lives today without access to the Internet, the same is true for most terrorist groups and lone wolves. From searching online for information on potential targets and weapons to posting various messages and manifestos, the Internet is used by practically every terrorist group and lone wolf in existence today. As prominent terrorism analyst Steven Emerson notes: "The Internet is a global communication medium that provides terrorist operatives and their organizations an often anonymous and instantaneous method of sending messages, images, intelligence, financial transaction, operational orders, training material, and any variety of their information to further their goals."[12]

But whereas terrorist groups, for the most part, have become more sophisticated in their counterintelligence methods regarding the Internet, including adopting various ways to elude detection by intelligence and law-enforcement agencies through changing Internet protocol addresses, using encryption and other stealth methods to communicate, and so forth, the lone wolves are lagging far behind. Whether it's due to a lack of sophisticated information technology capabilities or hubris in feeling they simply will not be caught by the authorities, lone wolves are most vulnerable when they surface via the Internet.

One of the lessons learned regarding lone wolf terrorism is that most lone wolves love to talk through the Internet. Whether it is by announcing to the world, as Colleen LaRose did, that she was ready, willing, and able to commit terrorist acts or by posting manifestos outlining various extremist beliefs, as Anders Breivik did, the Internet gives us clues about who the lone wolves may be. In addition, the chat rooms they frequent and the online searches they conduct can all be potential pitfalls for the lone wolf, if their activity is uncovered by law enforcement.

As noted in chapter 6, lone wolves need the Internet more than the Internet needs them. I discussed in the previous chapter how this is different from the symbiotic relationship between traditional media (television, radio, print) and terrorists, in which each uses the other for mutual benefit, the media to get ratings and produce interesting stories for their audience; and the terrorists, particularly terrorist groups, to generate publicity for their cause and create fear in the targeted country.

While terrorist groups also need the Internet more than the Internet needs them, the groups would undoubtedly still survive and be active even without the benefits that the Internet provides (i.e., websites, communications, and so forth). Not so for lone wolves. While there would still be lone wolves, as there had been in the past, their numbers would be greatly reduced without the presence of the Internet. Since access to the Internet cannot and should not be restricted, the challenge is to find legal ways to use the Internet against lone wolves. I outlined some of these in chapter 6, including the monitoring of extremist chat rooms, alerts for when inflammatory manifestos and other threatening messages appear on the Internet, the interception of communications between potential lone wolves and terrorists abroad, and the monitoring of suspicious online purchases of materials that can be used to produce bombs and other weapons, including biological warfare agents.

It is worth noting that the Internet may provide lone wolves with a false sense of anonymity. The savvy terrorist groups are aware of this, but not so for most lone wolves. Many think that they can hide behind their keyboards and computer screens and become invulnerable to discovery. The more they use the Internet, the better our chances will be to prevent their attacks.

DON'T BE FOOLED BY THE LULLS IN LONE WOLF ATTACKS

Throughout the history of terrorism, there have been periods when the public and the government in a particular country thought the worst was over because a certain amount of time had passed since the last major attack. In the United States, for example, the terrorism of the 1970s and 1980s, which was primarily aimed at US targets overseas, was believed to have been over with end of the Cold War and the return of American hostages from Lebanon. As the early 1990s progressed, even the Persian Gulf War in Iraq, with threats of Saddam Hussein–inspired retaliatory terrorist attacks against the United States, did not shatter the belief that a corner had been turned in the battle against terrorism.

That optimism came crashing down when a car bomb exploded at the World Trade Center in New York in February 1993, killing six people and injuring one thousand others, with most of the injuries due to smoke inhalation. But when there were no additional major terrorist attacks on US soil for a couple years, people once again breathed a sigh of relief. That, too, would be mistaken. A homegrown American lone wolf terrorist, Timothy McVeigh, set off a truck bomb at the federal building in Oklahoma City in April 1995, killing 168 people. There would be another lull before the next major attack on US soil occurred, more than six years later, with the 9/11 attacks. And as of the fall of 2012, there had yet to be another major terrorist attack within the United States, leading many Americans to once again assume that the worst is over.

The lulls in terrorist attacks, however, are part of terrorism's mystique. As noted earlier, terrorists, including lone wolves, always have the advantage of perpetrating just one major attack to put terrorism back on the front burner in the public's mind and reverse all perceptions of progress in the battle against terrorism. That is why we should never be fooled into thinking we are winning a "war" against terrorists. And if the incidence of lone wolf attacks should subside for a period of time, it would only take one major one, such as the 2011 Norway massacre, for the lone wolf threat to be front and center once again.

Lone wolves also have the ability to launch an attack or a series of attacks and then lay low for a long period of time before resurfacing again with renewed violence. This was the case with Theodore Kaczynski, the Unabomber, who began his reign of terror in May 1978 and continued sending or planting package bombs throughout the 1980s. However, after planting a bomb at the back entrance to a computer shop in Salt Lake City, Utah, in February 1987, which led to an eyewitness who provided the authorities with a composite sketch of Kaczynski that was widely circulated through the media, he stopped his terrorist attacks for more than six years, resuming with a package bomb sent to a University of California geneticist in June 1993. Another lone wolf who went a long period between attacks was George Metesky, the "Mad Bomber," who terrorized New York City during the 1940s and 1950s. As noted in chapter 6, after placing a bomb in the city in 1940 and then another one a year later, he suspended his attacks until 1950, explaining in letters he wrote that he was patriotic and didn't want to detract from the US effort during World War II.

Both Kaczynski and Metesky used their periods of inactivity to improve their bomb-making skills. Their later bombs were more sophisticated and more powerful than the earlier ones.[13] Time is indeed on the side of the patient lone wolves, who can set their own timetable for where and when they are going to strike. There is no pressure on them to immediately follow up one attack with another. Until a lone wolf is captured, therefore, we have to assume that he or she will strike again, no matter how long that may be. We also have to assume that, in some cases, they will become more violent as time goes on. Just like a terrorist group that needs to escalate its violence or do something different with each subsequent attack to ensure that the public and government in the targeted country do not become desensitized to the "normal" flow of terrorism, so, too, does a lone wolf have to keep the pot boiling with more sophisticated and more violent attacks. An escalation in violence may also allow the lone wolf to feel superior to the authorities, who appear helpless in catching the lone wolf and putting an end to the terrorism.

BE SKEPTICAL OF STATISTICS ON LONE WOLF TERRORISM

Just as we should not be fooled by lulls in lone wolf attacks, so, too, should we cast a skeptical eye toward any statistical reports or statements about terrorism. Statistics on terrorism can be misleading. The reason is terrorism's unique psychological hold on society and government, allowing just one major incident anytime, anywhere to change perceptions of the terrorist threat. That is why we need to be careful in interpreting government, research-institute, or academic reports utilizing statistics to explain various trends in terrorism. For example, at first look, a comparison of the number of international terrorism incidents in 2000 and 2001 would indicate that things were getting better in the battle against terrorism. In 2000, there were 426 international terrorist incidents. This number decreased to 355 in 2001.[14] Yet could we really state that things were getting better in 2001, given the 9/11 attacks? The number of casualties is also a poor indicator of whether things are getting better or worse in the world of terrorism. Some of the most important terrorist attacks in history had few or no casualties, such as the 1979–81 Iran hostage crisis that paralyzed the administration of President Jimmy Carter and had widespread international repercussions. In terrorism, it is the type of incident and its impact upon society and government that counts, not the frequency of incidents or even the number of casualties.

As misleading as statistics can be for overall terrorism, it is worse for lone wolf terrorism. That is because the database of lone wolf incidents is quite small. The study of lone wolf terrorism is still a relatively new field, and there is an understandable temptation to make generalizations based on very few cases. I noted earlier in this chapter how in one study the author concluded that lone wolves are likely to suffer from psychological disturbances even though the study was based on just five cases. In another study, the author came to similar conclusions, even though only six out of twenty-seven lone wolves who were studied had serious psychological problems.[15]

This is not to say that we can't gain some interesting insights about lone wolf terrorism from statistical analysis. For example, in one study that examined lone wolf incidents in fifteen countries from 1968 to 2010, it was found that the number of attacks had grown from thirty in the 1970s to seventy-three in the 2000s and that, out of a total of 198 attacks for the entire period, eighty-eight different lone wolves were responsible for the incidents. The total number of lone wolf attacks during this period was just 1.8 percent of all terrorist incidents from 1968 to 2010 in the fifteen countries examined. (These countries combined, which included the United States, Britain, France, Italy, Germany, Spain, and Canada, among others, experienced 11,235 non–lone wolf terrorist attacks during the same period).[16] These data points give us a nice picture of how lone wolf terrorism, while a growing threat, is still dwarfed in terms of numbers by the incidence of terrorism committed by groups and cells.

However, when the author of the study cited above concludes that "lone wolf terrorism is predominantly, though clearly not exclusively, a US phenomenon" because there were 113 incidents in the United States during this period, accounting for 57 percent of all lone wolf attacks in the fifteen countries, one has to wonder if this is yet another example of how statistics can be misleading.[17] As already noted, it is not the number of incidents that count in measuring terrorism's impact on a society. One or two incidents can have as much effect in terms of generating fear and reaction in a country as can multiple attacks. Countries other than the United States that experienced significant lone wolf attacks included Norway (the massacre by Anders Breivik in 2011, one year after the end period for the above-cited data study), the Netherlands (the assassinations of Pim Fortuyn and Theo van Gogh), Britain (the Nailbomber attacks), Italy (the "Italian Unabomber" attacks), Austria (the bombing campaign initiated by Franz Fuchs), and Israel (the assassination of Yitzhak Rabin and the massacre of Muslims at a mosque in the West Bank town of Hebron), to name just a few. Rather than being restricted to any one country, lone wolf terrorism is clearly a global phenomenon.

DO NOT UNDERESTIMATE THE CREATIVITY, INNOVATION, AND DANGER OF THE LONE WOLF AND THE IMPACT HE OR SHE CAN HAVE ON GOVERNMENTS AND SOCIETIES

This journey into the world of lone wolf terrorism has revealed a remarkable degree of creativity, innovation, and danger exhibited by the individual terrorist. From Mario Buda, who in 1920 set off the first vehicle bomb in US history, to Anders Breivik, who in 2011 was responsible for one of the first dual terrorist attacks ever by a lone wolf—a horrific massacre of youths in Norway that had followed by just a couple hours his detonating a car bomb in Oslo—lone wolves have proven to be just as dangerous as, and sometimes even more so than, the most formidable terrorist groups in existence.

In between the attacks by Buda and Breivik came as series of "firsts" in terrorism history, including the first use of anthrax letters to kill people and the first major midair plane bombing in the United States, all the work of lone wolves. As noted earlier, there are several reasons why lone wolves can be more creative and dangerous than many terrorist groups. First, since they are working alone, they do not have to answer to any higher-ups or colleagues. There is no leader of a group who may veto a lone wolf's ideas or other members who could ridicule or argue against a lone wolf's novel plans for an attack. Lone wolves are free to think up any type of terrorism scenario they want. Furthermore, since they only have to answer to themselves, lone wolves are usually not concerned about how many people they may kill or injure in an attack, unlike many terrorist groups, which have to consider potential backlashes from their supporters if they exceed a certain casualty total or commit a particularly gruesome attack. Terrorist groups also have to worry about a massive law-enforcement and government response following certain incidents, such as the use of a weapon of mass destruction or another type of high-casualty attack that could lead to the demise of the group through arrests and other measures, whereas this is not a concern for the lone wolf.

Lone wolves have also demonstrated that they can have a profound effect on governments and societies. We saw how, in the Netherlands, the lone wolf assassination of politician Pim Fortuyn shocked a nation not used to terrorism, causing one government official to proclaim that with the killing, "the Netherlands had lost its innocence."[18] The same was true for Norway, where, as noted in chapter 2, in the aftermath of the Breivik massacre, Norwegian prime minister Jens Stoltenberg stated: "I think what we have seen is that there is going to be one Norway before and one Norway after [the attacks of] July 22."[19] In the United States, Timothy McVeigh changed the way many Americans viewed terrorism with just one major attack in Oklahoma City, making people realize that homegrown American terrorists were as serious a threat as Islamic and other foreign-based extremists. And Bruce Ivins single-handedly shut down government buildings and mail-processing centers, and spread fear throughout the United States about a "new" form of terrorism—bioterrorism—with a wave of anthrax letter attacks.

The combination of danger, innovation, and impact that has characterized lone wolf terrorism in the past is destined to continue in the future. So, too, will the effort by governments and law enforcement to design ways to effectively combat this threat. While many lone wolf attacks, like those initiated by terrorist groups, will not be that significant in terms of the damage they cause or the reactions they elicit, others will undoubtedly have serious effects. What, then, can we expect to unfold regarding lone wolf terrorism in the coming years?

CHAPTER 8

A LOOK TOWARD THE FUTURE

Anticipating the future of terrorism is, of course, a speculative endeavor. There are no laws of nature or scientific principles that can guide one in stating with reasonable confidence that certain things will or will not unfold in the terrorist world. Yet trying to predict the future of terrorism is a very popular exercise, with scores of scholars, research institutes, government agencies, and the like all offering their prognoses on what the future may hold.[1]

I attempted to do this in a book I wrote in the early 1990s on America's experience with terrorism.[2] At that time, as noted in chapter 7, the optimism that the United States had turned a corner in the battle against terrorism, with the return of the hostages from Lebanon and the relative quiet in anti-US terrorist attacks around the world, was shattered with the 1993 World Trade Center bombing in New York City. Foreign terrorists had come to American shores and attacked one of the world's most famous business and financial structures in one of the country's most populated cities. The illusion of invulnerability to terrorism at home that many Americans had felt was now gone. But what lay ahead? As I looked toward the future then, I got some things right and some wrong. For example, I thought that a new type of terrorist threat would emerge, which I labeled "aerial terrorism," predicting that terrorists would begin crashing planes into buildings and other populated targets. However, I thought that, to avoid radar detection, their weapons would be low-flying, single-engine planes packed with explosives. I didn't foresee hijacked jets with thousands of gallons of fuel being the weapons, as turned out to be the case on 9/11. I also predicted that people in the coming years would be linked together through computer terminals and other devices anywhere in the world, and that this could be taken advantage of by terrorists to bypass traditional media when issuing threats and gathering information. But I didn't foresee the enormous impact that the Internet, which was still in its early stages, would eventually have on everyday life, including the lives of terrorists.

The task of predicting the future of terrorism is fraught with difficulties. The best one can hope for is to anticipate the broad outlines of where things seem headed so that law-enforcement and intelligence agencies, as well as policymakers and the public, are not caught off guard when terrorists strike next. With respect to lone wolf terrorism, several trends and developments point to it becoming more diversified, innovative, and dangerous in the years ahead.

THE EMERGING FIFTH WAVE OF GLOBAL TERRORISM

In chapter 1, I discussed how David C. Rapoport, in his classic study of the history of terrorism, observed that we have experienced four distinct waves of international terrorism since the late-nineteenth century: the Anarchist, Anti-Colonial, New Left, and Religious Waves.[3] Each wave, he noted, lasted approximately forty years, with the current fourth wave, the Religious Wave, beginning in 1979. While it is too early to determine if the Religious Wave will fade from prominence like its predecessors did after its forty-year period ends, many signs point to Rapoport being correct.

The end of US involvement in Iraq and Afghanistan will somewhat erode the appeal of Islamic extremism to impressionable youths around the world. Without the image of American troops occupying or involved in wars in Muslim nations, a major part of the Islamic extremists' current anti-US campaign will be stripped away. There will, of course, still be plenty of issues for Islamic extremists to exploit in the years ahead, including various policies and actions that the United

States and other Western nations may take on future developments around the world, as well as the extremists' continual animosity to moderate Islamic regimes. But the end of the wars in Iraq and Afghanistan, combined with the US killing of high-level al Qaeda operatives throughout the world, including, of course, Osama bin Laden, has left a void in the leadership structure of al Qaeda. According to renowned terrorism expert Brian Michael Jenkins, "Al Qaeda may remain lethal, but become increasingly irrelevant, confined to circulating its screeds from the edge, a reservoir of inchoate anger, a conveyer of individual discontents, which is its most likely fate."[4] Other Islamic terrorist organizations and cells, including al Qaeda affiliates such as al Qaeda in the Arabian Peninsula (AQAP), based in Yemen, and al Qaeda in the Islamic Maghreb (AQIM), based in Algeria, will undoubtedly continue to strike and carry on the struggle against all those they believe to be infidels. But it does appear that the glory days of the Religious Wave of terrorism, which was characterized by a seemingly endless flurry of incidents and threats made during the decade following the 9/11 attacks, may very well be in the past.

The Religious Wave is likely to be succeeded by a fifth wave of terrorism, which I have labeled the Technological Wave. As I discussed in chapter 1, this wave may have already emerged, as is evident by the growing impact that technology, and particularly the Internet, is having on virtually every aspect of terrorist and counterterrorist activity. The Technological Wave is empowering all types of terrorists with information and confidence to launch attacks and publicize their cause. It is creating a more level playing field, where no single religious or ideological agenda will dominate the world of terrorism. While much of the attention and effort to combat terrorism in the post-9/11 decade was aimed at Islamic extremists, other movements have been gathering steam, and they will continue to play an important role in this fifth wave of terrorism. Rob Wainwright, the director of Europol, the European Union's law-enforcement agency, put it best when he wrote the following in 2012 about the future of terrorism in Europol's annual report on trends in terrorism:

> The identified drivers [of terrorism] are not static . . . and can
> evolve or vanish over time in response to political or socio-economic
> developments, merge with other ideologies or convictions, or be
> the building blocks of new and sometimes very specific and highly
> individual motivations. Unclear or vague motives can blur the dis-
> tinction between a terrorist offence and other criminal acts.[5]

Terrorists of all persuasions will take even more advantage of
technology in the fifth wave than they have in the past, not just because
it will be available to them, but also because of the need to keep up
with other terrorists, as well as with the authorities, as they plan their
attacks. Terrorism is a competitive business, with groups, cells, and
lone wolves needing to outdo each other with more spectacular or
different types of attacks in order to ensure they achieve the publicity
and reaction they desire. More powerful and sophisticated weapons
and explosives will give them the opportunity to do just that. For
example, AQAP, after failing twice to blow up planes in midair (once
with bombs hidden in the cartridges of printers and the other time
with a bomb hidden in the underwear of a suicide bomber), decided
in 2012 to try again to set off an explosive with a more sophisticated
detonator. The plot was uncovered only because the "suicide
terrorist" who was to wear the "underwear" bomb turned out to be
working for Saudi intelligence, which then turned the bomb over to
the United States for forensic analysis.[6] Similarly, a technologically
sophisticated plot by Chechen extremists to sabotage the 2014
Winter Olympic Games in Russia was uncovered by Russian security
personnel in 2012. The plot involved using portable surface-to-air
missiles, anti-tank guided missiles, a mortar, and a flamethrower in
massive terrorist attacks during the Games.[7]

The next wave of terrorism will also see more groups use the
al Qaeda model for exploiting the Internet for maximum benefit,
including posting videos of terrorist attacks in order to attract recruits,
encouraging forums and chat rooms to keep people engaged in
the struggle, and calling for lone wolves to initiate their own operations. In fact, that trend may already be underway, as reflected in

the remarks of a German government official regarding a surge in left-wing terrorism in that country. "The leftists are putting out propaganda on the Internet detailing where the weak spots are in police body armour in order to wound officers," said Uwe Schünemann, the interior minister for the German state of Lower Saxony. "They are targeting police vehicles to set ablaze. They even have tips on how to attack police officers. We are in the preliminary stages of a new wave of leftist terror."[8] Right-wing extremists are also becoming more adept at using social media and the Internet to promote their cause. As one European terrorism expert noted: "More sophisticated propaganda structures—substantially empowered by the use of social media tools—means that such [right-wing] groups have nowadays the potential to spread their ideology among a specific target audience (younger generations) which would appear to be more receptive to their message."[9]

As other non-Islamic groups expand and improve their Internet presence, we can expect an even more diverse array of lone wolves in the years ahead. The lone wolf will have a plethora of issues and causes to choose from, ranging from environmental, ecological, and economic concerns to opposition to a wide range of various governments' policies and actions. Ethnic-nationalist and separatist causes are additional motivations for potential lone wolf activity. Self-radicalization over the Internet will remain a possibility for a lone wolf interested in any type of issue. And as Europol's Wainwright observed, the motivations for terrorist activity are never static; they can change at any time, as old issues recede and new ones arise.

Another likely development in the fifth wave of terrorism will be the global spread of individual skills and knowledge in making and using sophisticated IEDs. As noted in chapter 1, we can expect to find many former insurgents from the wars in Iraq and Afghanistan taking their skills and weapons to other countries and regions. Some will join existing terrorist groups, others will form their own cells, and still others may embark on individual attacks. The knowledge and skills they have in bomb making will eventually spread to other terrorists, who may use those skills for any cause they adopt. A harbinger of this might be the April 2011 discovery in a field in Northern Ireland of a type of IED that had been commonly used in Iraq and Afghanistan. That was the first time such a device had been found in Northern Ireland.[10]

The fifth wave will also likely see more women become lone wolf terrorists. Thus far, it has been a male-dominated activity, with the two most prominent female lone wolves being Colleen LaRose and Roshonara Choudhry. Both women were attracted to the jihadist cause, with Choudhry being influenced simply by downloading the sermons of Anwar al-Awlaki over the Internet. It may very well be the case that as the ability of al Qaeda recedes in terms of its face-to-face recruitment of female members (whom they then were able to turn into suicide bombers), these same women, who would have joined the extremist group or its affiliates, will instead act by themselves after heeding the online call to embark upon lone wolf attacks. And, as mentioned above, as other types of movements from all parts of the political spectrum increase their online presence and emulate the model set by Islamic extremists in attracting lone wolves via the Internet, there will likely be more lone wolf attacks by individuals, including women, who are sympathetic to all types of different causes.

FUTURE INNOVATIONS IN LONE WOLF TACTICS

I've discussed in this book how lone wolves have been among the most innovative of terrorists throughout history. From vehicle bombings to anthrax letters, they have many times been ahead of the curve in introducing new terrorist tactics. What, then, might be some of the future innovations in terrorist tactics that will originate with lone wolves? One that appears to be tailor-made for such individuals would be to commit the first major, successful cyberterrorism incident. After all, a lone wolf would not even have to leave his or her home to launch a computer-driven attack. It is somewhat surprising, then, given the technical computer knowledge that individuals possess around the world, that we have not yet seen a major lone wolf cyberterrorist attack. For that matter, considering that many terrorist groups and foreign governments are also quite knowledgeable regarding computer-software technology, it is surprising that a worst-case scenario cyberterrorist operation by anybody, such as the sabotaging of critical infrastructures through computer and information systems attacks, has not yet occurred. One explanation is that the technology that businesses and governments have put into protecting against such major attacks is still ahead of the capabilities of potential adversaries. Furthermore, since most terrorist groups rely upon the Internet for communications, recruitment, fundraising, targeting information, and such, they would be shooting themselves in the foot if they committed a major cyberterrorist attack that brought down the Internet or greatly disrupted their own use of interconnected computer systems. And a foreign government that launched a cyberterrorist attack against another state, targeting its critical infrastructures, would be susceptible to retaliatory measures from that state, if the attack could be traced back to them.[11]

The lone wolf, however, has none of these concerns. With the world filled with bright young people highly skilled in technical computer knowledge, it may only be a matter of time before one of them figures out a way to do what others thus far have not been able to do or have not been willing to attempt. We cannot expect that security against major cyberterrorism operations will always remain ahead of those who are trying to penetrate various computer and communications systems. It would not be surprising, therefore, if the first major cyberterrorist attack came from a creative, smart, and dangerous individual motivated by anything ranging from political, social, and religious issues to criminal or mischievous intent.

Another innovative lone wolf tactic in the coming years may involve bioterrorism. We have seen how a lone wolf was able to perpetrate the first anthrax letter attack in history. Although that's not considered a major attack, since the casualty total was relatively low (five people killed), the next time a lone wolf uses bioweapons, we may not be as lucky. I discussed some of the potential scenarios involving a mass-casualty bioterrorism attack perpetrated by a lone wolf in chapter 3. These range from dispersing anthrax spores from a low-flying airplane or crop-duster to releasing ricin in the heating, ventilation, air-conditioning (HVAC) system of a building.

There remain many doubters about the ability of not just a lone wolf but any type of terrorist to successfully launch a major bioterrorist attack, due to the technical and scientific knowledge required to handle and use biological agents. However, as I pointed out in chapter 3, former secretary of the navy Richard Danzig is correct when he writes that the hurdles for terrorists to obtain an effective bioweapon "are being lowered by the dissemination of knowledge, techniques, and equipment."[12] This dissemination is only likely to increase in the coming years, as the Internet continues to expand, providing even more detailed information than it does today on all types of weapons, including biological warfare agents. It should also be noted that if an innovative bioterrorist attack fails, or even if it is only a hoax, it can still be significant if it generates fear throughout a country, causes the closure of government buildings and other facilities, and, perhaps most importantly, gives new ideas to other terrorists, who then improve upon the failure or hoax and commit a successful attack.[13]

Lone wolves may also be among the first to design effective ways to evade or defeat the emerging biometrics that are being used around the world. The creativity of lone wolves will allow them to test their skills in matching wits with governments and other entities that are deploying biometric devices. For example, it was a researcher who decided to create a fake finger by using the gelatin found in gummy bears candy and a plastic mold. The fake finger was able to fool fingerprint detectors four times out of five.[14] Although the researcher was not a lone wolf terrorist, it still indicates that smart, creative individuals can at times succeed in evading or penetrating existing security measures.

NEW THINKING ON TERRORISM

The lone wolf is also forcing us to rethink some of our basic concepts about terrorism. This reevaluation will likely continue in the coming years, as lone wolves make their presence felt throughout the world. The individual terrorist has proven repeatedly that he or she can be as dangerous and have as much impact on societies and governments as the larger, better-financed, and better-trained terrorist organizations.

One area where the lone wolf is forcing new thinking about terrorism is with regard to the age-old problem of definitions. No longer can definitions of terrorism be restricted to actions taken by "sub-national groups or clandestine agents," as the US State Department continues to view the terrorist threat.[15] The definition needs to also include the activities of lone wolves. Similarly, the tendency to restrict definitions of terrorism to those violent acts or threats that have a political or religious motive, as many definitions do, also merits change, since there are some lone wolves who are motivated mainly by financial incentives, personal revenge, or psychological problems, yet the impact of their activities is no different than had they stated they were acting in the name of some political or religious cause. The case of Bruce Ivins, who perpetrated the anthrax letter attacks partly to increase interest in his new anthrax vaccine, illustrates that point.

The lone wolf is also making it clear why viewing antiterrorism activities as part of a "war" is unrealistic. A government cannot really be at war with an individual terrorist, and such declarations only raise the status of terrorists, since it puts them on equal footing with the government that declares such a war. Yet equating terrorism with war has occurred throughout history. As noted in the introduction, following the 1920 Wall Street bombing, which turned out to be the work of a lone wolf terrorist, the New York Chamber of Commerce described the bombing as an "act of war."[16] During the 1985 hijacking of TWA Flight 847 in Lebanon, Secretary of Defense Caspar Weinberger stated: "It is a war and it is the beginning of war."[17] One year later, Secretary of State George Shultz said that the

United States was "pretty darn close" to declaring war on Libya due to Moammar Gadhafi's terrorism activities.[18] And President George W. Bush, shortly after the 9/11 attacks, referred to them as "acts of war" and launched what became known as the "global war on terror."[19]

The problem with equating terrorism with war, however, is that it raises expectations for the public and others of an ultimate victory, which, as pointed out throughout this book, is unattainable, given the endless nature of terrorism. With respect to the recent global war on terror, many people in the Muslim world viewed it mainly as a war on Muslims, which Osama bin Laden and other Islamic extremists exploited to their advantage. Although the administration of President Barack Obama ended the "war" terminology in 2009 by instead referring to counterterrorism efforts as "overseas contingency operations,"[20] it may only be a matter of time before another administration in the United States or elsewhere brings back the "war" analogy after a major terrorist attack. Lone wolf incidents, though, will continue to serve as reminders of the fallacy of viewing terrorism as a war.

The lone wolf is also causing a reevaluation of basic counterterrorism policies. While traditional measures (such as cutting off the finances of terrorist groups, launching military strikes when necessary, and pressuring state sponsors of terrorism to end their support for various terrorists) will continue to be vital parts of any nation's battle against terrorism, these measures will not be effective against a lone wolf. However, by employing a range of preventive and responsive strategies, as discussed in chapter 6, progress can be made in dealing with the lone wolf terrorist threat.

Finally, the lone wolf is changing the way we think about how somebody becomes a terrorist. No longer can theories and concepts about the radicalization of individuals be limited to considering only sociopolitical and economic explanations like poverty, unemployment, a sense of hopelessness among youths in a given society, revenge against perceived injustices, oppression, and other conditions. Likewise, we must dispense with the notion that radicalization is solely due to the efforts of charismatic leaders and other group members who recruit or brainwash impressionable individuals with face-to-face meetings. Explanations must now also include the impact of the Internet on virtually anybody who is curious about the world and finds information, websites, chat rooms, and other material online that can somehow accelerate the process of taking violent action in the name of some cause. The lone wolf may also develop out of a combination of personal and psychological problems that make certain individuals more susceptible to engaging in terrorist activities.

The world of lone wolf terrorism will continue to evolve in the coming years. We cannot predict the new issues that may arise to propel certain people into terrorism. It could be global economic and political developments, certain policies by various governments, or just a local issue that angers a particular individual. But whatever the cause, the lone wolf will try to remain anonymous and in the background until he or she strikes. Uncovering the secret world of the lone wolf terrorist will remain one of the major challenges in the battle against this form of terrorism.

CONCLUSION

"T he really valuable thing in the pageant of human life," Albert Einstein once wrote, "seems to me not the political state, but the creative, sentient individual, the personality; it alone creates the noble and the sublime, while the herd as such remains dull in thought and dull in feeling."[1] Individualism has certainly been lauded by philosophers, politicians, writers, and others throughout history. Among the characteristics valued in the individual are uniqueness, free will, spirit, and, as Einstein noted, creativity.

The lone wolf, however, has taken the positive aspects of individuality and turned them into a frightening form of violence. The lone wolf is usually not "dull in thought" but rather strives to think up new ways to commit terrorist attacks. Free from "the herd" or any type of group or peer pressure, lone wolves march to their own beat. This has allowed them to commit some of the most creative and horrific terrorist attacks in history.

Many people assume that the lone wolf terrorist is a wildcard, unpredictable, and usually mentally ill, and because of that, there is little that anybody can do to prevent an attack. I believe I've demonstrated in this book why that perception is wrong. The lone wolves demand our attention not just because of what these types of terrorists are capable of doing, but also because of what they tell us about the world we're living in.

Lone wolf terrorism is about individuals blowing up airplanes, sending package bombs and anthrax spores through the mail, setting off car and truck bombs in front of government buildings, and massacring scores of youths at a summer camp. It is also, though, about people who seek a purpose in their lives, with some of them finding it by embracing a cause and then embarking upon a terrorist attack. Like every other terrorist who joins a group, the lone wolf, too, seeks camaraderie with others, but instead of through face-to-face contact, he or she finds it on the Internet, whether that be from online chat rooms, reading extremists' blogs and websites, or living vicariously from learning about the terrorist exploits of others, until he or she perpetrates an attack.

The lone wolf, in many respects, is no different from anyone who takes advantage of the revolutionary technological age we're living in, but at the same time, without even knowing it, we are all being taken advantage of by that very technology. The lone wolf surfs the web, just like many of us, to learn about things, but often receives an "exponentially increasing amount of unvetted and unverified information"[2] that can be biased, manipulative, and many times just plain wrong. The Internet, with its vast reach and many different components, including websites, blogs, and social networks, can influence all types of people, ranging from peaceful citizens to lone wolf terrorists. The Internet can also be used to learn the identities of lone wolves through their online postings, searches, and chat-room activities, just like it can be used by commercial enterprises to learn about our online activities so as to exploit them for profit.

Lone wolves also tell us a lot about terrorism. They symbolize the diversity of this endless phenomenon, with terrorists coming from different backgrounds and possessing a wide range of motivations. Just as there is no prototypical terrorist who is a member or leader of an extremist group, so, too, is there no prototypical lone wolf. The lone wolf could be a male or a female, a highly educated or an illiterate individual, or a person driven by various political, religious, or financial motives. Lone wolves also serve as a reminder of why terrorism can never be "defeated," since there will always be one person, somewhere, with a cause and a weapon to commit a terrorist attack.

When Timothy McVeigh acknowledged blowing up the federal building in Oklahoma City and stated, "Isn't it scary that one man could reap this kind of hell?" he got at the heart of the lone wolf terrorist threat. It seems mind-boggling that in a world where some terrorist groups have global networks of highly trained militants, a lone individual is capable of matching, and sometimes exceeding, the carnage, destruction, and grief that larger and better-financed extremist groups can inflict upon society. It is a somewhat discomforting thought that after all the resources, time, and personnel are expended in the fight against terrorism—usually terrorist groups, their affiliates, or their state sponsors—along can come a Timothy McVeigh or an Anders Breivik to reap their own "kind of hell" upon all of us.

Those who have been the target of lone wolves do not easily forget their traumatic experiences. Charles Epstein, who lost several fingers and suffered permanent hearing loss when he opened a package bomb that had been sent by Theodore Kaczynski, the Unabomber, put it best when he said that "there's never closure" to the emotional wounds. He could have been speaking for virtually anybody who has survived a terrorist attack or lost a loved one or friend to terrorism.

Although we cannot obviously prevent every lone wolf terrorist incident from occurring, we can employ a creative mix of strategies that may help reduce the threat. State-of-the-art technology in the form of detection systems, biometrics, and Internet monitoring tools will play a key role in accomplishing this, as will good old-fashioned police and intelligence work, including an alert public that reports suspicious packages and individuals to the authorities. But living with terrorism and its aftereffects will continue to be an unfortunate fact of life in the twenty-first century, just as it has been for previous generations.

Lone wolf terrorists are fascinating and frightening creatures—fascinating because they can be incredibly creative and innovative in their thinking and actions, frightening because they often exhibit no fear and have few, if any, constraints on the level of violence they're willing to inflict on their targets. "I am not a killer at heart," Bruce Ivins, the lone wolf terrorist whom the FBI determined to be responsible for sending the anthrax letters, told a former coworker in June

2008, less than two months before he committed suicide while being investigated. "I, in my right mind, wouldn't do it."[3] In the end, though, it really doesn't matter whether the lone wolf is in his or her "right mind." While some lone wolves are mentally ill, others are quite rational. Regardless of their mental state, based on their past actions and future potential, lone wolves have clearly demonstrated that they are important players in the world of terrorism and that they will have to be reckoned with both now and for the foreseeable future.

DEFINING *LONE WOLF TERRORISM*

In order to provide a definition of lone wolf terrorism, we first must have a definition of terrorism in general. The definitional problem, however, has plagued terrorism studies and counterterrorism policies for a long time. Different governments, institutions, scholars, and others all have their own criteria when it comes to deciding how to label violence that is linked to political, religious, social, and other causes. One study found more than one hundred different proposed definitions of terrorism, and that was only for the period from 1936 to 1981.[1] There have undoubtedly been many other definitions of terrorism offered in the post-9/11 world, with seemingly everybody now writing or talking about terrorism.

The US State Department itself could not decide from one year to the next how to define terrorism. For example, in its 2003 report on global terrorism, the State Department defined terrorism as "premeditated, politically motivated violence perpetrated against non-combatant targets by sub-national groups or clandestine agents, *usually intended to influence an audience.*"[2] The next year, however, they deleted the phrase "usually intended to influence an audience" without any explanation.[3] It has remained deleted in all subsequent reports.

The confusion over definitions of terrorism could also be seen in the interpretation of the term "non-combatant." In its 2003 report, the State Department wrote that noncombatants were "in addition to civilians, military personnel who at the time of the incident *are unarmed and/or not on duty.*"[4] That would mean any soldiers or other military personnel located anywhere in the world and not carrying

259

a weapon or on duty would be considered to be noncombatants. Violence against them would therefore be interpreted as an act of terrorism. If, however, they are carrying arms or are on duty, then no matter where the incident occurs, violence against them would not be considered terrorism. Yet, in its 2004 report, the State Department reversed itself and wrote that "the term 'non-combatant' . . . is interpreted to mean, in addition to civilians, military personnel (*whether or not armed or on duty*) who are not deployed in a war zone or a war-like setting."[5] Now the definition meant that soldiers or other military personnel would be considered to be noncombatants even if they were armed or on duty, provided they were in a country or area that was not considered to be a "war zone" or "war-like setting." The State Department has kept that interpretation in subsequent reports.

The changing meaning of "non-combatant" in the State Department's definition of terrorism was probably due to the wars in Iraq and Afghanistan. The Iraqi war, in particular, which began in 2003, caused considerable confusion within the US government about how to portray those who were fighting against the United States and its allies. At first, those who committed bombings and other violent acts in Iraq against US troops, Iraqi security forces, civilians, and others were described by the US government and most media outlets as "terrorists."[6] Eventually, though, the perpetrators of these attacks were described as "insurgents" or "militants," with the term *insurgents* usually reserved for Sunni extremists and the term *militants* usually used to refer to Shiite extremists.

The FBI also struggled with its definition of terrorism, changing it from one year to the next as it tried to decide if a single individual (lone wolf) should be considered a terrorist. In 1994, the FBI defined domestic terrorism as "the unlawful use of force or violence, committed by a group(s) or two or more individuals, against persons or property to intimidate or coerce a government, the civilian population, or any segment thereof, in furtherance of political or social objectives."[7] This definition excluded the single individual, such as Theodore Kaczynski, the infamous Unabomber, who had yet to be caught and was still sending package bombs to victims. In fact, in December 1994 an advertising executive, Thomas Mosser, was killed when he opened a package bomb that was sent by Kaczynski to his New Jersey home. The FBI reported zero incidents of domestic terrorism for that year.[8] The next year, the words "group(s) or two or more individuals" was replaced with "groups or individuals."[9] This seemed to include lone wolves, since the plural "individuals" could be interpreted to mean different individuals perpetrating different attacks rather than multiple individuals teaming up to perpetrate an attack. Finally, in 1999, the wording was again changed, this time to "a group or individual," which left no doubt that a lone wolf could be considered a terrorist.[10]

However, the FBI noted in its 1999 report that it still did not view Kaczynski's activities or those of Amil Kanzi, who killed two CIA employees and wounded three others in a shooting spree outside the agency's headquarters in Langley, Virginia, in January 1993, as constituting acts of terrorism:

> While views vary widely concerning whether Theodore Kaczynski (the UNABOMBER) and Amil Kanzi . . . are terrorists, the FBI does not classify the acts committed by these individuals as incidents of terrorism. When the series of deadly bombings perpetrated by the "UNABOMBER" began in the 1970s, the subject's motivations were unclear. It was not known, for example, whether the subject's targets were chosen randomly or as part of some personal vendetta. Due to the lack of information regarding the subject's motivation, the FBI investigated the case as a criminal, rather than as a terrorism, matter.
>
> Although an attack on vehicles outside the entrance of a U.S. Government facility may raise the specter of terrorist intent, FBI investigation into the January 1993 shooting outside CIA headquarters did not support speculation that the attack was an act of terrorism. Amil Kanzi, the individual ultimately identified as the lone assailant in the shooting, was determined by the FBI to be acting on personal, rather than ideological, motivations.[11]

The FBI never indicated in subsequent years whether it had changed its view of Kaczynski and Kanzi as not being terrorists. Yet both individuals were indeed motivated by political objectives to some degree. Kaczynski demanded that a rambling, thirty-five-thousand-word manifesto calling for a revolution against the industrial-technological society be published in the *New York Times* or the *Washington Post* or he would continue to send package bombs. (It was published in September 1995 in the *Washington Post*, with the *New York Times* sharing the printing cost.) When one perpetrates violence in the name of a revolution, whatever type of revolution that may be, it would seem to qualify as a political or ideological motivation. In the case of Kanzi, his violent actions were based on his desire to protest American foreign policy, which he believed was harming Muslims around the world. He told FBI special agent Brad Garrett on a flight from Pakistan to the United States (he had fled the country after the shootings and was arrested in Pakistan in 1997) that he wanted to "teach a lesson" to the US government. According to Garrett, Kanzi thought his actions would change US policies. "It was almost illogic logic," Garrett told a reporter. "It wasn't personal. It wasn't like hating individuals. It was more institutional."[12]

The issue of motivations again came up in the case of an Egyptian immigrant, Hesham Mohamed Hadayet, who shot and killed two people at an Israeli El Al Airlines ticket counter at Los Angeles International Airport on July 4, 2002. After several months of investigation, the FBI determined that Hadayet, who was killed by an El Al security guard at the airport, acted alone and that his violence constituted an act of terrorism. Although Hadayet was depressed over personal issues, including a failing business, he targeted the El Al ticket counter due to his anger over Israel's treatment of Palestinians. He had also told people close to him that he believed in jihad and in the targeting of innocent civilians. "The barrier to calling it a terrorist event earlier than now was that we did not know his motivations," a Los Angeles FBI spokesman said. "We think we have a very good handle on that now."[13]

What, though, if somebody's motivation for violence is indeed personal, with no political, ideological, or religious objective in mind? Are there circumstances in which those acts of violence can be considered terrorism? One example would be the hijacking of a plane for money. Imagine a lone wolf or a group of individuals hijacking a plane and demanding a large sum of money in exchange for the lives of the passengers and crew. There is no political or other motivation except monetary gain. The effect on government and society, however, would be the same as if the motivation and objective were political, ideological, or religious. The government would still have to initiate negotiations with the hijacker or hijackers, launch a potential hostage-rescue operation, increase security at airports, and take other measures to reduce the risk of future hijackings. There would be fear among the public concerning the safety of air travel, as other criminals, or even the same group, might commit additional hijackings. There would also be widespread media coverage and statements by high-level government officials, all adding to the crisis atmosphere of the hijacking. Under virtually all definitions of terrorism, this would not qualify as a terrorist incident, even though it has the same effects as a "terrorist" attack. And if the group simply stated that their action was done in the name of some cause rather than for monetary gain, there would be little debate as to whether the incident qualifies as a terrorist event.

Monetary gain, in fact, was the motive for the first major midair plane bombing in the United States. John Gilbert Graham (who was mentioned in the introduction and discussed in further detail in chapter 2) put several sticks of dynamite and a timer in his mother's luggage before she boarded a United Airlines flight out of Denver on November 1, 1955. Graham was hoping to collect a $37,500 insurance policy on her life. Forty-four people, including Graham's mother, were killed in the bombing. President Dwight Eisenhower, as was the case for most Americans, expressed outrage at this new form of violence. There were also reactions from Congress, which soon afterward passed a bill that established the death penalty for anyone convicted of causing loss of life by damaging an airplane, bus, or commercial vehicle. (An existing statute covered the sabotage of trains).

Graham was executed in 1957 under Colorado law for murder. The FBI and the Civil Aviation Administration began conducting studies on measures that might be taken to detect explosives in luggage. There was also an increase in bomb threats to US airlines following the Graham attack. Thus, in many respects, there was little difference in government and societal reactions to the Graham bombing, which had a purely financial motive, than there would have been had Graham or an extremist group perpetrated the violence in the name of some political, social, or religious cause.[14]

The requirement in many definitions of terrorism that there be a political, social, or religious objective associated with the act of violence would also exclude those terrorists who suffer from various types of mental illness and commit their violence for no apparent reason beyond their own psychological problems. If Kaczynski, the Unabomber, did not have as his motive a "revolution" against the technological-industrial society but rather sent the package bombs and made threats for no apparent reason, it would still be "terrorism," based on the effect it had on the United States. The Unabomber's activities caused fear and anxiety among the public, frustrated the government in its search for the perpetrator, and led to changes in the way packages were allowed to be sent through the mail.

There are many other aspects of definitions of terrorism that could be challenged, such as the "innocent victims" or "non-combatant" phrases used by many observers to denote a terrorist attack. As pointed out earlier, the US State Department changed its interpretation of who qualified as a noncombatant. Several scholarly and other definitions of terrorism over the years have used the innocent-victims distinction, yet terrorists oftentimes do not recognize that classification. As noted in chapter 2, a French anarchist, Émile Henry, coined a phrase in the late-nineteenth century that many terrorists still use today. Henry hurled a homemade bomb (or in today's jargon, an IED) into a crowded café in Paris in 1894 to avenge the recent execution of a fellow anarchist.

The bombing resulted in several injuries and one death. When the judges at his trial expressed bewilderment at the crime, pointing out that most of the victims were small shopkeepers, clerks, and workers— people who were innocent of any wrongdoing—Henry simply replied, "There are no innocent bourgeois."[15] That was basically the same view of Faisal Shahzad, the man who placed a bomb that failed to detonate in Times Square in New York City in May 2010. During submission of his guilty plea, the judge asked him if he was aware that there were innocent people walking around Times Square that night who could have been killed by his bomb. Shahzad replied, "Well, the people select the government; we consider them all the same."[16]

So how, then, should we define terrorism? As I crafted the wording, I focused on what I thought to be the main challenge in creating a meaningful definition of terrorism—namely, how to account for those tactics that appear to be terrorism but are not perpetrated by a "terrorist" or do not have the same motives as those of a terrorist yet have virtually the same impact on government and society as a "terrorist" act. An adequate definition of terrorism also needs to exclude violence that may occur during the course of a protest, demonstration, popular uprising, or guerrilla insurgency against a government's troops. Taking all of these factors into account requires a rather long-worded definition of terrorism:

> Terrorism is the use or threat of violence or nonviolent sabotage, including cyber attacks, against government, society, business, the military (when the military is not an occupying force or involved in a war, insurgency, or state of hostilities), or any other target, by individual(s) or group(s) (but not including actions taken during popular uprisings, riots, or violent protests), to further a political, social, religious, financial, or other related goal, or, when not having such an objective, nevertheless has the same effect, or potential effect, upon government, society, business, or the military in terms of creating fear and/or disrupting daily life and/or causing government, society, business, or the military to react with heightened security and/or other responses.

A definition of lone wolf terrorism would be exactly the same as the above general definition of terrorism, but to qualify as a lone wolf, an individual would have to be working alone or have just minimal assistance from one or two other people (such as Timothy McVeigh receiving assistance from Terry Nichols in preparing the bomb that was used to blow up the federal building in Oklahoma City). Therefore, lone wolf terrorism can be defined as follows:

> Lone wolf terrorism is the use or threat of violence or nonviolent sabotage, including cyber attacks, against government, society, business, the military (when the military is not an occupying force or involved in a war, insurgency, or state of hostilities), or any other target, by an individual acting alone or with minimal support from one or two other people (but not including actions taken during popular uprisings, riots, or violent protests), to further a political, social, religious, financial, or other related goal, or, when not having such an objective, nevertheless has the same effect, or potential effect, upon government, society, business, or the military in terms of creating fear and/or disrupting daily life and/or causing government, society, business, or the military to react with heightened security and/or other responses.

Any definition of terrorism, whether it is lone wolf terrorism or terrorism in general, will naturally have many gray areas. For example, from the definition of both general and lone wolf terrorism, I have chosen to exclude all violent actions taken during a protest, demonstration, or mass uprising. Yet one could make the case that somebody throwing a bomb, shooting a gun, or setting fire to a building during a mass demonstration is perpetrating an act of terrorism. To do so, though, would seem to open up the floodgates on incidents of terrorism, as virtually every violent action occurring during a demonstration or protest would be counted as a terrorist act. That is why definitions of terrorism are problematic and will always be open to debate.

NOTES

PREFACE TO THE PAPERBACK

1. Jennifer Levitz, "Boston Marathon Bomber Dzhokhar Tsarnaev Sentenced to Death, Apologizes to Victims," *Wall Street Journal,* June 24, 2015, http://www.wsj.com/articles/dzhokhar-tsarnaev-apologizes-before-being-sentenced-to-death-for-boston-bombing-1435170191 (accessed June 13, 2016); Richard Fausset, Richard Pérez-Peña, and Matt Apuzzo, "Slain Troops in Chattanooga Saved Lives Before Giving Their Own," *New York Times,* July 22, 2015, http://www.nytimes.com/2015/07/23/us/chattanooga-tennessee-shooting-investigation-mohammod-abdulazeez.html (accessed June 13, 2016); Laura Wagner and Bill Chappell, "FBI: San Bernardino Shooting Is Being Investigated as a Terrorist Act," *NPR,* December 4, 2015, http://www.npr.org/sections/thetwo-way/2015/12/04/458464907/alleged-san-bernardino-attacker-pledged-allegiance-to-isis (accessed June 13, 2016); Ralph Ellis, Ashley Frantz, Faith Karimi, and Eliott C. McLaughlin, "Orlando Shooting: 49 Killed, Shooter Pledged ISIS Allegiance," CNN, June 13, 2016, http://www.cnn.com/2016/06/12/us/orlando-nightclub-shooting/ (accessed June 13, 2016).

2. Julie Turkewitz and Jack Healy, "3 Are Dead in Colorado Springs Shootout at Planned Parenthood Center," *New York Times,* November 27, 2015, http://www.nytimes.com/2015/11/28/us/colorado-planned-parenthood-shooting.html (accessed June 13, 2016); Michael S. Schmidt, "Charleston Suspect Was in Contact With Supremacists, Officials Say," *New York Times,* July 3, 2015, http://www.nytimes.com/2015/07/04/us/dylann-roof-was-in-contact-with-supremacists-officials-say.html (accessed June 13, 2016); Polly Mosendz, "Dylann Roof Confesses: Says He Wanted To Start 'Race War,'" *Newsweek,* June 19, 2015, http://www.newsweek.com/dylann-roof-confesses-church-shooting-says-he-wanted-start-race-war-344797 (accessed June 13, 2016); Dan Weikel, Scott Gold, Richard Winton, Brian Bennett, Joel Rubin, Joseph Serna, Ari Bloomkatz, Samantha Schaefer, Kate Mather, Matt Stevens, Jill Cowan, Alicia Banks, and Laura J. Nelson, "LAX Shooting: Gunman Targeted TSA Officers, Wrote Anti-Government Note," *Los Angeles Times,* November 1, 2013, http://articles.latimes.com/2013/nov/01/local/la-me-ln-lax-shooting-multiple-tsa-agents-shot-by-gunman-with-rifle-20131101 (accessed June 13, 2016).

INTRODUCTION

1. Paul Avrich, *Sacco and Vanzetti: The Anarchist Background* (Princeton, NJ: Princeton University Press, 1991), pp. 196–97.

2. Mike Davis, *Buda's Wagon: A Brief History of the Car Bomb* (London: Verso, 2007), p. 2.

3. Avrich, *Sacco and Vanzetti*, p. 207.

4. The first reported midair plane bombing in the United States occurred near Chesterton, Indiana, on October 10, 1933. A United Airlines transcontinental passenger plane exploded, killing all seven people aboard. No motive or suspects were uncovered. The higher number of casualties caused by the Graham bombing and the reaction it elicited across the country, including front-page coverage in the *New York Times*, would seem to qualify that incident as the first "major" midair plane bombing in US history.

5. Mark Juergensmeyer, "Religious Terror and the Secular State," *Harvard International Review* (Winter 2004): 5.

6. Avrich, *Sacco and Vanzetti*, p. 206.

7. Among the few systematic studies of lone wolves are Dennis Pluchinsky, *The Global Jihad: Leaderless Terrorism?* (Washington, DC: Woodrow Wilson International Center for Scholars, 2006); *Lone-Wolf Terrorism*, COT, Institute voor Veiligheids- en Crisismanagement, Final draft, June 7, 2007, Case Study for Work Package 3, http://www.scribd.com/doc/34968770/Lone-Wolf-Terrorism (accessed June 10, 2011); Ramon Spaaij, *Understanding Lone Wolf Terrorism: Global Patterns, Motivations, and Prevention* (New York: Springer, 2012); Raffaello Pantucci, "A Typology of Lone Wolves: Preliminary Analysis of Lone Islamist Terrorists," *Developments in Radicalisation and Political Violence*, March 2011; and George Michael, *Lone Wolf Terror and the Rise of Leaderless Resistance* (Nashville, TN: Vanderbilt University Press, 2012).

8. Ricardo A. Martinez, "Partners in the Battle," *FBI Law Enforcement Bulletin*, February 2011, http://www.fbi.gov/stats-services/publications/law-enforcement-bulletin/february2011/notable-speech (accessed November 8, 2012).

CHAPTER 1. THE GROWING THREAT OF LONE WOLF TERRORISM

1. Aamer Madhani, "Obama: 'Lone Wolf' Attack Is Biggest Concern," *National Journal*, August 17, 2011, http://www.nationaljournal.com/whitehouse/obama-lone-wolf-attack-is-biggest-concern-20110816 (accessed August 23, 2011).

2. "Intelligence Officials Warn Attempted al Qaeda Attack Months Away," Fox News, February 2, 2010, http://www.foxnews.com/politics/2010/02/02/

intelligence-officials-warn-attempted-al-qaeda-attack-months-away/ (accessed April 16, 2010).

3. Matt Wade, "Game On," *Age*, March 1, 2010, http://www.theage.com.au/world/game-on-20100228-pbc0.html (accessed April 14, 2010).

4. "Kevin Rudd Says Australia Faces Major Terror Threat," BBC News, February 23, 2010, http://news.bbc.co.uk/2/hi/8529613.stm (accessed April 14, 2010).

5. Brynjar Lia and Katja H-W Skjolberg, *Why Terrorism Occurs—A Survey of Theories and Hypotheses on the Causes of Terrorism*, FFI/RAPPORT-2000/02769, p. 8.

6. David C. Rapoport, "The Four Waves of Modern Terrorism," in *Attacking Terrorism: Elements of a Grand Strategy*, ed. Audrey Kurth Cronin and James M. Ludes (Washington, DC: Georgetown University Press, 2004), pp. 46–73.

7. Ibid., p. 47.

8. Ibid., p. 48.

9. Ibid., p. 50.

10. Ibid., p. 70, n. 23.

11. Ibid., pp. 52–53.

12. Ibid., p. 56.

13. Ibid., p. 62.

14. Ibid.

15. For a discussion of the fifth wave of terrorism, see Jeffrey D. Simon, "Technological and Lone Operator Terrorism: Prospects for a Fifth Wave of Global Terrorism," in *Terrorism, Identity, and Legitimacy: The Four Waves Theory and Political Violence*, ed. Jean E. Rosenfeld (London: Routledge, 2011), pp. 44–65.

16. Jeff Shogol, "DOD Report Says EFP Attacks Are Up in Iraq," *Stars and Stripes*, September 19, 2007, http://www.stripes.com/news/dod-report-says-efp-attacks-are-up-in-iraq-1.68998 (accessed June 19, 2011).

17. Scott Shane, "Killings in Norway Spotlight Anti-Muslim Thought in U.S.," *New York Times*, July 24, 2011, http://www.nytimes.com/2011/07/25/us/25debate.html?pagewanted=all (accessed July 28, 2011).

18. David Cay Johnston, "Tax Law Was Cited in Software Engineer's Suicide Note," *New York Times*, February 18, 2010, http://www.nytimes.com/2010/02/19/us/19tax.html (accessed May 2, 2011).

19. Asher Price, "Suicide Pilot Joe Stack Had History of Shutting Doors on People," *Statesman*, March 7, 2010, http://www.statesman.com/news/local/suicide-pilot-joe-stack-had-history-of-shutting-326300.html (accessed May 6, 2011).

20. "RAW DATA: Joseph Stack Suicide Manifesto," Fox News, February 18, 2010, http://www.foxnews.com/us/2010/02/18/raw-data-joseph-stack-suicide-manifesto/ (accessed May 2, 2011).

21. "Richard Poplawski: The Making of a Lone Wolf," Anti-Defamation

League, April 8, 2009, http://www.adl.org/learn/extremism_in_the_news/White_Supremacy/poplawski%20report.htm (accessed August 13, 2009).

22. Jon Schmitz, "Poplawski Bought Guns through Shop in Wilkinsburg," *Pittsburgh Post-Gazette*, April 7, 2009, http://www.post-gazette.com/pg/09097/961071-53.stm (accessed June 8, 2010).

23. *Lone-Wolf Terrorism*, COT, Instituut voor Veiligheids- en Crisismanagement, Final draft, June 7, 2007, Case Study for Work Package 3, p. 43, http://www.scribd.com/doc/34968770/Lone-Wolf-Terrorism (accessed June 10, 2011).

24. Duncan Gardham, "'Al-Qaeda' Terrorists Who Brainwashed Exeter Suicide Bomber Still on the Run," *Daily Telegraph*, October 15, 2008, http://www.telegraph.co.uk/news/uknews/law-and-order/3204139/Al-Qaeda-terrorists-who-brainwashed-Exeter-suicide-bomber-still-on-the-run.html (accessed June 28, 2010).

25. Louis Beam, quoted in "Extremism in America: Louis Beam," Anti-Defamation League, 2005, http://www.adl.org/learn/ext_us/beam.asp?xpicked=2&item=beam (accessed July 4, 2010).

26. Mark Sageman, "The Next Generation of Terror," *Foreign Policy* (March/April 2008): 37–38.

27. Ibid., p. 41.

28. "'Lone Wolf' Attacks: A Developing Islamist Extremist Strategy?" Integrated Threat Assessment Centre, June 29, 2007: 2, http://www.nefafoundation.org/miscellaneous/FeaturedDocs/ITAC_lonewolves_062007.pdf (accessed April 26, 2010).

29. "Securing Australia/Protecting Our Community," counterterrorism white paper, Australian government, 2010, p. 8.

30. *EU Terrorism Situation and Trend Report (TE-SAT) 2010*, Europol, p. 37.

31. *Rightwing Extremism: Current Economic and Political Climate Fueling Resurgence in Radicalization and Recruitment*, Office of Intelligence and Analysis, US Department of Homeland Security, April 7, 2009, http://www.fas.org./irp/eprint/rightwing.pdf (accessed April 22, 2009).

32. Jeffrey D. Simon, *The Terrorist Trap: America's Experience with Terrorism*, 2nd ed. (Bloomington: Indiana University Press, 2001), pp. 383–85.

CHAPTER 2. WHO ARE THE LONE WOLVES?

1. Walter Laqueur, *The Age of Terrorism* (Boston: Little, Brown, 1987), p. 70.

2. Yoram Schweitzer and Sari Goldstein Ferber, "Al-Qaeda and the Internationalization of Suicide Terrorism," Memorandum 78, Jaffee Center for Strategic Studies, November 2005, p. 39.

3. Jessica Stern, *Terror in the Name of God: Why Religious Militants Kill* (New York: HarperCollins, 2003), p. 172.

4. David Johnston and James Risen, "Lone Terrorists May Strike in the U.S., Agencies Warn," *New York Times*, February 23, 2003, http://query.nytimes.com/gst/fullpage.html?res=9F0CE1DC113DF930A15751C0A9659C8B63 (accessed April 3, 2011).

5. Ehud Sprinzak, "The Lone Gunman," *Foreign Policy* (November/December 2001): 72–73.

6. Ibid.

7. See chapter 5 of this book for a detailed discussion of lone wolf assassins.

8. James W. Clarke, *American Assassins: The Darker Side of Politics*, rev. ed. (Princeton, NJ: Princeton University Press, 1990); R. Hrair Dekmejian, *Spectrum of Terror* (Washington, DC: CQ Press, 2007), pp. 25–38.

9. Carolyn Tuft and Joe Holleman, "Inside the Christian Identity Movement," *St. Louis Post-Dispatch*, March 5, 2000, http://www.rickross.com/reference/christian_identity/christianidentity7.html (accessed April 24, 2011); "Extremism in America: Christian Identity," Anti-Defamation League, 2005, http://www.adl.org/learn/ext_us/Christian_Identity.asp?xpicked=4&item=Christian_ID (accessed April 24, 2011).

10. Scott Brown, "Interview with Oklahoma City Bomber Timothy McVeigh Released as Part of MSNBC Special," WGRZ/MSNBC, April 19, 2010, http://www.wgrz.com/news/local/story.aspx?storyid=76090&catid=13 (accessed May 1, 2011). *Buffalo News* reporters Lou Michel and Dan Herbeck spent parts of seven days interviewing McVeigh as he awaited his execution. They published a book on McVeigh in 2001 titled *American Terrorist: Timothy McVeigh and the Oklahoma City Bombing* (New York: Regan Books, 2001).

11. Ibid.

12. "Testimony of Jennifer McVeigh," University of Missouri–Kansas City, May 5, 1997, http://law2.umkc.edu/faculty/projects/ftrials/mcveigh/jennifertestimony.html (accessed May 2, 2011).

13. *PrimeTime: McVeigh's Own Words*, ABC News, March 29, 2001, http://abcnews.go.com/Primetime/story?id=132158&page=1 (accessed May 2, 2011).

14. Brown, "Interview with Oklahoma City Bomber Timothy McVeigh."

15. "McVeigh Remorseless about Bombing," Associated Press, March 29, 2001, http://www.rickross.com/reference/mcveigh/mcveigh6.html (accessed May 2, 2011).

16. Ibid.

17. Ibid.

18. *PrimeTime.*

19. Timothy Stenovec, "Oslo Terror Attacks: A History of Terrorism in Norway,"

Huffington Post, July 22, 2011, http://www.huffingtonpost.com/2011/07/22/oslo-terrorism-history_n_907380.html (accessed July 31, 2011).

20. Michael Schwirtz, "Norway's Premier Vows to Keep an Open Society," *New York Times,* July 27, 2011, http://www.nytimes.com/2011/07/28/world/europe/28norway.html (accessed August 2, 2011).

21. "Norway's Black Friday: A Chronology of the Twin Attacks," *Spiegel Online International,* July 25, 2011, http://www.spiegel.de/international/europe/0,1518,776437,00.html (accessed August 1, 2011).

22. Ian MacDougall and Karl Ritter, "Norway Suspect Was Considering Other Targets," Associated Press, July 30, 2011, http://www.tulsaworld.com/site/printerfriendly story.aspx?articleid=20110730_298_0_OSLONo914857 (accessed November 8, 2012).

23. Karl Ritter, "Gunman's Background Puzzles Police in Norway," Associated Press, July 23, 2011, http://news.yahoo.com/gunmans-background-puzzles-police-norway-044701742.html (accessed July 23, 2011).

24. Chris Slack, "Anders Breivik 'Was on Norwegian Secret Service Watchlist' after Buying Chemical Haul from Polish Retailer," *Mail Online,* http://www.daily mail.co.uk/news/article-2018646/Norway-shooting-Anders-Behring-Breivik-secret-service-watchlist.html (accessed July 26, 2011).

25. Ibid.

26. Victoria Klesty and Gwladys Fouche, "Norway Mourns Victims of Anti-Islam 'Crusader,'" Reuters, July 24, 2011, http://www.reuters.com/article/2011/07/24/us-norway-idUSL6E7IN00C20110724 (accessed July 24, 2011).

27. Ibid.

28. Victoria Klesty and Gwladys Fouche, "Norway Suspect Deems Killings Atrocious but Needed," Reuters, July 24, 2011 http://www.abs-cbnnews.com/global-filipino/world/07/24/11/norway-suspect-deems-killings-atrocious-needed (accessed July 24, 2011).

29. MacDougall and Ritter, "Norway Suspect Was Considering Other Targets."

30. Bjoern Amland and Sarah DiLorenzo, "Suspect: Norway Attacks 'Marketing' for Manifesto," Associated Press, July 24, 2011, http://abclocal.go.com/wpvi/story?section=news/national_world&id=8268226 (accessed August 2, 2011).

31. Michael Schwirtz and Matthew Saltmarsh, "Oslo Suspect Cultivated Parallel Life to Disguise 'Martyrdom Operation,'" *New York Times,* July 24, 2011, http://www.nytimes.com/2011/07/25/world/europe/25breivik.html (accessed July 26, 2011).

32. "As Horrors Emerge, Norway Charges Christian Extremist," *New York Times,* July 24, 2011.

33. Balazs Koranyi and Walter Gibbs, "Norway Killer Picked Victims Who Had 'Leftist' Look," Reuters, http://uk.reuters.com/article/2012/04/23/uk-norway-attacks-trial-idUKBRE83M0GT20120423 (accessed April 24, 2012).

34. Scott Stewart, "Norway: Lessons from a Successful Lone Wolf Attacker," Stratfor Global Intelligence, July 28, 2011, http://www.stratfor.com/weekly/20110727-norway-lessons-successful-lone-wolf-attacker (accessed August 2, 2011).

35. Monte Kuligowski, "Anders Breivik: A Teachable Moment on Fundamentalism," *American Thinker*, August 2, 2011, http://www.americanthinker.com/2011/08/anders_breivik_a_teachable_moment_on_fundamentalism.html (accessed August 2, 2011).

36. Scott Shane, "Killings in Norway Spotlight Anti-Muslim Thought in U.S.," *New York Times*, July 24, 2011, http://www.nytimes.com/2011/07/25/us/25debate.html?pagewanted=all (accessed July 28, 2011).

37. Ibid.

38. Nicholas Kulish, "Shift in Europe Seen in Debate on Immigrants," *New York Times*, July 27, 2011, http://www.nytimes.com/2011/07/28/world/europe/28europe.html (accessed August 1, 2011).

39. Ibid.

40. Steven Erlanger and Scott Shane, "Oslo Suspect Wrote of Fear of Islam and Plan for War," *New York Times*, July 23, 2011, http://www.nytimes.com/2011/07/24/world/europe/24oslo.html?pagewanted=all (accessed August 2, 2011).

41. Tad Tietze, "The Importance of the Anders Breivik Verdict Reaches beyond Norway," *Guardian*, August 24, 2012, http://www.guardian.co.uk/commentisfree/2012/aug/24/anders-breivik-verdict-norway1 (accessed November 9, 2012).

42. Mark Townsend, "Breivik Verdict: Norwegian Extremist Declared Sane and Sentenced to 21 Years," *Guardian*, August 24, 2012, http://www.guardian.co.uk/world/2012/aug/24/breivik-verdict-sane-21-years (accessed November 9, 2012). Breivik himself indicated shortly after his arrest that he was quite aware of what he had done. According to his lawyer, Breivik said that "he believed the actions were atrocious, but that in his head they were necessary." See Klesty and Fouche, "Norway Suspect Deems Killings Atrocious but Needed."

43. Laura Smith-Spark, "Norway Killer Anders Breivik Ruled Sane, Given 21-Year Prison Term," CNN, August 24, 2012, http://www.cnn.com/2012/08/24/world/europe/norway-breivik-trial/index.html (accessed November 9, 2012).

44. Stewart, "Norway."

45. Gavin Hewitt, "Analysis," BBC News, July 25, 2011, http://www.bbc.co.uk/news/world-europe-14280210 (accessed August 4, 2011).

46. "Bin Laden Death Could Inspire Lone Wolf Attacks, Feds Say," CBS News, May 10, 2011, http://www.cbsnews.com/8301-503543_162-20061417-503543.html (accessed May 10, 2011).

47. James Dao, "Suspect Was 'Mortified' about Deployment," *New York Times*, November 5, 2009, http://www.nytimes.com/2009/11/06/us/06suspect.html (accessed May 11, 2011).

48. Chris McGreal, "Fort Hood Shootings: Nidal Hasan's Quiet Manner Hid Hostility to US Army," *Guardian,* http://www.guardian.co.uk/world/2009/nov/06/fort-hood-shootings-nidal-hasan (accessed May 11, 2011).

49. Daniel Pipes, "Maj. Hasan's Islamist Life," FrontPageMagazine.com, November 20, 2009, http://www.danielpipes.org/7763/major-nidal-hasan-islamist-life (accessed May 11, 2011).

50. Ibid.

51. Joseph I. Lieberman and Susan M. Collins, *A Ticking Time Bomb: Counterterrorism Lessons from the U.S. Government's Failure to Prevent the Fort Hood Attack,* United States Senate Committee on Homeland Security and Government Affairs, February 3, 2011, p. 8.

52. Pipes, "Maj. Hasan's Islamist Life."

53. Lieberman and Collins, *Ticking Time Bomb,* p. 9

54. Del Quentin Wiber, "Von Brunn, White Supremacist Holocaust Museum Shooter, Dies," *Washington Post,* January 7, 2010, http://www.washingtonpost.com/wp-dyn/content/article/2010/01/06/AR2010010604095.html (accessed May 14, 2011).

55. "Extremism in America: Christian Identity," Anti-Defamation League, 2005, http://www.adl.org/learn/ext_us/Christian_Identity.asp?xpicked=4&item=Christian_ID (accessed April 24, 2011).

56. "James von Brunn: An ADL Backgrounder," Anti-Defamation League, 2009, http://www.adl.org/main_Extremism/von_brunn_background.htm?Multi_page_sections=sHeading_2 (accessed April 24, 2011).

57. Ibid.

58. David Stout, "Museum Gunman a Longtime Foe of Government," *New York Times,* June 10, 2009, http://www.nytimes.com/2009/06/11/us/11shoot.html (accessed May 14, 2011); "Law Center: Shooting Suspect Has 'Long History' with Neo-Nazis," CNN Justice, June 10, 2009, http://articles.cnn.com/2009-06-10/justice/dc.museum.shooting.suspect_1_white-supremacist-jews-and-blacks-von-brunn?_s=PM:CRIME (accessed May 14, 2011).

59. "James von Brunn."

60. Neal Augenstein, "Separatist Describes Von Brunn as Depressed," WTOP, June 11, 2009, http://www.wtop.com/?nid=25&sid=1694189 (accessed May 15, 2011).

61. "White Supremacists Celebrate Holocaust Museum Shooter Suspect as a Martyr and Hero," Anti-Defamation League, June 11, 2009, http://www.adl.org/main_Extremism/White-Supremacists-Celebrate-Shooter.htm (accessed May 14, 2011).

62. "Full Text of Eric Rudolph's Confession," NPR, April 14, 2005, http://www.npr.org/templates/story/story.php?storyId=4600480 (accessed May 17, 2011).

63. Ibid.

64. Ibid.

65. Jeffrey Gettleman, "Ambivalence in the Besieged Town of 'Run, Rudolph, Run,'" *New York Times*, June 1, 2003, http://www.nytimes.com/2003/06/01/national/01SCEN.html (accessed May 18, 2011).

66. "Atlanta Olympic Bombing Suspect Arrested," CNN, May 31, 2003, http://articles.cnn.com/2003-05-31/us/rudolph.main_1_eric-robert-rudolph-george-nordmann-atlanta-olympic-bombing?_s=PM:US (accessed May 19, 2011).

67. "Full Text of Eric Rudolph's Confession."

68. Ibid.

69. Shaila Dewan, "Olympics Bomber Apologizes and Is Sentenced to Life Terms," *New York Times*, August 23, 2005, http://www.nytimes.com/2005/08/23/national/23bomber.html?pagewanted=print (accessed May 19, 2011).

70. Henry Schuster with Charles Stone, *Hunting Eric Rudolph* (New York: Berkeley, 2005).

71. Thad Anderson, "Notes on Eric Rudolph's Manifesto & Postscript," *Blogcritics*, http://blogcritics.org/politics/article/notes-on-eric-rudolphs-manifesto-postscript/ (accessed May 20, 2011).

72. Blake Morrison, "Special Report: Eric Rudolph Writes Home," *USA Today*, July 5, 2005, http://www.usatoday.com/news/nation/2005-07-05-rudolph-cover-partone_x.htm (accessed May 22, 2011).

73. Peter Jan Margry, "The Murder of Pim Fortuyn and Collective Emotions: Hype, Hysteria, and Holiness in the Netherlands?" *Etnofoor:antropologisch tijdschrift* 16 (2003): 106–31, http://www.meertens.knaw.nl/meertensnet/file/edwinb/20050420/PF_webp_Engels_lang.pdf (accessed May 25, 2011).

74. Rod Dreher, "Murder in Holland," National Review Online, May 7, 2002, http://old.nationalreview.com/dreher/dreher050702.asp (accessed May 24, 2011).

75. "Crisis Talks over Dutch Killing," BBC News, May 7, 2002, http://news.bbc.co.uk/2/hi/europe/1971943.stm (accessed May 25, 2011).

76. "Dutch Election to Go Ahead," BBC News, May 7, 2002, http://news.bbc.co.uk/2/hi/europe/1972454.stm (accessed May 25, 2011).

77. Ibid.

78. "The Political Legacy of Pim Fortuyn," *Economist*, May 9, 2002, http://www.economist.com/node/1125205 (accessed May 24, 2011); Dreher, "Murder in Holland."

79. *Lone-Wolf Terrorism*, COT, Instituut voor Veiligheids- en Crisismanagement, Final draft, June 7, 2007, Case Study for Work Package 3, p. 24, http://www.scribd.com/doc/34968770/Lone-Wolf-Terrorism (accessed June 10, 2011).

80. Ibid., p. 35.

81. Ibid., p. 44.

82. Ibid., p. 46.

83. Ibid., pp. 64–65.

84. Ibid., pp. 24–25.

85. Marlise Simons, "Dutch Court Sentences Killer of Politician to 18-Year Term," *New York Times*, April 16, 2003, http://www.nytimes.com/2003/04/16/world/dutch-court-sentences-killer-of-politician-to-18-year-term.html?ref=pimfortuyn (accessed May 24, 2011).

86. *Lone-Wolf Terrorism*, p. 25.

87. "Fortuyn Gunman Spared Life Term," BBC News, April 15, 2003, http://news.bbc.co.uk/2/hi/europe/2948555.stm (accessed May 24, 2011).

88. Margry, "Murder of Pim Fortuyn."

89. Ibid.

90. *Lone-Wolf Terrorism*, p. 79.

91. Ibid., p. 80. The Netherlands experienced another assassination in November 2004 when controversial filmmaker Theo van Gogh was shot and stabbed to death in Amsterdam by a Dutch Moroccan man upset with Van Gogh's anti-Islamic views as well as with a recent film that portrayed violence against women in Islamic societies.

92. Jeffrey D. Simon, *The Terrorist Trap: America's Experience with Terrorism*, 2nd ed. (Bloomington: Indiana University Press, 2001), pp. 49–51.

93. Ibid., p. 49.

94. Ibid., pp. 49–50.

95. Ibid., p. 50.

96. "What Kind of Man Is This?" *Rocky Mountain News*, November 16, 1955, p. 44.

97. "Famous Cases and Criminals: Jack Gilbert Graham," Federal Bureau of Investigation, http://www.fbi.gov/about-us/history/famous-cases/jack-gilbert-graham (accessed May 31, 2011); "Graham Paying Back Check Forgery Fund," *Denver Post*, November 14, 1955, p. 1.

98. "Graham Paying Back Check Forgery Fund."

99. "Graham Faces Charge of Murder," *Denver Post*, November 14, 1955, p. 3.

100. "Famous Cases and Criminals."

101. Ibid.

102. Ibid.

103. This discussion of Panos Koupparis ("Commander Nemo") is drawn from Simon, *Terrorist Trap*, pp. 335–37, and from Jeffrey D. Simon, "Lone Operators and Weapons of Mass Destruction," in *Hype of Reality: The "New Terrorism" and Mass Casualty Attacks*, ed. Brad Roberts (Alexandria, VA: Chemical and Biological Arms Control Institute, 2000), pp. 75–76, 78–79. I have included Koupparis in this discussion of criminal lone wolves even though he had help from more than one or two

other people. However, since that support came entirely from his family members, it seems to be a special case of an individual who uses close relatives to assist him in threatening a terrorist attack.

104. Pericles Solomides, "Blackmailers Had Plans for Bombings," *Cyprus Mail*, May 19, 1987, p. 1.

105. Simon, *Terrorist Trap*, p. xii.

106. Ted Ottley, "Ted Kaczynski: The Unabomber," TruTV Crime Library, http://www.trutv.com/library/crime/terrorists_spies/terrorists/kaczynski/15.html (accessed June 9, 2011).

107. For a discussion of the Croatian hijacking, see Simon, *Terrorist Trap*, pp. 110–19.

108. Ibid., p. xii.

109. *Lone-Wolf Terrorism*, pp. 27–28.

110. Ibid., pp. 39–40.

111. Ottley, "Ted Kaczynski."

112. Kevin Fagan, "Victims React to Kaczynski's Plea Deal/They're Sad, Angry But Glad It's Over," SFGate, January 24, 1998, http://articles.sfgate.com/1998-01-24/news/17710993_1_hugh-scrutton-unabomber-theodore-kaczynski-unabomber-explosion (accessed June 10, 2011). Epstein died in 2011 at the age of seventy-seven.

113. "Psychological Evaluation of Theodore Kaczynski," 1998, http://www.paulcooijmans.com/psychology/unabombreport2.html (accessed June 10, 2011).

114. This discussion of Muharem Kurbegovic (the "Alphabet Bomber") is drawn from Jeffrey D. Simon, "The Alphabet Bomber," in *Toxic Terror: Assessing Terrorist Use of Chemical and Biological Weapons*, ed. Jonathan B. Tucker, BCSIA Studies in International Security (Cambridge, MA: MIT Press, 2000), pp. 71–94; Simon, *Terrorist Trap*, pp. xxvi–xxvii; and Simon, "Lone Operators and Weapons of Mass Destruction," pp. 76–79.

115. Transcript of tape recovered on August 9, 1974, in Maywood, California, following call to CBS (Los Angeles Police Department Item No. 1340, Files, Los Angeles County District Attorney's Office).

116. Transcript of tape recovered August 16, 1974, at 11th and Los Angeles Streets (Los Angeles Police Department Item No. 1345, Files, Los Angeles County District Attorney's Office).

117. Simon, "Alphabet Bomber," p. 92.

118. Transcript of tape recovered August 20, 1974, at Sunset and Western, the site of Kurbegovic's arrest (Los Angeles Police Department Item No. 1337 and Item No. 1338, Files, Los Angeles County District Attorney's Office).

119. Simon, "Alphabet Bomber," p. 92.

120. Ibid., pp. 92–93.

CHAPTER 3. WHY LONE WOLVES ARE SO DANGEROUS

1. *Proliferation of Weapons of Mass Destruction: Assessing the Risks*, US Congress, Office of Technology Assessment, OTA-ISC-559 (Washington, DC: US Government Printing Office, 1993), p. 54.

2. Jeffrey D. Simon, *Terrorists and the Potential Use of Biological Weapons: A Discussion of Possibilities* (Santa Monica, CA: RAND Corporation, 1989).

3. Milton Leitenberg, *The Problem of Biological Weapons* (Stockholm: Swedish National Defense College, 2004), pp. 27–29; David C. Rapoport, "Terrorism and Weapons of the Apocalypse," in *Twenty-First Century Weapons Proliferation*, ed. Henry Sokolski and James M. Ludes (London: Frank Cass, 2001), p. 22.

4. David E. Kaplan and Andrew Marshall, *The Cult at the End of the World: The Incredible Story of Aum* (London: Arrow Books, 1996), pp. 93–112, 289.

5. Jeffrey D. Simon, "Technological and Lone Operator Terrorism: Prospects for a Fifth Wave of Global Terrorism," in *Terrorism, Identity, and Legitimacy: The Four Waves Theory and Political Violence*, ed. Jean E. Rosenfeld (London: Routledge, 2011), p. 58.

6. Rebecca L. Frerichs, Reynolds Mathewson Salerno, Kathleen Margaret Vogel, et al., *Historical Precedence and Technical Requirements of Biological Weapons Use: A Threat Assessment*, Sandia National Laboratories, SAND2004-1854, May 2004, p. 3.

7. Simon, *Terrorists and the Potential Use of Biological Weapons*; Jeffrey D. Simon, "Nuclear, Biological, and Chemical Terrorism: Understanding the Threat and Designing Responses," *International Journal of Emergency Mental Health* 1, no. 2 (Spring 1999): 81–89.

8. The following discussion is drawn from Simon, "Nuclear, Biological, and Chemical Terrorism," pp. 83–84.

9. Jessica Eve Stern, "The Covenant, the Sword, and the Arm of the Lord," in *Toxic Terror: Assessing Terrorist Use of Chemical and Biological Weapons, BCSIA Studies in International Security*, ed. Jonathan B. Tucker (Cambridge, MA: MIT Press, 2000), pp. 139–57.

10. "Evidence of Anthrax Labs near Kandahar," ABC News, March 25, 2002, http://abcnews.go.com/International/story?id=80052&page=1 (accessed September 9, 2011).

11. Graham Allison, *Nuclear Terrorism: The Ultimate Preventable Catastrophe* (New York: Times Books, 2004), p. 26.

12. Jeffrey D. Simon, "The Forgotten Terrorists: Lessons from the History of Terrorism," *Journal of Terrorism and Political Violence* 20, no. 2 (April/June 2008): 207.

13. Richard Preston, *The Hot Zone* (New York: Random House, 1994); "Fort Detrick, Maryland," GlobalSecurity.org, http://www.globalsecurity.org/wmd/facility/fort_detrick.htm (accessed September 22, 2011).

14. Noah Shachtman, "Anthrax Redux: Did the Feds Nab the Wrong Guy?"

WIRED, April 2011, http://www.wired.com/magazine/2011/03/ff_anthrax_fbi/all/1 (accessed September 30, 2011).

15. Ibid.

16. *Amerithrax Investigative Summary*, United States Department of Justice, February 19, 2010, p. 10.

17. Shachtman, "Anthrax Redux."

18. Ibid.

19. *Amerithrax Investigative Summary*, p. 61.

20. David Willman, *The Mirage Man: Bruce Ivins, the Anthrax Attacks, and America's Rush to War* (New York: Bantam Books, 2011), p. 13.

21. Ibid., p. 48.

22. Ibid., p. 9.

23. Ibid., pp. 55–56.

24. Ibid., p. 72.

25. *Amerithrax Investigative Summary*, p. 39.

26. Ibid.

27. Willman, *Mirage Man*, pp. 49–50.

28. Ibid., pp. 62–63.

29. Ibid., p. 61.

30. Ibid., p. 67.

31. Ibid., p. 65.

32. Scott Shane, "Panel on Anthrax Inquiry Finds Case against Ivins Persuasive," *New York Times*, March 23, 2011, http://www.nytimes.com/2011/03/24/us/24anthrax.html?_r=1&hp (accessed October 16, 2011).

33. *Amerithrax Investigative Summary*, p. 8.

34. Ibid., p. 10.

35. Ibid., p. 9.

36. Ibid,

37. Ibid., pp. 2–3.

38. "Amerithrax or Anthrax Investigation," Famous Cases and Criminals, Federal Bureau of Investigation, http://www.fbi.gov/about-us/history/famous-cases/anthrax-amerithrax (accessed September 9, 2011).

39. Shachtman, "Anthrax Redux."

40. Ibid.

41. Ibid.

42. *Amerithrax Investigative Summary*; see also "Amerithrax or Anthrax Investigation."

43. Scott Shane, "Expert Panel Is Critical of F.B.I. Work in Investigating Anthrax Letters," *New York Times*, February 15, 2011, http://www.nytimes.com/2011/02/16/us/16anthrax.html (accessed October 17, 2011).

44. Shane, "Panel on Anthrax Inquiry."

45. Ibid. Regarding Ivins's animosity toward the news media, the panel wrote that the *New York Post*, which was one of the targets of the anthrax letters, "represented [to Ivins] the media and New York City, [and] appeared to have been [a] symbolic stand-in . . . for broader targets." See *Report of the Expert Behavioral Analysis Panel*, Gregory Saathoff, chairman, August 23, 2010, p. 9. The panel's report was not made public until March 2011.

46. Simon, "Forgotten Terrorists," p. 207.

47. Beverly Gage, *The Day Wall Street Exploded: A Story of America in Its First Age of Terror* (New York: Oxford University Press, 2009), p. 326.

48. "Sixteen Individuals Arrested in the United States for Alleged Roles in Cyber Attacks," Department of Justice, July 19, 2011, http://www.justice.gov/opa/pr/2011/July/11-opa-944.html, (accessed January 7, 2012).

49. Jeffrey D. Simon, "The Alphabet Bomber," in *Toxic Terror: Assessing Terrorist Use of Chemical and Biological Weapons*, ed. Jonathan B. Tucker, BCSIA Studies in International Security (Cambridge, MA: MIT Press, 2000), p. 86.

50. Nassim Nicholas Taleb, *The Black Swan: The Impact of the Highly Improbable* (New York: Random House, 2007), pp. xvii–xviii.

51. Taleb views the 9/11 attacks, which were committed by a terrorist group, al Qaeda, and not by a lone wolf, as a black-swan event, since they served as evidence that "some events, owing to their dynamics, stand largely outside the realm of the predictable" and were an example of the "built-in defect of conventional wisdom" (*Black Swan*, p. xxi). However, I do not view the 9/11 attacks as a black-swan event, since while they certainly had an extreme impact in the United States and elsewhere, it is questionable whether they were beyond our realm of normal expectations. There had been suicide terrorist attacks on the ground in Lebanon and elsewhere during the 1980s as well as a suicide attack at sea on the USS *Cole* in Yemen in 2000. It was therefore just a matter of time before terrorists escalated to suicide attacks from the air.

52. *Proliferation of Weapons of Mass Destruction*, p. 3.

53. *Technologies Underlying Weapons of Mass Destruction*, US Congress, Office of Technology Assessment, OTA-BP-ISC-115 (Washington, DC: US Government Printing Office, December 1993), p. 71.

54. David A. Relman, "Bioterrorism—Preparing to Fight the Next War," *New England Journal of Medicine* 354, no. 2 (2006): 113–15; cited in Richard J. Danzig, *A Policymaker's Guide to Bioterrorism and What to Do about It*, Center for Technology and National Security Policy, National Defense University, December 2009, p. 9.

55. Danzig, *Policymaker's Guide*, pp. 9–10.

56. *Proliferation of Weapons of Mass Destruction*, pp. 2–3.

57. Ibid., p. 3.

58. "Safety of Nuclear Power Reactors," World Nuclear Association, October 31, 2011, http://www.world-nuclear.org/info/inf06.html (accessed November 28, 2011).

59. Allison, *Nuclear Terrorism*, p. 46.

60. Brian Michael Jenkins, *Will Terrorists Go Nuclear?* (Amherst, NY: Prometheus Books, 2008), p. 372.

CHAPTER 4. WHERE ARE THE WOMEN?

1. David C. Rapoport, "The Four Waves of Modern Terrorism," in *Attacking Terrorism: Elements of a Grand Strategy*, ed. Audrey Kurth Cronin and James M. Ludes (Washington, DC: Georgetown University Press, 2004), p. 51.

2. Amy Knight, "Female Terrorists in the Russian Socialist Revolutionary Party," *Russian Review* 38, no. 2 (April 1979): 139.

3. Ibid.

4. Walter Laqueur, *The Age of Terrorism* (Boston, MA: Little, Brown, 1987), p. 79.

5. Knight, "Female Terrorists," p. 139.

6. Eileen MacDonald, *Shoot the Women First* (New York: Random House, 1991), p. 91.

7. All the hostages from the other hijacked planes were also eventually released in exchange for Palestinian militants in prisons in Switzerland, West Germany, and Britain. Israel also released a number of Palestinian and Libyan prisoners after the hostages were freed but denied that this was part of any deal with the hijackers. All the planes (with the exception of one) had been diverted to Jordan, where, after taking the hostages and crew off the planes, the terrorists blew the planes up on the ground. They did the same thing in Cairo with the Pan Am jet that they hijacked and forced to land there. See Jeffrey D. Simon, *The Terrorist Trap: America's Experience with Terrorism*, 2nd ed. (Bloomington: Indiana University Press, 2001), pp. 97–106.

8. Ibid, pp. 110–19. Before surrendering in Paris, the hijackers cut up pieces of the fake clay bombs and gave them to the passengers as souvenirs!

9. Ibid., p. 117.

10. MacDonald, *Shoot the Women First*, pp. 127–28.

11. Simon, *Terrorist Trap*, p. 118.

12. Thomas Strentz, "The Stockholm Syndrome: Law Enforcement Policy and Hostage Behavior," *Victims of Terrorism*, ed. Frank M. Ochberg and David A. Soskis (Boulder, CO: Westview Press, 1982), pp. 149–63.

13. Simon, *Terrorist Trap*, p. 114.

14. Ibid., p. 343.

15. MacDonald, *Shoot the Women First*, p. 104.

16. Ibid., pp. 104–105.

17. Ibid., p. xiv.

18. Simon, *Terrorist Trap*, pp. 339–40.

19. Cindy D. Ness, "In the Name of the Cause: Women's Work in Secular and Religious Terrorism," in *Female Terrorism and Militancy: Agency, Utility, and Organization*, ed. Cindy D. Ness (London: Routledge, 2008), p. 13.

20. MacDonald, *Shoot the Women First*, p. 198. Both Baader and Meinhof committed suicide while in prison in the 1970s.

21. Margaret Gonzalez-Perez, *Women and Terrorism: Female Activity in Domestic and International Terror Groups* (London: Routledge, 2008), pp. 117–18.

22. Simon, *Terrorist Trap*, p. 320.

23. "'The Urban Guerrilla Is History': The Final Communiqué from the Red Army Faction (RAF)," German Guerilla, March 1998, http://www.germanguerilla.com/red-army-faction/documents/98_03.html (accessed September 5, 2009).

24. One of the members of the Weather Underground was Judith Clark, who was a classmate of mine at Midwood High School in Brooklyn, New York, in the 1960s. Clark is currently serving three consecutive twenty-five-years-to-life sentences in a New York state prison for her participation in a Brinks armored truck robbery and murders that occurred in Nyack, New York, in 1981. During the trial, she and her two codefendants claimed that the robbery was an "expropriation" needed to finance a revolution against the United States. Another classmate of mine had a different experience with terrorism. Miriam Beeber was one of the hostages taken by the Popular Front for the Liberation of Palestine when it hijacked four planes on the same day in September 1970. She was eventually freed after spending several weeks in captivity in Jordan. When I looked at my high-school yearbook for the first time in decades, I was surprised to discover that Clark, Beeber, and I appeared together in a group photo for the honor society. When I related that story during a radio call-in show, a person called the show and wanted to know if the name of my high school was Terror High!

25. This religious wave, as noted in chapter 1, was characterized by David Rapoport as the fourth wave of modern terrorism.

26. The fervent belief that God is on one's side is also the reason why it is more difficult to bring about an end, whether negotiated or forced, to a religious-inspired terrorist movement than it is to bring about an end to a secular one. In the case of political and ethnic-nationalist terrorist movements, several things can happen to end the hostilities. For example, a group that is driven by a desire for a homeland, a separate state, or the overthrow of a government will end its terrorist acts once that home-

land or state is achieved or the government overthrown. A political terrorist group can also fade from the scene as members are arrested and it becomes difficult to find new recruits, or when the issues for which it fought are either resolved or are no longer seen as important by members of the group. Political terrorists may also decide, once they get older, to simply retire from the terrorist life. This is not likely to happen in the case of the religious terrorist. Religious terrorism cannot be resolved by political agreements (like the Northern Ireland conflict, which was more of a political than a religious conflict). Compromise is not in the vocabulary of the religious extremist, who may view anything short of a complete victory as failing in the eyes of God.

27. Hezbollah also bombed the barracks of the French contingent of the Multinational Force in Lebanon the same day it attacked the US Marine barracks (October 23, 1984).

28. Yoram Schweitzer, "Suicide Terrorism: Development & Characteristics," International Institute for Counter-Terrorism, April 21, 2000, http://www.ict.org.il/Articles/tabid/66/Articlsid/42/Default.aspx (accessed December 23, 2011).

29. Ness, "In the Name of the Cause," p. 19.

30. "The Role of Palestinian Women in Suicide Terrorism," Israel Ministry of Foreign Affairs, January 30, 2003, http://www.mfa.gov.il/MFA/MFAArchive/2000_2009/2003/1/The%20Role%20of%20Palestinian%20Women%20in%20Suicide%20Terrorism (accessed December 24, 2011).

31. Ibid.

32. Ibid.

33. Alissa J. Rubin, "Despair Drives Suicide Attacks by Iraqi Women," *New York Times*, July 5, 2008, http://www.nytimes.com/2008/07/05/world/middleeast/ 05 diyala.html?pagewanted=all (accessed December 25, 2011).

34. Rohan Gunaratna, "Suicide Terrorism: A Global Threat," *PBS Frontline/World*, October 2000, http://www.pbs.org/frontlineworld/stories/srilanka/global threat.html (accessed December 25, 2011).

35. Steve Emerson, "Female Suicide Bombers Raise Deadly Stakes," *Newsmax*, March 29, 2010, http://www.newsmax.com/Emerson/femalesuicidebombers-terrorists -Hamas/2010/03/29/id/354164 (accessed December 24, 2011).

36. Mia Bloom, *Bombshell: Women and Terrorism* (Philadelphia: University of Pennsylvania Press, 2011), pp. 233–49. Bloom notes that another "R," which stands for rape, can be added to the list. She points out (p. 236) that in Iraq and Chechnya rape was used "to coerce women to participate in combat."

37. See chapter 1 and the appendix for my definition of *lone wolf terrorism*.

38. *Lone-Wolf Terrorism*, COT, Instituut voor Veiligheids- en Crisismanagement, Final draft, June 7, 2007, Case Study for Work Package 3, p. 24, http://www.scribd .com/doc/34968770/Lone-Wolf-Terrorism (accessed June 10, 2011), pp. 98–111.

The only female lone wolf attack recorded for this period occurred in Wichita, Kansas, when Rachelle Shannon shot and wounded George Tiller, a late-term abortion doctor, outside his clinic in August 1993. Tiller would again be the target of an anti-abortion lone wolf when Scott Roeder assassinated him in Wichita in July 2009.

39. Cristen Conger, "What Is a Lone Wolf?" Animal Planet, http://animals.howstuffworks.com/mammals/lone-wolf.htm (accessed December 27, 2011).

40. Alison Jamieson, "Entry, Discipline, and Exit in the Italian Red Brigades," *Terrorism and Political Violence* 2, no. 1 (Spring 1990): 18–19.

41. Christine R. Harris, Michael Jenkins, and Dale Glaser, "Gender Difference in Risk Assessment: Why Do Women Take Fewer Risks Than Men?" *Judgment and Decision Making* 1, no. 1 (July 2006): 48–63.

42. Ibid, p. 49.

43. David Weidner, "Women Are Better Investors, and Here's Why," *Wall Street Journal*, June 24, 2011, http://www.marketwatch.com/story/women-are-better-investors-and-heres-why-2011-06-14?pagenumber=1 (accessed December 27, 2011).

44. Nigel Barber, "Why Women Live Longer Than Men," *Psychology Today*, August 10, 2010, http://www.psychologytoday.com/blog/the-human-beast/201008/why-women-live-longer-men (accessed December 27, 2011).

45. Paola Sapienza, Luigi Zingales, and Dario Maestripieri, "Gender Differences in Financial Risk Aversion and Career Choices Are Affected by Testosterone," *Proceedings of the National Academy of Sciences of the United States of America*, August 24, 2009, http://www.pnas.org/content/early/2009/08/20/0907352106 (accessed December 28, 2011).

46. Laura Madson and David Trafimow, "Gender Comparisons in the Private, Collective, and Allocentric Selves," *Journal of Social Psychology* 141, no. 4 (2001): 552.

47. Stephanie S. Covington, "The Relational Theory of Women's Psychological Development: Implications for the Criminal Justice System," in *Female Offenders: Critical Perspectives and Effective Interventions*, 2nd ed., ed. Ruth T. Zaplin (Sudbury, MA: Jones and Bartlett, 2007), pp. 135–64.

48. Sarah Ben-David, "The Two Facets of Female Violence: The Public and the Domestic Domains," *Journal of Family Violence* 8, no. 4 (December 1993): 352.

49. See chapter 7 for a further discussion of the role of psychology in explaining lone wolf terrorism.

50. Jennie Jacobs Kronenfeld, "Gender and Health Status," in *Handbook of the Sociology of Gender*, ed. Janet Saltzman Chafetz (New York: Springer), p. 476.

51. "Paranoid Schizophrenia: Definition," Mayo Clinic, December 16, 2010, http://www.mayoclinic.com/health/paranoid-schizophrenia/DS00862 (accessed December 29, 2011).

52. "Health Guide: Schizophrenia," *New York Times*, January 27, 2011, http://

health.nytimes.com/health/guides/disease/schizophrenia/risk-factors.html
(accessed December 26, 2011).

53. "Paranoid Schizophrenia: Symptoms," Mayo Clinic, December 16, 2010, http://
www.mayoclinic.com/health/paranoid-schizophrenia/DS00862/DSECTION
=symptoms (accessed December 29, 2011).

54. Richard Howard and Conor Duggan, "Mentally Disordered Offenders:
Personality Disorders," in *Forensic Psychology*, ed. Graham J. Towl and David
A. Crighton (Chichester, West Sussex, UK: Wiley-Blackwell, 2010), p. 321.

55. "Antisocial Personality Disorder: Definition," Mayo Clinic, October 8,
2010, http://www.mayoclinic.com/health/antisocial-personality-disorder/DS00829
(accessed December 29, 2011).

56. "Antisocial Personality Disorder: Symptoms," Mayo Clinic, October 8, 2010,
http://www.mayoclinic.com/health/antisocial-personality-disorder/DS00829/
DSECTION=symptoms (accessed December 29, 2011).

57. "Schizoid Personality Disorder: Causes," Mayo Clinic, December 8, 2010,
http://www.mayoclinic.com/health/schizoid-personality-disorder/DS00865/
DSECTION=causes (accessed January 1, 2012).

58. Michael H. Stone, *The Anatomy of Evil* (Amherst, NY: Prometheus Books,
2009), p. 190; Anna Motz, *The Psychology of Female Violence: Crimes against the Body*, 2nd
ed. (London and New York: Routledge, 2008), p. 271.

59. Ben-David, "Two Facets of Female Violence," p. 347.

60. Shauna Bottos, "Women and Violence: Theory, Risk, and Treatment
Implications," Research Branch, Correctional Service Canada, July 2007, p. 22.

61. Simon, *Terrorist Trap*, p. 23.

62. Most of the following account of LaRose's Internet activity (unless other-
wise noted) is derived from the text of her federal indictment and a superseding
indictment. See *In the United States District Court for the Eastern District of Pennsylvania,
United States of America v. Colleen R. LaRose, a/k/a "Fatima LaRose," a/k/a "JihadJane,"*
Case 2:10-cr-00123-PBT, Document 23, Criminal No. 10, Date Filed: March 4, 2010;
*In the United States District Court for the Eastern District of Pennsylvania, United States of
America v. Colleen R. LaRose, a/k/a "Fatima LaRose," a/k/a "JihadJane,"* [and defen-
dant] *Jamie Paulin-Ramirez*, Case 2:10-cr-00123-PBT, Document 31, Criminal No.
10-123, Date Filed: April 1, 2010.

63. Ian Urbina, "Views of 'JihadJane' Were Unknown to Neighbors," *New York
Times*, March 10, 2010, http://www.nytimes.com/2010/03/11/us/11pennsylvania
.html (accessed June 22, 2010).

64. David Sapsted, "'Jihad Jane' Was Tracked by Amateur Internet Sleuths,"
National, March 18, 2010, http://www.thenational.ae/apps/pbcs.dll/article?AID
=/20100317/FOREIGN/703169948/1013/ART (accessed June 22, 2010).

65. Maryclaire Dale, "'Jihad Jane' Terror Suspect Pleads Guilty in PA," Associated Press, February 1, 2011, http://www.msnbc.msn.com/id/41374247/ns/us _news-security/t/jihad-jane-terror-suspect-pleads-guilty-pa/#.TwOhkRw0jw5 (accessed January 3, 2012); Peter Hall, "'Jihad Jane' Codefendant Pleads Guilty to Terrorism Charge," *Los Angeles Times*, March 10, 2011, http://articles.latimes.com/2011/mar/ 10/nation/la-na-terror-plea-20110310 (accessed January 3, 2012).

66. Urbina, "Views of 'JihadJane' Were Unknown to Neighbors"; Sapsted, "'Jihad Jane' Was Tracked by Amateur Internet Sleuths"; Eamon McNiff, "Net Posse Tracked 'Jihad Jane' for Three Years," ABC News, March 11, 2010, http:// abcnews.go.com/TheLaw/Technology/internet-monitors-tracked-jihad-jane-years/ story?id=10069484 (accessed June 14, 2010).

67. Raffaello Pantucci, "Trial of Would-Be Assassin Illustrates al-Awlaki's Influence on the British Jihad," Jamestown Foundation, December 2, 2010, http:// www.jamestown.org/programs/gta/single/?tx_ttnews%5Btt_news%5D=37234&c Hash=873daf2211 (accessed January 3, 2012).

68. Vikram Dodd, "Profile: Roshonara Choudhry," *Guardian*, November 2, 2010, http://www.guardian.co.uk/uk/2010/nov/02/profile-roshonara-choudhry -stephen-timms (accessed January 3, 2012).

69. Vikram Dodd, "Roshonara Choudhry: Police Interview Extracts," *Guardian*, November 3, 2010, http://www.guardian.co.uk/uk/2010/nov/03/roshonara -choudhry-police-interview (accessed December 29, 2011). Choudhry also told police that she was influenced by a YouTube video she watched in April 2010 by Sheikh Abdullah Azzam, who was a Palestinian Islamic militant killed in 1989. Choudhry told the detectives that Azzam said that "when a Muslim land is attacked it becomes obligatory on every man, woman and child and even slave to go out and fight and defend the land and the Muslims."

70. Paul Avrich, *Anarchist Voices: An Oral History of Anarchism in America* (Edinburgh: AK Press, 2005), pp. 107, 111, 120, 132, 157, 158, 316; cited in Jeffrey D. Simon, "The Forgotten Terrorists: Lessons from the History of Terrorism," *Terrorism and Political Violence* 20, no. 2 (April/June 2008): 196.

71. Dodd, "Roshonara Choudhry: Police Interview Extracts."

72. Pantucci, "Trial of Would-Be Assassin."

73. Vikram Dodd, "Roshonara Choudhry: I Wanted to Die . . . I Wanted to be a Martyr," *Guardian*, November 3, 2010, http://www.guardian.co.uk/uk/2010/ nov/04/stephen-timms-attack-roshonara-choudhry (accessed December 29, 2011).

74. Dodd, "Roshonara Choudhry: Police Interview Extracts."

75. Dodd, "Profile: Roshonara Choudhry."

76. Dodd, "Roshonara Choudhry: Police Interview Extracts."

77. "Student Jailed for Stabbing of MP Stephen Timms," Channel 4 News,

November 3, 2010, http://www.channel4.com/news/student-jailed-for-stabbing-of -mp-stephen-timms (accessed January 4, 2012).

CHAPTER 5. LONE WOLF ASSASSINS

1. Maximilien Robespierre gave birth to the term *terrorism* by unleashing his Reign of Terror between 1793 and 1794 upon all strata of French society. The Committee on Public Safety that ruled France following the French Revolution can be considered the first case of state terror imposed upon a people. It was the forerunner of twentieth-century terror governments such as Stalin's Russia, Hitler's Germany, and Pol Pot's Cambodia. Robespierre viewed terror as the only way to save the revolution from anarchy at home and the threat of invasion from abroad by European monarchs. More than seventeen thousand people, ranging from peasants and workers to aristocrats and moderate revolutionaries, met their deaths by the guillotine, while approximately twenty-five thousand others were shot or killed by different methods throughout the country. There were more than one hundred thousand political prisoners taken, while several hundred thousand others were declared suspects. Robespierre did not view terrorism as an evil or immoral act but instead thought of it as a virtuous deed. "If the basis of popular government in time of peace is virtue," he argued, "the basis of popular government in time of revolution is both virtue and terror: virtue without which terror is murderous, terror without which virtue is powerless." See Jeffrey D. Simon, *The Terrorist Trap: America's Experience with Terrorism,* 2nd ed. (Bloomington: Indiana University Press, 2001), pp. 27–29. The word *terrorism* first appeared in the 1798 supplement of the *Dictionnaire de l'Académie Française,* as meaning a "système, régime de la terreur." See Walter Laqueur, *The Age of Terrorism* (Boston, MA: Little, Brown, 1987), p. 11

2. Bernard Lewis, *The Assassins: A Radical Sect in Islam* (New York: Oxford University Press, 1987), p. 134.

3. Quoted in ibid., p. 5.

4. A poison-tipped umbrella was used to assassinate Bulgarian dissident Georgi Markov on a London street in 1978. Markov was waiting for a bus when a man poked him in the thigh with the umbrella and then apologized as though it had been an accident. What he had actually done, however, was fire a platinum pellet from the umbrella containing ricin, a poison derived from the castor bean plant for which there is no antidote. Markov died a few days later. Bulgarian agents working with the Soviet KGB had designed the plot.

5. Philip B. Heymann, *Terrorism and America: A Commonsense Strategy for a Democratic Society* (Cambridge, MA: MIT Press), p. 6.

6. R. Hrair Dekmejian, *Spectrum of Terror* (Washington, DC: CQ Press, 2007), p. 25.

7. Franklin L. Ford, *Political Murder: From Tyrannicide to Terrorism* (Cambridge, MA: Harvard University Press, 1985), p. 381.

8. See, for example, Nancy Jo Sales, "Click Here for Conspiracy," *Vanity Fair*, August 2006, http://www.vanityfair.com/ontheweb/features/2006/08/loose change200608 (accessed February 25, 2012); "Debunking the 9/11 Myths: Special Report—The World Trade Center," *Popular Mechanics*, March 2005, http://www .popularmechanics.com/technology/military/news/debunking-911-myths-world -trade-center (accessed February 25, 2012).

9. Lindsay Porter, *Assassination: A History of Political Murder* (New York: Overlook Press, 2010), p. 154.

10. Ibid., p. 143.

11. David C. Rapoport, *Assassination and Terrorism* (Toronto: Canadian Broadcasting Company, 1971), p. 19.

12. Ibid.

13. Ford, *Political Murder*, pp. 383–84.

14. See for example, Trevor Burrus, "Get Rid of the Spoils System," *Washington Times*, March 11, 2011, http://www.washingtontimes.com/news/2011/mar/11/ run-democrats-run/ (accessed March 26, 2012); "Garfield, James A.: Assassination," *Encyclopedia Britannica*, 2012, http://www.britannica.com/presidents/article-302 549 (accessed March 26, 2012); "History through the Decades, United States Census Bureau," http://www.census.gov/history/www/through_the_decades/fast _facts/1880_fast_facts.html (accessed March 26, 2012).

15. James W. Clarke, *American Assassins: The Darker Side of Politics* (Princeton, NJ: Princeton University Press, 1982), pp. 198–99, 206–207. During his trial, Guiteau continually referred to the need to "remove the President of the United States for the good of the American people." See Douglas O. Linder, "Excerpts from the Trial Transcript: Cross-Examination of Charles Guiteau," University of Missouri–Kansas City School of Law, http://law2.umkc.edu/faculty/projects/ftrials/guiteau/guiteau transcriptguiteaucrossx.html (accessed January 22, 2012).

16. Clarke, *American Assassins*, pp. 209–10; Alan Peskin, "Charles Guiteau of Illinois: President Garfield's Assassin," *Journal of the Illinois State Historical Society* 70, no. 2 (May 1977): 130–31; Charles Guiteau Collection, Georgetown University, http:// gulib.georgetown.edu/dept/speccoll/cl133.htm (accessed January 22, 2012).

17. Clarke, *American Assassins*, pp. 199–200; Peskin, "Charles Guiteau of Illinois," pp. 130–32.

18. Clarke, *American Assassins*, pp. 201–202; Peskin, "Charles Guiteau of Illinois," p. 132.

19. Peskin, "Charles Guiteau of Illinois," p. 132.

20. Candice Millard, *Destiny of the Republic: A Tale of Madness, Medicine, and the Murder of a President* (New York: Doubleday, 2011), pp. 30–47.

21. Ibid., p. 57.

22. Clarke, *American Assassins*, p. 204.

23. Ibid.

24. Peskin, "Charles Guiteau of Illinois," p. 135.

25. Clarke, *American Assassins*, pp. 206–207.

26. Peskin, "Charles Guiteau of Illinois," p. 136.

27. Millard, *Destiny of the Republic*, p. 113.

28. Peskin, "Charles Guiteau of Illinois," p. 136.

29. Clarke, *American Assassins*, p. 207.

30. Ibid.

31. "Guiteau's Day of Torture: The Assassin Driven into Maze of Contradictions," *New York Times*, December 2, 1881, http://query.nytimes.com/mem/archive-free/pdf?res=F60A17FB3A581B7A93C0A91789D95F458884F9 (accessed January 22, 2012).

32. Millard, *Destiny of the Republic*, pp. 119–24.

33. Ibid., pp. 125–37.

34. Douglas O. Linder, "The Trial of Charles Guiteau: An Account," University of Missouri–Kansas City School of Law, http://law2.umkc.edu/faculty/projects/ftrials/guiteau/guiteauaccount.html (accessed January 22, 2012).

35. Millard, *Destiny of the Republic*, p. 215.

36. Ibid., p. 253.

37. Ibid., p. 236.

38. *Guiteau Trial, Closing Speech to the Jury of John K. Porter of New York, In the Case of Charles J. Guiteau, the Assassin of President Garfield*, Washington, January 23, 1882 (New York: John Polhemus, 1882), p. 54.

39. "Guiteau's Day of Torture."

40. Ibid.

41. Ibid.

42. "Pendleton Act (1883)," Our Documents, http://www.ourdocuments.gov/doc.php?flash=true&doc=48 (accessed January 27, 2012).

43. Millard, *Destiny of the Republic*, p. 249.

44. Ibid.

45. The Boxer Rebellion was a peasant uprising against foreign presence in China. The United States and several other nations sent troops to China to suppress the rebellion and protect their interests in the country.

46. Clarke, *American Assassins*, p. 44.

47. Scott Miller, *The President and the Assassin: McKinley, Terror, and Empire at the Dawn of the American Century* (New York: Random House, 2011), p. 57.

48. Clarke, *American Assassins*, pp. 44–49.

49. Miller, *President and the Assassin*, p. 246.

50. Ibid., pp. 273–75.

51. Clarke, *American Assassins*, p. 55.

52. Ibid., p. 56.

53. Ibid., pp. 56–57.

54. Porter, *Assassination*, p. 154.

55. "'Lights Out in the City of Light': Anarchy and Assassination at the Pan-American Exposition," Libraries, University of Buffalo, June 2004, http://library.buffalo.edu/exhibits/panam/law/trial.html (accessed January 29, 2012).

56. Miller, *President and the Assassin*, p. 323.

57. "'Lights Out in the City of Light.'"

58. Clarke, *American Assassins*, pp. 10–11. The M'Naghten Rule derived from a case in Britain in 1843. Daniel M'Naghten, a Scottish woodworker, believed that he was the target of a conspiracy between the pope and British prime minister Robert Peel. He attempted to assassinate Peel but instead shot and killed the prime minister's private secretary, Edward Drummond. M'Naghten was acquitted based on his lawyers' successful argument that their client was insane. The verdict infuriated the British public and government as well as Queen Victoria, who, a few years earlier, had herself been the target of an assassin who was also found not guilty by reason of insanity. The House of Lords and the queen, along with many other people, felt that Britain needed a clear and strict definition of criminal insanity. Therefore, the British Supreme Court ruled, just four months after the M'Naghten verdict, that a defendant could use an insanity defense only if "at the time of committing of the act, the party accused was labouring under such a defect of reason, from a disease of the mind, as not to know the nature and quality of the act he was doing; or, if he did know it, that he did not know he was doing what was wrong." See Millard, *Destiny of the Republic*, p. 237.

59. All the doctors who examined Czolgosz found him to be sane. One group of doctors wrote in its report that "the most careful questioning failed to discover any hallucinations of sight or hearing. He had received no special command; he did not believe he had been specially chosen to do the deed. He always spoke of his motive for the crime as duty; he always referred to the Anarchists' belief that killing of rulers was a duty. . . . He is the product of anarchy, sane and responsible." See Miller, *President and the Assassin*, pp. 347–48.

60. Clarke, *American Assassins*, pp. 58–59.

61. Ibid., p. 59.

62. Ibid.

63. Ibid.

64. Theodore Roosevelt, "State of the Union Message," December 3, 1901,

Primary Speeches, Addresses, and Essays by Theodore Roosevelt, Almanac of Theodore Roosevelt, http://www.theodore-roosevelt.com/trspeeches.html (accessed February 3, 2012). While many anarchists condemned the assassination and denounced Czolgosz, Emma Goldman came to his defense. In an article in *Free Society* one month after the assassination, she wrote, "Some people have hastily said that Czolgosz's act was foolish and will check the growth of progress. Those worthy people are wrong in forming hasty conclusions. What results the act of September 6 will have no one can say; one thing, however, is certain: he has wounded government in its most vital spot." See Jewish Women's Archive, "Article by Goldman about Leon Czolgosz's Assassination of President McKinley and the Use of Violence," http://jwa.org/media/article-by-goldman-about-leon-czolgoszs-assassination-of-president-mckinley-and-use-of-violenc (accessed January 29, 2012).

65. Paul Avrich, *Sacco and Vanzetti: The Anarchist Background* (Princeton, NJ: Princeton University Press, 1991), p. 130.

66. Porter, *Assassination*, p. 154.

67. Gerald Posner, *Case Closed: Lee Harvey Oswald and the Assassination of JFK* (New York: Anchor Books, 2003), p. xii. Posner wrote the first edition of the book for Random House in 1993.

68. Ibid., pp. 5–7.

69. Ibid., pp. 10–11.

70. Clarke, *American Assassins*, p. 108.

71. Ibid.

72. Porter, *Assassination*, pp. 140–41.

73. Clarke, *American Assassins*, pp. 109–10.

74. Ibid., pp. 110–11.

75. Ibid., pp. 113–20.

76. There has been speculation that Oswald might have changed his mind about killing Kennedy had his wife, Marina, given him assurances that their rocky relationship would improve. Oswald visited her the night before the assassination. They had been living apart, and Marina was staying with friends in Irving, Texas, while Oswald stayed in Dallas during the week for his job. Marina was surprised to see Oswald on a Thursday and rebuffed his pleas for her to come live with him. She even turned her back on him when he spoke. A panel of doctors told the Warren Commission that if Marina had been warm and affectionate to Oswald during that last visit, he might have changed his mind about the assassination. One doctor said, "I think what Marina had a chance to do unconsciously that night was to veto his plan without ever knowing of its existence, but she didn't. She really stamped it down hard." See Posner, *Case Closed*, pp. 220–21.

77. Simon, *Terrorist Trap*, pp. 262–63.

78. Marshall McLuhan, *Understanding Media: The Extensions of Man* (New York: Mentor/Penguin, 1964), pp. 292–93.

79. Porter, *Assassination*, p. 143.

80. Mark Lane, *Rush to Judgment* (New York: Holt, Rinehart & Winston, 1966).

81. Posner, *Case Closed*, pp. 412–13.

82. Porter, *Assassination*, pp. 143–45.

83. Ibid., pp. 145–48.

84. Posner, *Case Closed*, p. 477.

85. James G. Blight, Janet M. Lang, and David A. Welch, *Vietnam If Kennedy Had Lived: Virtual JFK* (Lanham, MD: Rowman & Littlefield, 2009), p. xiii.

86. Sean Wilentz, "What If Kennedy Had Lived?" *New York Times*, November 21, 2003, http://www.nytimes.com/2003/11/21/opinion/what-if-kennedy-had-lived .html (accessed January 16, 2012). The Cuban missile crisis occurred in October 1962, when the world stood on the brink of nuclear war due to a US-Soviet confrontation over the placement of Soviet intermediate-range nuclear missiles in Cuba and a subsequent US naval blockade of Cuba to prevent Soviet vessels from delivering additional weapons to the island. The crisis ended when the Soviets agreed to remove the missiles already there and dismantle the missile sites in exchange for a US promise not to invade Cuba.

87. Blight et al., *Vietnam*, pp. 17–20.

88. Ibid., pp. 107–108.

89. Ehud Sprinzak, "Israel's Radical Right and the Countdown to the Rabin Assassination," in *The Assassination of Yitzhak Rabin*, ed. Yoram Peri (Stanford, CA: Stanford University Press, 2000), p. 122.

90. *Oslo I Accords (Declaration of Principles on Interim Self-Government Arrangements)*, Council on Foreign Relations, Essential Documents, http://www.cfr.org/israel/ oslo-accords-declaration-principles-interim-self-government-arrangements/p9674 (accessed February 16, 2012).

91. Michael Karpin and Ina Friedman, *Murder in the Name of God: The Plot to Kill Yitzhak Rabin* (New York: Metropolitan Books, 1998), pp. 19–20.

92. Sprinzak, "Israel's Radical Right," pp. 121–23.

93. Karpin and Friedman, *Murder in the Name of God*, pp. 105–106.

94. Sprinzak, "Israel's Radical Right," p. 121.

95. Karpin and Friedman, *Murder in the Name of God*, p. 27.

96. Sprinzak, "Israel's Radical Right," p. 123.

97. Serge Schmemann, "Rabin Killer and 2 Others Guilty of Related Plots against Leader," *New York Times*, September 12, 1996, http://www.nytimes.com/ 1996/09/12/world/rabin-killer-and-2-others-guilty-of-related-plots-against-leader.html (accessed February 14, 2012).

98. Sprinzak, "Israel's Radical Right," p. 126.

99. Nadav Gabay, "Peace Begins at Home: Toleration, Identity Politics, and the Changing Conception of Peacemaking in Israel after Yitzhak Rabin's Assassination," *Social Identities* 12, no. 3 (May 2006): 358.

100. Sprinzak, "Israel's Radical Right," p. 121.

101. Yoram Peri, ed., "The Assassination: Causes, Meaning, Outcomes," in *The Assassination of Yitzhak Rabin* (Stanford, CA: Stanford University Press, 2000), p. 49.

102. Bill Clinton, "Finish Rabin's Work," *New York Times*, November 4, 2010, http://www.nytimes.com/2010/11/04/opinion/04clinton.html (accessed February 17, 2012).

103. Peri, "Assassination," p. 57.

104. Dan Perry, "Rabin's Assassin Convicted of Murder by Israeli Court," Associated Press, March 27, 1996, http://www.apnewsarchive.com/1996/Rabin-s -Assassin-Convicted-Of-Murder-By-Israeli-Court/id-2121d3a0c955c801ad444fa5b0d80 c9d (accessed February 17, 2012).

105. Sprinzak, "Israel's Radical Right," p. 125.

106. Karpin and Friedman, *Murder in the Name of God*, p. 28.

107. Joel Greenberg, "Rabin Assassin's Testimony: My Goal Was to Paralyze Him," *New York Times*, January 24, 1996, http://www.nytimes.com/1996/01/24/world/rabin -assassin-s-testimony-my-goal-was-to-paralyze-him.html (accessed February 14, 2012).

108. Dekmejian, *Spectrum of Terror*, pp. 25–38.

109. Clarke, *American Assassins*, pp. 14–17.

CHAPTER 6. STRATEGIES FOR DEALING WITH LONE WOLF TERRORISM

1. Marc Sageman, *Leaderless Jihad: Terror Networks in the Twenty-First Century* (Philadelphia: University of Pennsylvania Press, 2008), p. vii.

2. Ibid., pp. vii–viii.

3. Ibid., pp. 147–78.

4. Paul Cruickshank and Tim Lister, "The 'Lone Wolf'—The Unknowable Terror," CNN, September 7, 2011, http://security.blogs.cnn.com/2011/09/07/the -lone-wolf-the-unknowable-face-of-terror/ (accessed March 4, 2012).

5. *Tenth Anniversary Report Card: The Status of the 9/11 Commission Recommendations*, National Security Preparedness Group, Bipartisan Policy Center, Washington, DC, September 2011, p. 7.

6. Geraldo Rivera, "Are We Any Safer?" Fox News, September 9, 2011, http:// www.foxnews.com/on-air/geraldo/blog/2011/09/09/are-we-any-safer (accessed March 4, 2012).

7. John Mueller and Mark G. Stewart, *Terror, Security, and Money: Balancing the Risks, Benefits, and Costs of Homeland Security* (New York: Oxford University Press, 2011), p. 3.

8. Jeffrey D. Simon, *The Terrorist Trap: America's Experience with Terrorism*, 2nd ed. (Bloomington: Indiana University Press, 2001), pp. 396–97.

9. Paul Cruickshank, Nic Robertson, and Ken Shiffman, "How Safe Is the Cargo on Passenger Flights?" CNN, February 19, 2012, http://www.cnn.com/2012/02/16/travel/cargo-terror-concerns/index.html (accessed March 8, 2012).

10. Ibid.

11. Ibid.

12. Ibid.

13. *Semiannual Report on the Audit, Investigative, and Security Activities of the United States Postal Service, April 1–September 30, 2008*, United States Postal Service, pp. 30–31.

14. "Postal Strike: Spotting Mailbombs," Global Security Solutions, http://www.global-securitysolutions.com/scanna-msc-ltd-security-screening-and-detection/postal-strike-spot ting-mailbombs.html (accessed March 10, 2012).

15. Barry Zellen, "Special Delivery: After Two Centuries, Letter-Bombs Continue Their Lethal Legacy," Security Innovator, March 6, 2009, http://securityinnovator.com/index.php?articleID=15842&sectionID=27 (accessed March 9, 2012).

16. Marcus Wohlsen, "Scientists Man Bioterror Front Lines Post-9/11," Associated Press, http://www.rdmag.com/News/2011/08/Life-Science-Biotechnology-Analytical-Scientists-man-bioterror-front-lines/ (accessed March 12, 2012). The deployment of the air monitors is known as the national BioWatch system. However, it was revealed in October 2012 that tests of the system by scientists found that BioWatch "operated with defective components that left it unable to detect lethal germs." See David Willman, "BioWatch Technology Couldn't Detect Lethal Germs, Tests Found," *Los Angeles Times*, October 22, 2012, http://www.latimes.com/news/nationworld/nation/la-na-biowatch-faulty-assays-20121023,0,6634110.story (accessed November 16, 2012).

17. There is, however, x-ray technology that has been developed to specifically visualize and enhance powders inside packages. These are being used to inspect suspicious letters and packages. See "Postal Strike."

18. Ian Evans, "Report: London No Safer for All Its CCTV Cameras," *Christian Science Monitor*, February 22, 2012, http://www.csmonitor.com/World/Europe/2012/0222/Report-London-no-safer-for-all-its-CCTV-cameras (accessed March 12, 2012).

19. Christopher Hope, "1,000 CCTV Cameras to Solve Just One Crime, Met Police Admits," *Telegraph*, August 25, 2009, http://www.telegraph.co.uk/news/uknews/crime/6082530/1000-CCTV-cameras-to-solve-just-one-crime-Met-Police-admits.html (accessed March 12, 2012).

20. *Lone-Wolf Terrorism*, COT, Instituut voor Veiligheids-en Crisismanagement, Final draft, June 7, 2007, Case Study for Work Package 3, p. 22, http://www.scribd.com/doc/34968770/Lone-Wolf-Terrorism (accessed June 10, 2011).

21. Ibid., pp. 77–78.

22. "Real Crime—Nailing the Nailbomber," Real Crime, June 4, 2007, http://www.throng.co.nz/real-crime/real-crime-nailing-the-nailbomber (accessed March 13, 2012).

23. *Lone-Wolf Terrorism*, p. 77.

24. Ian Evans, "London Riots Caught on CCTV Camera: 'We Will Pursue You' Say Police," *Christian Science Monitor*, August 9, 2011, http://www.csmonitor.com/World/Europe/2011/0809/London-riots-caught-on-CCTV-camera-We-will-pursue-you-say-police-VIDEO (accessed March 16, 2012).

25. Fred Burton, "The Challenge of the Lone Wolf," Stratfor, May 30, 2007, http://www.stratfor.com/challenge_lone_wolf (accessed December 23, 2011).

26. Scott Stewart and Fred Burton, "Lone Wolf Lessons," Stratfor, 2009, http://www.trapwire.com/stratforreport4.htm (accessed March 15, 2012).

27. Jeff Salton, "Smarter CCTV System to Be Used to Recognize and Prevent Crime," *Gizmag*, September 29, 2009, http://www.gizmag.com/intelligent-cctv-system-recognizes-prevents-crime/12971/ (accessed March 15, 2012).

28. Michael Pollitt, "Surveillance: The Next Generation," *Guardian*, February 18, 2009, http://www.guardian.co.uk/technology/2009/feb/19/cctv-behaviour-patterns (accessed March 15, 2012).

29. "Could 'Smart CCTV Surveillance' Help in Fight against Terror," PRNewswire, July 18, 2011, http://www.prnewswire.co.uk/cgi/news/release?id=150279 (accessed March 15, 2012).

30. Mimi Hall, "Feds Focus on Detecting Bombs," *USA Today*, November 27, 2007, http://www.usatoday.com/news/nation/2007-11-26-bomb-detection_N.htm (accessed March 9, 2012).

31. Retired Department of Defense intelligence analyst, telephone interview with author, March 2, 2012.

32. "Introduction to Biometrics," National Science and Technology Council (NSTC), Committee on Technology, Committee on Homeland and National Security, Subcommittee on Biometrics, August 7, 2006, http://www.biometrics.gov/ReferenceRoom/Introduction.aspx (accessed March 19, 2012); "History of Biometrics," Global Security, July 13, 2011, http://www.globalsecurity.org/security/systems/biometrics-history.htm (accessed March 18, 2012).

33. "The Bertillon System," US National Library of Medicine, National Institutes of Health, February 16, 2006, http://www.nlm.nih.gov/visibleproofs/galleries/technologies/bertillon.html (accessed March 19, 2012).

34. "History of Biometrics."

35. "The FBI and the American Gangster, 1924–1938," Federal Bureau of Investigation, http://www.fbi.gov/about-us/history/a-centennial-history/fbi_and_the_american_gangster_1924-1938 (accessed March 17, 2012).

36. *The National Biometrics Challenge*, National Science and Technology Council, Subcommittee on Biometrics and Identity Management, September 2011, p. 6; "Introduction to Biometrics."

37. *National Biometrics Challenge*, p. 5.

38. Ibid., p. 6.

39. Ibid., pp. 5, 16.

40. *CJIS Annual Report 2011*, US Department of Justice, Federal Bureau of Investigation, Criminal Justice Information Services Division, p. 20.

41. William M. Casey, interview with author, February 22, 2012, Clarksburg, West Virginia.

42. "The Biometric News Portal," http://www.biometricnewsportal.com/biometrics_definition.asp (accessed February 20, 2012); "Introduction to Biometrics"; *National Biometrics Challenge*, pp. 11–15; *CJIS Annual Report 2011*, p. 24; "Biometrics," Global Security, July 13, 2011, http://www.globalsecurity.org/security/systems/biometrics.htm (accessed March 20, 2012).

43. Stephen G. Fischer Jr., interview with author, February 22, 2012, Clarksburg, West Virginia.

44. "Biometric News Portal"; "Biometrics."

45. Rym Momtaz and Lee Ferran, "French School Shooter Was on US No Fly List," ABC News, http://abcnews.go.com/Blotter/french-school-shooter-us-fly-list/story?id=15981115#.T24CfxxBnw4 (accessed March 23, 2012); Scott Sayare, "Suspect in French Killings Slain as Police Storm Apartment after 30-Hour Siege," *New York Times*, March 22, 2012, http://www.nytimes.com/2012/03/23/world/europe/mohammed-merah-toulouse-shooting-suspect-french-police-standoff.html (accessed March 23, 2012).

46. *National Biometrics Challenge*, p. 20.

47. Margit Sutrop and Katrin Laas-Mikko, "From Identity Verification to Behavior Prediction: Ethical Implications of Second Generation Biometrics," *Review of Policy Research* 29, no. 1 (2012): 21–36; Ellen Messmer, "Can Behavioral Biometrics Help Detect Terrorists Entering the U.S.?" Network World, September 22, 2010, http://www.networkworld.com/news/2010/092210-biometrics.html (accessed March 19, 2012).

48. *Privacy Impact Assessment for the Future Attribute Screening Technology (FAST) Project*, Science and Technology Directorate, Department of Homeland Security, December 15, 2008, p. 2.

49. Declan McCullagh, "Real-Life 'Minority Report' Program Gets a Try-Out,"

CBS News, October 7, 2011, http://www.cbsnews.com/2100-503063_162-20117207 .html (accessed March 26, 2012).

50. *Privacy Impact Assessment,* p. 4.

51. Sharon Weinberger, "Terrorist 'Pre-Crime' Detector Field Tested in United States," *Nature,* May 27, 2011, http://www.nature.com/news/2011/110527/full/ news.2011.323.html (accessed March 24, 2012); McCullagh, "Real-Life 'Minority Report' Program"; Wilmer Heck, "EU to Monitor Deviant Behavior in Fight against Terrorism," *Spiegel Online International,* October 21, 2009, http://www.spiegel.de/ international/europe/0,1518,656468,00.html (accessed March 24, 2012).

52. Elizabeth Montalbano, "Homeland Security Tests Crime Prediction Tech," *Information Week,* October 11, 2011, http://www.informationweek.com/news/gov ernment/security/231900555 (accessed March 24, 2012).

53. Weinberger, "Terrorist 'Pre-Crime' Detector."

54. Joseph A. Bernstein, "Big Idea Seeing Crime before It Happens," *Discover Magazine,* January 23, 2012, http://discovermagazine.com/2011/dec/02-big-idea-seeing -crime-before-it-happens/article_view?b_start:int=1&-C (accessed March 26, 2012).

55. Steven Cherry and Anne-Marie Corely, "Loser: Bad Vibes: A Quixotic U.S. Government New Security System Seeks to Look into Your Soul," *IEEE Spectrum,* January 2010, http://spectrum.ieee.org/computing/embedded-systems/loser-bad -vibes (accessed March 24, 2012).

56. Sageman, *Leaderless Jihad,* p. 114.

57. Ibid., pp. 115–16.

58. Ibid., p. 122.

59. Charlie Savage, "Homeland Analysts Told to Monitor Policy Debates in Social Media," *New York Times,* February 22, 2012, http://www.nytimes.com/2012/02/23/ us/house-questions-homeland-security-program-on-social-media.html (accessed March 27, 2012).

60. Ibid.

61. Lori Andrews, "Facebook Is Using You," *New York Times,* February 4, 2012, http://www.nytimes.com/2012/02/05/opinion/sunday/facebook-is-using-you .html? pagewanted=all (accessed March 31, 2011).

62. Mark F. Giuliano, interview with author, October 1, 2009, Washington, DC.

63. David Johnston and James Risen, "Lone Terrorists May Strike in the U.S., Agencies Warn," *New York Times,* February 23, 2003, http://www.nytimes .com/2003/ 02/23/world/threats-responses-domestic-security-lone-terrorists-may-strike-us -agencies -warn.html?pagewanted=all&src=pm (accessed April 1, 2012).

64. Michael Brick, "Man Crashes Plane into Texas I.R.S. Office," *New York Times,* February 18, 2010, http://www.nytimes.com/2010/02/19/us/19crash.html?_r=1 (accessed April 2, 2012).

65. Matthew Harwood, "Tripping up Terrorists," *Security Management*, January 2012, http://www.securitymanagement.com/print/9356 (accessed April 1, 2012).

66. Sageman, *Leaderless Jihad*, pp. 156–57.

67. Ibid., pp. 151–54; Liat Shetret, "Use of the Internet for Counter-Terrorist Purposes," Policy Brief, Center on Global Counterterrorism Cooperation, February 2011, pp. 6–7.

68. Shetret, "Use of the Internet," p. 6.

69. "Empowering Local Partners to Prevent Violent Extremism in the United States," Office of the Press Secretary, White House, August 2011, http://www.white house.gov/the-press-office/2011/08/03/empowering-local-partners-prevent-violent -extremism-united-states (accessed April 2, 2012).

70. Benjamin Weiser and Colin Moynihan, "A Guilty Plea in Plot to Bomb Times Square," *New York Times*, June 22, 2010, http://query.nytimes.com/gst/full page.html?res=9B05E0DA1030F931A15755C0A9669D8B63&pagewanted=allAft (accessed April 10, 2012).

71. Carl Franzen, "How Faisal Shahzad Was Apprehended, Step by Step," AOL News, May 4, 2010, http://www.aolnews.com/2010/05/04/how-faisal-shahzad-was -apprehended-step-by-step/ (accessed April 10, 2012); "FBI Team 'Lost' Suspected Times Square Bomber during Critical Hours," Fox News, May 5, 2010, http://www .foxnews.com/us/2010/05/05/fbi-team-lost-suspected-times-square-bomber-crucial -hours/ (accessed April 10, 2012). After learning Shahzad's identity, the FBI placed him on the no-fly list and alerted other federal agencies that he was a suspect in the attempted bombing in Times Square. An updated no-fly list, however, had not yet been activated in computer systems. That was how Shahzad was able to board the plane. It wasn't until Shahzad was already on the plane that Customs and Border Protection officials received the final passenger list with his name from Emirates Airlines. Had the authorities been just a few minutes late before notifying air-traffic control at Kennedy Airport to not allow the plane to take off, Shahzad would have safely fled the country.

72. *CJIS Annual Report 2011*, p. 18.

73. Yanjun Yan and Lisa Ann Osadciw, "Bridging Biometrics and Forensics," in *Security, Forensics, Steganography, and Watermarking of Multimedia Contents X*, ed. Edward J. Delp, Ping Wah Wong, Jana Dittmann, and Nasir D. Memon (San Jose, CA: Proceedings—SPIE, 2008).

74. Fischer Jr., interview.

75. *CJIS Annual Report 2011*, p. 24.

76. Casey, interview.

77. *Lone-Wolf Terrorism*, pp. 26, 66; Adrian Bridge, "Austria's 'Unabomber' Taunts Police with History and Myth," *Independent*, December 15, 1996, http://www

.independent.co.uk/news/world/austrias-unabomber-taunts-police-with-history-and -myth-1314636.html (accessed April 11, 2012).

78. *Lone-Wolf Terrorism*, pp. 80–82; Ramon Spaaij, *Understanding Lone Wolf Terrorism: Global Patterns, Motivations and Prevention* (New York: Springer, 2012), pp. 84–86.

79. Ibid.

80. Ibid.

81. Michael M. Greenburg, *The Mad Bomber of New York: The Extraordinary True Story of the Manhunt That Paralyzed a City* (New York: Union Square Press, 2012), p. 79; Spaaij, *Understanding Lone Wolf Terrorism*, pp. 23–24; Melissa Ann Madden, "George Metesky: New York's Mad Bomber (City Under Siege)," TruTV Crime Library, http://www.trutv.com/library/crime/terrorists_spies/terrorists/metesky/1.html (accessed April 12, 2012).

82. Don DeNevi and John H. Campbell, *Into the Minds of Madmen: How the FBI's Behavioral Science Unit Revolutionized Crime Investigation* (Amherst, NY: Prometheus Books, 2004), pp. 60–65; Lyn Bixby, "'Mad Bomber' of Waterbury Terrorized New York for 17 Years," *Hartford Courant*, July 2, 1995, http://articles.courant.com/1995 -07-02/news/9507020146_1_unabomber-s-signature-first-bomb-george-metesky (accessed April 12, 2012); Madden, "George Metesky (Small Beginnings)," TruTV Crime Library, http://www.trutv.com/library/crime/terrorists_spies/terrorists/ metesky/2.html (accessed April 12, 2012).

83. DeNevi and Campbell, *Into the Minds of Madmen*, pp. 60–65.

84. Madden, "George Metesky (The Game Begins)," TruTV Crime Library, http://www.trutv.com/library/crime/terrorists_spies/terrorists/metesky/5 .html (accessed April 12, 2012); Madden, "George Metesky (Revelations)," TruTV Crime Library, http://www.trutv.com/library/crime/terrorists_spies/terrorists/ metesky/7.html (accessed April 12, 2012); DeNevi and Campbell, *Into the Minds of Madmen*, pp. 60–65.

85. Madden, "George Metesky (Aftermath)," TruTV Crime Library, http:// www.trutv.com/library/crime/terrorists_spies/terrorists/metesky/9.html (accessed April 12, 2012); Alexander Feinberg, "Edison Clerk Finds Case in File; Bomber's Words Alerted Her," *New York Times*, January 23, 1957, p. 18; "The Bomber's Grievances Came to Light in a Series of Letters," *New York Times*, January 23, 1957, p. 19; Malcolm Gladwell, "Dangerous Minds: Criminal Profiling Made Easy," *New Yorker*, November 12, 2007, http://www.newyorker.com/reporting/2007/11/12/071112fa _fact_gladwell (accessed April 12, 2012); Michael T. Kaufman, "'Mad Bomber,' Now 70, Goes Free Today," *New York Times*, December 13, 1973, p. 1.

86. "Bomber's Grievances Came to Light."

87. "Extremist Chatter Praises Eric Rudolph as 'Hero,'" Anti-Defamation League,

June 3, 2003, http://www.adl.org/presrele/asus_12/4264_72.htm (accessed April 14, 2012).

88. Edecio Martinez, "Joe Stack Is a 'True American Hero': Facebook Groups Support Domestic Terrorist," CBS News, February 19, 2010, http://www.cbsnews.com/8301-504083_162-6223132-504083.html (accessed May 8, 2011).

89. Andrea Canning and Lee Ferran, "Stack's Daughter Retracts 'Hero,' Statement," ABC News, February 22, 2010, http://abcnews.go.com/GMA/joe-stacks-daughter-samantha-bell-calls-dad-hero/story?id=9903329#.T4svwBxBnw5 (accessed April 14, 2012).

90. Jeffrey D. Simon, "Biological Terrorism: Preparing to Meet the Threat," *Journal of the American Medical Association* 278, no. 5 (August 6, 1997): 428–30.

CHAPTER 7. UNCOVERING THE LESSONS LEARNED

1. George Santayana, *Reason in Common Sense*, vol. 1, *The Life of Reason, or, The Phases of Human Progress* (New York: Scribner's, 1905), p. 284.

2. Matthew Cole, "New Al Qaeda Video: American Muslims Should Buy Guns, Start Shooting People," ABC News, June 3, 2011, http://abcnews.go.com/Blotter/al-qaeda-video-buy-automatic-weapons-start-shooting/story?id=13704264#.T5bzKxxLmfc (accessed April 24, 2012).

3. David Ljunggren, "Al Qaeda Challenges with Lone Wolf Tactics: Canada," Reuters, April 23, 2012, http://www.reuters.com/article/2012/04/23/us-alqaeda-idUSBRE83M1HP20120423 (accessed April 23, 2012).

4. Claire Sterling, *The Terror Network* (New York: Henry Holt, 1981).

5. Jerry S. Piven, "On the Psychosis (Religion) of Terrorists," in *Terror and the Apocalypse: Psychological Undercurrents of History, Volume II*, ed. Jerry S. Piven, Paul Zilio, and Henry W. Lawton (Lincoln, NE: Bloomusalem Press, 2002), p. 186.

6. Jeffrey D. Simon, *The Terrorist Trap: America's Experience with Terrorism*, 2nd ed. (Bloomington: Indiana University Press, 2001), pp. 5–6.

7. See, for example, Martha Crenshaw, "The Causes of Terrorism," in *International Terrorism*, ed. Charles W. Kegley Jr. (New York: St. Martin's Press, 1990), p. 121; John Horgan, *The Psychology of Terrorism* (London: Routledge, 2005), pp. 62–79; Marc Sageman, *Leaderless Jihad: Terror Networks in the Twenty-First Century* (Philadelphia: University of Pennsylvania Press, 2008), pp. 62–65; Jerrold M. Post, *The Mind of the Terrorist: The Psychology of Terrorism from the IRA to al-Qaeda* (New York: Palgrave Macmillan, 2007), pp. 3–4.

8. Christopher Hewitt, *Understanding Terrorism in America: From the Klan to al Qaeda* (London: Routledge, 2003), p. 80.

9. Ibid.

10. Ramon Spaaij, "The Enigma of Lone Wolf Terrorism: An Assessment," *Studies in Conflict & Terrorism* 33, no. 9 (2010): 862.

11. Horgan, *Psychology of Terrorism*, p. 48.

12. Steven Emerson, *Jihad Incorporated: A Guide to Militant Islam in the US* (Amherst, NY: Prometheus Books, 2006), p. 479.

13. John H. Campbell and Don DeNevi, *Profilers: Leading Investigators Take You inside the Criminal Mind* (Amherst, NY: Prometheus Books, 2004), p. 194; Malcolm Gladwell, "Dangerous Minds: Criminal Profiling Made Easy," *New Yorker*, November 12, 2007, http://www.newyorker.com/reporting/2007/11/12/071112fa_fact_gladwell (accessed April 12, 2012); Melissa Ann Madden, "George Metesky: New York's Mad Bomber," Dinge en Goete (Things and Stuff), http://dingeengoete.blogspot.com/2012/03/george-metesky-new-yorks-mad-bomber.html (accessed April 29, 2012).

14. "Patterns of Global Terrorism: 2002," United States Department of State, April 2003, appendix H, p. 161. International terrorism refers to "terrorism involving citizens or the territory of more than one country" (p. xiii). In other words, it involves terrorist incidents "in which terrorists go abroad to strike their targets, stay at home but select victims because of their connections to a foreign state (e.g., diplomats or the executives of foreign corporations), or attack international lines of commerce (e.g., airliners). It excludes the considerable amount of terrorist violence carried out by terrorists operating within their own country against their own nationals and in many countries by governments against their own citizens." (Brian Michael Jenkins, *International Terrorism: The Other World War*, Rand Corp, R-3302-AF, November 1985, p. 4.) Domestic terrorist incidents are now combined with international ones in the annual US government statistics on terrorism, bringing the numbers to staggering totals. For example, the number of terrorist incidents in 2011 was 10,283! See *Country Reports on Terrorism: 2011*, United States Department of State, National Counterterrorism Center: Annex of Statistical Information, July 2012, p. 2.

15. Spaaij, "Enigma of Lone Wolf Terrorism," p. 862; Hewitt, *Understanding Terrorism in America*, p. 80.

16. Ramon Spaaij, *Understanding Lone Wolf Terrorism: Global Patterns, Motivations, and Prevention* (New York: Springer, 2012), pp. 27–33.

17. Ibid., p. 31.

18. *Lone-Wolf Terrorism*, COT, Instituut voor Veiligheids- en Crisismanagement, Final draft, June 7, 2007, Case Study for Work Package 3, p. 80, http://www.scribd.com/doc/34968770/Lone-Wolf-Terrorism (accessed June 10, 2011).

19. Michael Schwirtz, "Norway's Premier Vows to Keep an Open Society," *New York Times*, July 27, 2011, http://www.nytimes.com/2011/07/28/world/europe/28norway.html (accessed August 2, 2011).

CHAPTER 8. A LOOK TOWARD THE FUTURE

1. See, for example, Marvin J. Cetron and Owen Davies, *55 Trends Now Shaping the Future of Terrorism* (n.p.: CreateSpace, 2008); *Report of the Future of Terrorism Task Force*, Homeland Security Advisory Council, January 2007; Harvey W. Kushner, ed., *The Future of Terrorism: Violence in the New Millennium* (Thousand Oaks, CA: Sage, 1998); Max Taylor and John Horgan, eds., *The Future of Terrorism* (London: Routledge, 2000); Jon Meacham, ed., *Beyond bin Laden: America and the Future of Terror* (New York: Random House, 2011).

2. Jeffrey D. Simon, *The Terrorist Trap: America's Experience with Terrorism* (Bloomington: Indiana University Press, 1994), pp. 347–73.

3. David C. Rapoport, "The Four Waves of Modern Terrorism," in *Attacking Terrorism: Elements of a Grand Strategy*, ed. Audrey Kurth Cronin and James M. Ludes (Washington, DC: Georgetown University Press, 2004), pp. 46–73.

4. Brian Michael Jenkins, *Al Qaeda in Its Third Decade: Irreversible Decline or Imminent Victory?* (Santa Monica, CA: RAND Corporation, 2012), p. 16.

5. *EU Terrorism Situation and Trend Report (TE-SAT) 2012*, Europol, 2012, p. 4.

6. Nic Robertson and Paul Cruickshank, "Sources: Saudi Counterterrorism Work Broke up New AQAP Plane Plot," CNN, May 9, 2012, http://www.cnn .com/2012/0 5/09/world/meast/al-qaeda-plot/index.html (accessed May 10, 2012).

7. "Russia Foils 2014 Winter Olympics Terror Plot, State Media Reports," CNN, May 10, 2012, http://www.cnn.com/2012/05/10/world/europe/russia -terror-plot/index.html (accessed May 10, 2012).

8. Allan Hall, "Germans Fear Rise in Left-Wing Terrorism after Seven Petrol Bombs Found in Berlin Rail Tunnel," *Dailymail*, October 11, 2011, http://www .dailymail.co.uk/news/article-2047791/Germans-fear-rise-left-wing-terrorism-seven -petrol -bombs-Berlin-rail-tunnel.html (accessed May 8, 2012).

9. Valentina Soria, "Not Welcome Here: The Resurgence of Far-Right Wing Extremism in Europe," Royal United Services Institute, January 9, 2012, http://www .rusi.org/analysis/commentary/ref:C4F0AD7935C9BD/ (accessed May 9, 2012).

10. "Dungannon Man Patrick Carty Charged over 'Iraq-Style IED,'" BBC News, February 13, 2012, http://www.bbc.co.uk/news/uk-northern-ireland-17013837 (accessed May 11, 2012).

11. There have, however, been "low level" types of cyber attacks by many governments in recent years.

12. Richard J. Danzig, *A Policymaker's Guide to Bioterrorism and What to Do about It*, Center for Technology and National Security Policy, National Defense University, December 2009, p. 10.

13. Jeffrey D. Simon, "Technological and Lone Operator Terrorism: Prospects for

a Fifth Wave of Global Terrorism," in *Terrorism, Identity, and Legitimacy: The Four Waves Theory and Political Violence*, ed. Jean E. Rosenfeld (London: Routledge, 2011), pp. 58–59.

14. Ibid., p. 60.

15. *Country Reports on Terrorism: 2011*, United States Department of State, July 2012, p. 269.

16. Paul Avrich, *Sacco and Vanzetti: The Anarchist Background* (Princeton, NJ: Princeton University Press, 1991), p. 206.

17. Jeffrey D. Simon, "Misunderstanding Terrorism," *Foreign Policy* 67 (Summer 1987): 111.

18. Ibid.

19. Katharine Q. Seelye and Elisabeth Bumiller, "Bush Labels Aerial Terrorist Attacks 'Acts of War,'" *New York Times*, September 13, 2001, http://www.nytimes.com/2001/09/13/national/13BUSH.html (accessed May 14, 2012).

20. Scott Wilson and Al Kamen, "'Global War on Terror' Is Given New Name," *Washington Post*, March 25, 2009, http://www.washingtonpost.com/wp-dyn/content/article/2009/03/24/AR2009032402818.html (accessed May 14, 2012).

CONCLUSION

1. Albert Einstein, "The World as I See It," *Forum and Century* 84 (1931): 193–94.

2. Rory O'Connor, *Friends, Followers, and the Future: How Social Media Are Changing Politics, Threatening Big Brands, and Killing Traditional Media* (San Francisco: City Lights Books, 2012), p. 264.

3. David Willman, *The Mirage Man: Bruce Ivins, the Anthrax Attacks, and America's Rush to War* (New York: Bantam Books, 2011), p. 297.

APPENDIX

1. Alex Schmid, *Political Terrorism: A Research Guide to Concepts, Theories, Data Bases, and Literature* (Amsterdam: North-Holland, 1984), pp. 119–58.

2. *Patterns of Global Terrorism: 2003*, United States Department of State, April 2004, p. xii (italics added). The State Department's reports on terrorism are published during the subsequent year, so that the 2003 report on terrorism was issued in 2004, the 2004 report on terrorism was issued in 2005, and so forth. The title of the reports were changed from "Patterns of Global Terrorism" to "Country Reports on Terrorism" in April 2005, when the State Department issued its report for 2004. The new title has stayed in effect for subsequent reports.

3. *Country Reports on Terrorism: 2004*, United States Department of State, April 2005, p. 1.

4. *Country Reports on Terrorism: 2003*, United States Department of State, April 2004, p. xii (italics added).

5. *Country Reports on Terrorism: 2004*, United States Department of State, April 2005, p. 1 (italics added).

6. Secretary of Defense Donald Rumsfeld used the term "dead-enders" to describe the initial violent attacks against US troops in Iraq. See Donald Rumsfeld, "Remarks as Delivered by Secretary of Defense Donald H. Rumsfeld," San Antonio, TX, Monday, August 25, 2003, to the Veterans of Foreign Wars, US Department of Defense, http://www.defenselink.mil/speeches/speech.aspx?speechid=513 (accessed June 3, 2008). President Bush, however, preferred to use the term "terrorists." In October 2003, Bush said that "the best way to describe the people who are conducting these attacks are cold-blooded killers, terrorsts [*sic*]. That's all they are. They're terrorists." See George W. Bush, "President Bush, Ambassador Bremer Discuss Progress in Iraq," White House Press Release, October 27, 2003, http://merln.ndu.edu/merln/pfiraq/archive/wh/20031027-1.pdf (accessed June 3, 2008).

7. *Terrorism in the United States: 1994*, Terrorist Research and Analytical Center, National Security Division, US Department of Justice, Federal Bureau of Investigation, p. 24.

8. Ibid., p. 26.

9. *Terrorism in the United States: 1995*, Terrorist Research and Analytical Center, National Security Division, US Department of Justice, Federal Bureau of Investigation, p. ii.

10. *Terrorism in the United States: 1999*, Counterterrorism Threat Assessment and Warning Unit, Counterterrorism Division, US Department of Justice, Federal Bureau of Investigation, p. ii.

11. Ibid., p. 26. The FBI report used the spelling "Amil Kanzi." The name has also been spelled as "Aimal Kasi" and "Aimal Kansi" in many other references.

12. Patricia Davis and Maria Glod, "CIA Shooter Kasi, Harbinger of Terror, Set to Die Tonight," *Washington Post*, November 14, 2002, http://www.washingtonpost.com/ac2/wp-dyn/A55638-2002Nov14 (accessed July 9, 2010).

13. Greg Krikorian, "No Link to Extremists in LAX Shootings," *Los Angeles Times*, April 12, 2003, p. B3.

14. Jeffrey D. Simon, *The Terrorist Trap: America's Experience with Terrorism*, 2nd ed. (Bloomington: Indiana University Press, 2001), pp. 49–51.

15. Walter Laqueur, *The Age of Terrorism* (Boston: Little, Brown, 1987), p. 70.

16. Benjamin Weiser, "A Guilty Plea in Plot to Bomb Times Square," *New York Times*, June 22, 2010, p. A2.